The Gee Years, 2007–2013

The Gee Years, 2007–2013

HERBERT B. ASHER

The Ohio State University Press
Columbus

Copyright © 2021 by The Ohio State University.
All rights reserved.

Library of Congress Cataloging-in-Publication Data
Names: Asher, Herbert B., author.
Title: The Gee years, 2007–2013 / Herbert B. Asher.
Description: Columbus : The Ohio State University Press, [2021] | Includes index. | Summary: "Chronicles E. Gordon Gee's second tenure as president of The Ohio State University, which ran from 2007 to 2013"—Provided by publisher.
Identifiers: LCCN 2021012323 | ISBN 9780814214756 (cloth) | ISBN 0814214754 (cloth) | ISBN 9780814281451 (ebook) | ISBN 0814281451 (ebook)
Subjects: LCSH: Gee, E. Gordon (Elwood Gordon), 1944- | Ohio State University—History—21st century.
Classification: LCC LD4230 .A84 2021 | DDC 378.771/57—dc23
LC record available at https://lccn.loc.gov/2021012323
Other identifiers: ISBN 9780814258590 (paper) | ISBN 081425859X (paper)

Type set in Adobe Minion Pro

Contents

Foreword vii

1 The 1981 to 2007 Era at Ohio State 1
2 The Gee Return and Transition 7
3 Building a Team 16
4 Shaping a University Culture 32
5 The Face of the University: Organizing the Calendar 37
6 The Internal Constituencies 59
7 Old Issues and New Outcomes: Semester Conversion and Arts and Sciences Consolidation 75
8 From Development to Advancement 85
9 From Redevelopment to Revitalization: On Campus and Off 99
10 Signature Buildings, the North Campus Residential District, and the Two-Year Residency Rule 117
11 Other Initiatives and Actions 131
12 Alternative Resource Strategies 157
13 Ohio State by the Numbers: Trends in Quality and Performance 177
14 Athletics 199
15 The Ohio State University Wexner Medical Center 209
16 The Changing Dimensions of Diversity at Ohio State 226
17 Gee and the Governors 241
18 The Ohio State University and the Gee Legacy 254

Appendix A Gee's Rules of Engagement 265
Appendix B Gee and Alutto Memos to the Board of Trustees 273

CONTENTS

Appendix C   *Ohio State University Enrollment Report*   280

Appendix D   *Commencement Speakers and Honorary Degree Recipients in the Second Gee Presidency*   286

Appendix E   *Members of the Board of Trustees in the Second Gee Presidency*   288

Index   291

Foreword

This book is the fifteenth in a series of volumes sponsored by The Ohio State University Board of Trustees showcasing the history of The Ohio State University. The first book in the series is a general history of the university overall, while the other volumes each focus on a particular university president and what happened at Ohio State during his or her administration. This volume focuses on the second administration of Gordon Gee, who served as president between 2007 and 2013. There was actually a first Gee administration between 1990 and 1997; Malcolm Baroway wrote a wonderful chronicle of those years.

My approach to the book was thematic; it is organized around major events, developments, and successes of the university. The book is not a chronological summary of events that occurred during the second Gee administration. I also took some liberties with the time span covered by this book. Although Gee was president between 2007 and 2013, in many instances I went further back in time prior to his return and in some cases noted developments in the administration of his successor Michael Drake. My major reason for going further back in time was the recognition that the beginning and end dates of a particular administration are arbitrary constraints in discussing and analyzing university events. Instead, there is a broader history that shapes future developments, and to truly appreciate what has happened at the university, some knowledge of that history is essential.

Many Ohio State colleagues and community citizens and institutions contributed to this manuscript, but before acknowledging them, I want to say a bit about my qualifications to write this book. I worked for Gordon Gee throughout his first and his second term in various capacities, always reporting directly to him. This was a wonderful asset for me in writing this book, but it also had its challenges. I knew too much. I had too many materials and notes and documents and communications. I had perspectives on events and experiences that sometimes differed from what the official university communications offices put out for mass consumption.

I also had the privilege of working for other university presidents, starting with Ed Jennings, for whom I worked in the last seven years of his presidency between 1983 and 1990. I also worked for Brit Kirwan throughout his presidency from 1997 to 2002 and for Karen Holbrook between 2002 and 2003. After Gee's departure in 2013, I worked for interim President Joe Alutto from 2014–2015 and then stayed on to work for the newly selected President Michael Drake in the first five months of his administration until I retired in January of 2015. This experience supporting multiple presidents was rewarding and enlightening in many ways. I clearly had the opportunity to witness firsthand their administrative and decision-making styles. More importantly, it reinforced my belief that university events and developments are better understood when there is an appreciation of what transpired in earlier years. Finally, I had the privilege of being a member of the faculty of the department of political science as a professor and professor emeritus for over four decades.

I am grateful to many university citizens for their contributions to this book. First and foremost is Gordon Gee, not simply because of the experiences working for him, but also because of the extensive oral history interview in excess of seven hours that we conducted for this book. Although numerous interviews were conducted, I want to mention a few individuals who were especially helpful in a variety of ways. Steven Sterrett was an excellent source of information about the history of Campus Partners and its early and subsequent accomplishments. Jerry Friedman was a valuable contributor to my understanding of the politics and policies of the medical center. The materials produced by the Office of Institutional Research headed by Julie Carpenter-Hubin were very helpful, as were the enrollment reports prepared by Dolan Evanovich and his colleagues. Randy Smith, vice provost in the Office of Academic Affairs, was also a valuable resource, particularly in his contributions to the accreditation report he shepherded to completion; this report covered many key events of the second Gee administration. Randy was also very helpful in moving the book through the publication process. David Frantz, retired English professor and former secretary of the Board of Trustees, was a constant source of advice and a wonderful calming influence as the writing of this book went far beyond my initial time estimates. Tracy Stuck and Sue Jones were excellent sources of information on Gee's interactions with students and on his state tours. In addition, they were both very generous in sharing materials from their files about Gee's travels and his interactions with students and with the broader community. Katie Reed was very helpful in various aspects of manuscript preparation logistics. Jo McCulty provided invaluable assistance in selecting the photographs for this volume. Jessica Melfi was a wonderfully constructive copyeditor who enhanced the readability of the book. Finally, Dick

FOREWORD

Stoddard was a consistently insightful resource about the history of Ohio State and its presidents.

As mentioned above, I conducted many interviews for this book. I also had conversations with many people; in some cases, I would have difficulty distinguishing a conversation from an interview except that the interviews tended to be more formal, structured and lengthier, and the conversations more casual, free ranging, and shorter. Let me cite some of these wonderful sources, knowing that I will inevitably commit sins of omission: Javaune Adams-Gaston, Joe Alutto, Michael Caligiuri, Geoff Chatas, Melinda Church, Chris Culley, AJ Douglas, Mike Eicher, Steve Gabbe, Tim Gerber, Archie Griffin, Richard Gunther, Jack Hershey, Jeff Kaplan, Jay Kasey, Tom Katzenmeyer, Bruce McPheron, Tom Near, Stacy Rastauskas, Robert Schottenstein, Alex Shumate, Gene Smith, Joe Steinmetz, Blake Thompson, and Carol Whitacre. Jeff Kaplan was especially helpful in reviewing a draft version of this manuscript. University Archives and various university publications such as *onCampus* and numerous press releases and reports issued by University Communications were also important sources of information as were the *Columbus Dispatch, Columbus Monthly, Columbus Business First,* and the *Chronicle of Higher Education.*

1
The 1981 to 2007 Era at Ohio State

The Ohio State University is one of America's most comprehensive universities, with a strong Arts and Sciences core, a set of outstanding professional colleges, and a medical center and collection of health sciences colleges that are increasingly growing in prominence and impact. The undergraduate student body at Ohio State is among the largest in the country, while the graduate and professional students bring great intellectual and research strengths to the campus along with a major international representation. Although Ohio State has always been a prominent university with major contributions to teaching, research, public service and engagement, and educational opportunities for first generation college students, the university witnessed a qualitative transformation that began in the 1980s under the leadership of President Edward Jennings (see Figure 1.1). It was during the Jennings administration that the university began the process of moving from an open admissions institution to a selective admissions university, a process that accelerated in the first Gordon Gee presidency and the subsequent presidency of William "Brit" Kirwan. Also during the Jennings era, the university moved to enhance its research profile across the university's academic departments. Selective investments were made in outstanding departments and in those departments that with a boost in university support could move from good to excellent. And it was in the Jennings era that the medical center, long known for its outstanding patient and clinical care, strategically enhanced its research science profile in carefully chosen areas such as cancer, cardiology, and others.

All of these positive trends in student quality and research proficiency gained momentum in the subsequent presidencies of Gordon Gee (Gee One,

CHAPTER 1

FIGURE 1.1. Former OSU President Ed Jennings meets with President Gee on a return trip to campus. Credit: The Ohio State University.

1990–1997) and Brit Kirwan (1997–2002). The aspirations of the university grew, as did the expectations that the university would be a more significant, impactful player in the life of the community, the state of Ohio, and the nation. This was at a time when the industrial Midwest was undergoing a wrenching transformation as the older manufacturing and extraction economies were declining and their replacements were still emerging. On campus, there was a growing sense of expanding possibilities and opportunities—that Ohio State could indeed be one of the top ten public universities in the country, that excellence could thrive at Ohio State just as it did at more prestigious private and public universities.

Throughout the Jennings, Gee One, and Kirwan years, OSU athletics enjoyed much success, particularly the football program, which regularly competed for Big 10 championships, earned spots in prestigious post-season college bowl games, and was in the mix for potential national championships. In this era, men's and women's basketball also enjoyed success and visibility, and the overall athletic program was the rare breed in intercollegiate athletics: it was one of the few programs in the nation that was financially self-sufficient and did not rely on university subsidies or student fees to fund the program.

Indeed, this financial stability enabled Ohio State to be a leader in offering a wide range of intercollegiate activities in major and minor sports, including an impressive array of women's sports.

Throughout the 1990 to 2007 era, one continuing challenge facing Ohio State and public higher education throughout the nation was the gradual divestments by state governments in their support for public higher education. In most (but not all) cases, this was not because of any hostility toward higher education. Instead, it was due to budgetary pressures—the need to fund primary and secondary education, health care, especially Medicaid, and the penal system. Prisons were a rapidly growing part of state budgets during this era, in part because state legislatures, under the rubric of law and order, were criminalizing more activities and raising the penalties for already illegal activities. Thus, the prison population was growing, more prisons were built, more prison guards were hired, and in some states the cost of the corrections system approached the cost of higher education. At that time, many state legislatures believed that colleges and universities did not have to rely so heavily on state appropriations, that higher education had another source of support it directly controlled—student tuition. A decade later, tuition increases would become politically unpopular, and universities were sharply criticized for raising tuition. But for a while tuition increases enabled state governments to diminish their support of higher education. Thus, in many states, including Ohio, if state dollars had once paid 70 percent of the cost of educating an in-state, undergraduate student and tuition paid the other 30 percent, fifteen years later it was very common for tuition to bear 70 percent of the cost and state dollars pick up the other 30 percent. With universities raising tuition every year (but not Ohio State, which kept resident undergraduate tuition flat for four years in the second Gee administration), the chorus of criticism directed toward universities by elected officials and the public grew enormously.

As pressures on state budgets increased, OSU presidents, especially Jennings and Gee One, recognized that the institution would need to generate more of its own resources even as it continued to lobby the state and federal governments for financial support. One important approach was to initiate major capital (fundraising) campaigns targeted to friends and supporters of the university, be they alumni, friends, businesses, foundations, etc. Capital campaigns had not been common at public institutions, and Ohio State's first such major campaign was in the late 1980s during the Jennings administration. Since that time, private fundraising became an integral part of Ohio State's resource acquisition strategy, and one of the major reasons for Gee's return in 2007 was to lead the next and largest capital campaign in Ohio State's history.

Chapter 1

While these capital campaigns could never fully compensate for shortfalls in state and federal support, they were often described in terms such as "the critical difference" or the "margin of excellence."

Prior to this era, Ohio State and many other major public universities, despite having significant and well-led alumni associations, did not do as good a job staying connected to and seeking support from its alumni as did the major private universities. This situation had developed for a number of reasons, including heavy reliance on state and federal support as well as tuition and a belief by some that private dollars should be the domain of the private universities since public universities received so much governmental support. Moreover, the number of alumni of public institutions was huge, which made for difficulty in staying connected with such a huge population. And many of the alumni were not graduates, but simply attendees who did not complete a degree program. In this era, many public institutions were open enrollments universities, including Ohio State University. Admission was easy, but graduation was difficult, with dropout rates in the freshman year approaching 30 to 40 percent. Remediation rates in English and mathematics for entering freshmen were appallingly high, as discussed in chapter 13. But the admissions standards at many public institutions such as Ohio State changed, and the importance of staying connected with their graduates became a higher priority. And thus, the advancement model was established during the second Gee presidency. (See chapter 8.)

Brit Kirwan's presidency at Ohio State ended in 2002 when he returned to Maryland to become the Chancellor of the University of Maryland System; prior to coming to Ohio State, he had been the head of the College Park campus of the University of Maryland. During his tenure at Ohio State, Kirwan was widely regarded by the university community as a visionary leader who understood the complexities of the university and the challenges facing it. He had built strong relationship with deans, faculty, and students, and was widely respected in higher education circles in Ohio and nationally.

Kirwan (see Figure 1.2) was succeeded by Karen Holbrook in fall 2002. Holbrook (see Figure 1.3) had been the research vice president at the University of Florida and the provost at the University of Georgia before becoming the thirteenth president of Ohio State. And while many of the positive trends that had begun in the Jennings years and accelerated in the Gee and Kirwan presidencies continued during the Holbrook administration (including winning the national championship in football in Holbrook's first year), there was a growing feeling that momentum was waning, that the university itself was playing a lesser role in state and national policy deliberations, and

FIGURE 1.2. Former OSU President Brit Kirwan chats with OSU Board of Trustee member Alex Shumate (right) on a return visit to campus. Credit: The Ohio State University.

FIGURE 1.3. President Karen Holbrook preparing to preside over the commencement ceremony. Walking behind her is Vice President for Student Life Bill Hall. Credit: The Ohio State University.

CHAPTER 1

that many of the functional units such as development and fundraising (later to become advancement) were lagging.

Thus, when Holbrook's contract expired, the OSU Board of Trustees sought to find a new, dynamic, visionary leader for Ohio State. And while there was a well-designed search process to seek out and attract the best candidates, it was clear from the outset that some key trustees and former trustees were endeavoring to get former OSU president Gordon Gee to return to Ohio State University. Although it was very unusual for a university president to do a second stint at an institution he had previously led, many influential university and community leaders believed that bringing Gee back to Columbus was just the shot in the arm that the campus needed.

2

The Gee Return and Transition

The Recruitment

Gordon Gee had left Ohio State in 2007 to become president of Brown University, where he stayed for only two years before being recruited by Vanderbilt University to become its Chancellor in 2000. Gee was very successful, very happy, and highly regarded at Vanderbilt, but that did not prevent Ohio State trustees and others from asking the question, "Could Gee be persuaded to return to Ohio State?" Gee himself gave signals, even while at Brown and Vanderbilt, of his love for his Ohio State experience. He had maintained close contacts with his many friends on campus, in Columbus, and throughout Ohio. And many of his friends, faculty, and students remembered their deep sense of loss they felt when Gee left for Brown.

Many Ohioans also felt they had lost a friend who clearly relished being the university president and who was proud and happy to be a Buckeye. Gee's enthusiasm for the university spilled over to the internal constituencies of faculty, staff, and students, and to the external constituencies of alumni, business and civic leaders, donors, and the people of Ohio in general. Gee always related well to his audiences. At a large event he would work the room and make every person in attendance feel that he or she were special. Gee had a wonderful sense of humor (that later would get him in trouble) that he would often turn on himself, thus making him a more accessible and more human person. He certainly was not an "ivory tower" president. There is little he would not do in order to promote the university and to relate to the university's friends and supporters. He loved the students of Ohio State, and the students recipro-

Chapter 2

cated that feeling in many ways. Any walk across the Oval for Gee took longer because students would constantly stop him and ask to have their picture taken with him. He, of course, obliged, and the students would post these photos on Facebook and other sites. It became an important Buckeye tradition for students to have their picture taken with Gordon Gee. (We'll say more about Gee and the student body in chapters 5 and 18.) One humorous anecdote about the pervasiveness of photos occurred on a late Sunday afternoon at Marcella's, a restaurant in the Short North section of Columbus. Earlier in the day, Gee had taken United States Senator Rob Portman and Mrs. Portman to a basketball game at the Schottenstein Center. After the game, the three of them went to Marcella's for dinner. As they entered the restaurant, many of the customers and the serving staff, some of whom were students, recognized Gee and said hello. Gee proudly introduced his guests: "This is United States Senator Rob Portman and his spouse Jane." At this point, many of the customers and staff began clamoring to have their picture taken and both Gee and Portman readily agreed. The students then handed their phones/cameras to the Senator, asking him to take pictures of them with President Gee. With great grace and humor, Senator Portman played the role of photographer while President Gee was the rock star in the photos.

Gee had a fantastic memory so that once he met someone, he knew them forever. And when he first met someone, especially a student, he would do the interrogation: "Where are you from?," "What does your family do?," "What are you studying?," "What should Ohio State be doing better?" It was absolutely flattering and surprising to people that upon meeting them for a second time, he could recite what he had learned about them in their first meeting. It was so clear to people that Gee loved OSU and felt privileged to be the leader of the institution. He regularly thanked others for allowing him to be president of Ohio State.

So even though it was rare for a university president to return to his former institution, many people were not surprised to see Gee return to Columbus. It was "where he belonged," "it was home," "he never should have left in the first place." At the official event at the Longaberger Alumni House on July 12, 2007, confirming Gee's designation as the next president of Ohio State (Gee officially took office on October 1, 2007), the mood was festive, emotional, and optimistic. David Frantz, an emeritus professor in the Department of English and former secretary to the Board of Trustees, said that Gee's return "opened up new possibilities for the university; that once again people could think big about their university and where it was going." This notion of Gee lifting spirits, of energizing people, of making people feel better about Ohio State, was a

THE GEE RETURN AND TRANSITION

recurrent them in the many interviews I conducted. Chris Culley, the university general counsel, emphasized how Gee's return energized the university. Culley argued that Gee served as a catalyst that got many things moving again. Ohio State had gotten sleepy, and Gee jump-started it. Culley believed that Gee "inspired us to think about who we were and who we could be," and in Culley's experience very few university presidents were able to accomplish this.

The actual recruitment of Gee from Vanderbilt to Ohio State had elements of humor, drama, chess, and surprises that were well documented by Eric Lyttle and Ray Paprocki in their September 2007 story in *Columbus Monthly* titled "The Stealing of a President." The lead-in to the story read:

> How a determined Titan, a persistent friend, a relentless daughter, the Gang of Three and a cast of thousands persuaded Gordon Gee to return to Ohio State. A tale about "a vast conspiracy," secret plane trips into enemy territory . . . and a tear or two.

All of these elements were indeed a central part of Gee's return. I was in regular contact with Gee throughout this courtship and knew firsthand the turmoil he was experiencing in deciding whether to return to Ohio State or stay at Vanderbilt, an institution that he deeply valued and which, in turn, valued him. I expected that Gee would ultimately base his decision on what his heart told him, and this made me optimistic that he would return to Ohio State, a place he continued to love even after he left for Brown and Vanderbilt. His daughter Rebekah urged her father to return to Ohio State, arguing that OSU was his true home.

Key university players in recruiting Gee back to Ohio State were Gil Cloyd, chair of the OSU Board of Trustees (see Figure 2.1); trustee Alex Shumate, chair of the presidential search committee; and former trustee Jack Kessler (see Figure 2.2) and trustee Les Wexner, both close friends of Gee.

A key community leader in getting Gee back to Ohio State was John F. Wolfe (see Figure 2.3). Wolfe was the publisher of the *Columbus Dispatch*, a longtime supporter of Ohio State, and a personal friend of Gordon Gee. It was Wolfe who organized the effort in 1995 to keep Gee at Ohio State when the University of California tried to recruit him to head the UC system. Wolfe mobilized the Columbus community to convince Gee to stay at Ohio State; Wolfe and his colleagues succeeded. Thus, when the possibility arose that Gee might return to Ohio State from Vanderbilt, Wolfe was fully engaged behind the scenes to achieve that outcome. Gee would often talk about what a wonderful friend, colleague, and advisor John F. Wolfe was. Wolfe was always focused

FIGURE 2.1. The composition of the Board of Trustees that brought Gordon Gee back to Ohio State. From left first row: Dimon McPherson, Karen Hendricks, Gordon Gee, Board Chair Gil Cloyd, Brian Hicks, Douglas Borror. Second row from left: Leslie Wexner, student trustee Christopher Alvarez-Breckenridge, Walden O'Dell, Ronald Ratner, John Ong, Jo Ann Davidson, Alex Shumate, Algenon Marbley, Alan Brass, student trustee Debra Van Kamp, Robert Schottenstein, Board Secretary David Frantz, John Fisher. Credit: The Ohio State University.

FIGURE 2.2. Gordon Gee and his close friend Jack Kessler. Credit: The Ohio State University.

THE GEE RETURN AND TRANSITION

FIGURE 2.3. (from left) Annie Glenn, Ann Wolfe, John F. Wolfe, John Glenn, Gordon Gee. The Glenns and the Wolfes were very close friends of Gee. Credit: The Ohio State University.

on what was best for the Columbus community and the university. Gee felt that Wolfe was one of the most honorable people he had met, someone that could be trusted in the most sensitive and challenging situations.

The courtship to recruit Gee had its ups and downs, including a secret trip to Nashville by Wexner and Kessler, who believed that Gee would return to Ohio. But then followed a statement that Gee would not be leaving Vanderbilt, which in turn inspired a broad-based campaign led by Wexner, Kessler, and Rebekah Gee to convince him to "come home." The clincher was a secret visit by Gee to Columbus and the OSU campus on July 8 orchestrated by Kessler.

Thus, on July 12, 2007, the OSU Board of Trustees unanimously welcomed Gordon Gee back as the fourteenth president of The Ohio State University in a very joyous, emotional, and optimistic meeting held at the Longaberger Alumni House (see Figure 2.4). Gee's comments touched all the appropriate points, thanking those who had been instrumental in his recruitment and thanking his former colleagues at Vanderbilt who had made his experience

FIGURE 2.4. A very happy Gordon Gee leaving the Board of Trustees meeting after his well-received remarks. Behind him is Gil Cloyd, chair of the board and chair of the search committee that selected Gee. Behind Cloyd and to the left is Gee's daughter Rebekah, and behind her and to the left is her late husband Allan. Credit: The Ohio State University.

there so uplifting. Probably the most revealing and pointed comment Gee made was his commitment to public higher education; he stated:

> Perhaps the most compelling reason I am here, I can now sleep at night. I have spent 10 years, not in the wilderness, because I love those institutions [Brown and Vanderbilt], but I woke up every morning, I said why am I here? A private institution has a particular role to play, but 80 percent of the students in this country are educated in our public universities. They are the front door to the American dream. They represent what life is about. They represent what this nation is about, and I have returned to the great opportunity that exists. I believe, I believe in every fiber of my being, in the public university, in the land-grant mission of this public university.

Later in his remarks, Gee previewed some of the dominant themes of his new administration:

But the fundamental challenge, I believe, centers around people and ideas. We must capture the hearts and minds of the people Of Ohio . . .

. . . we must create a climate of dignity and respect for each and we must not be pugilistic with each other. We must . . . understand the value of this great university. We must engage and win the battle of talent. It's all about talent. We will win that battle for talent. And the corollary is that we must win the battle of ideas . . . There can't be a great university unless we are a place of great ideas . . .

. . . we must not think of our size as an impediment, but as an opportunity . . . We are the most massive intellectual platform in America, gathered on one campus.

We will only be that if we can think and act and operationalize ourselves as one university. We can't be eighteen colleges connected by a heating plant. We can't be a series of departments connected by telephone lines. We have to act—and you're going to hear this theme from me a lot—we have to be one university.

The Transition

Gee was named president on July 12, but his first official day as the leader of the university was October 1 Thus, Gee had a transition period of almost three months, and he vowed to use that time well. He knew that the clock started counting not on your first official day on the job, but on the day you were named. Throughout this transition period, Joe Alutto served as interim president, but Gee was very active talking with OSU personnel on campus, off campus, on the phone, and by e-mail.

He began the process of reconnecting with the people of Ohio and with the political leadership of the state. He began to build his administration by bringing back some people who had worked for him in his first administration, such as Jeff Kaplan and Herb Asher, and decided early on that interim president Alutto would be the provost.

Gee also commissioned a distinguished group of academic leaders led by Dr. C. Peter Magrath to review the state of the university and to advise Gee on both the opportunities and challenges that faced the university. They spent three days on campus in September and completed their work in short order so that Gee was able to distribute their report in November 2007 to the President's Council and other university entities. The report was an optimistic one, but with aspirational goals that would be difficult to accomplish. The report stated that Ohio State "is well positioned to emerge as a premier public Land-Grant University building on the energy and vision of a new president and the unprecedented enthusiasm of the Ohio State community and the citizens of the state. This is a unique leadership moment at Ohio State." The report laid out four policy objectives along with associated implementation targets. The policy objectives were:

1. Ohio State commits itself to being one of America's top three land-grant universities in the next five years.
2. Ohio State commits itself as a state leader to being one of Ohio's principal drivers in building a stronger, vibrant, state economy.
3. Ohio State commits itself to becoming one of the top internationalized universities in the next five years by developing a focused and coordinated set of innovative educational and research programs.
4. Ohio State commits itself to leading a policy discussion on access and diversity.

These policy objectives along with the specific recommendations to accomplish them became important guideposts for the second Gee administration.

In this interim period, Gee was also highly active and visible to the student body. He participated in the freshman convocation, helped students move into the residence halls, and attended football games. At the convocation, Gee offered inspirational comments, linking his return and the freshman arrival on campus: "We are here—you and I—because Ohio State is a remarkable institution, without peer in the breadth of its academic programs and the depth of their quality."

He later remarked to the students:

> You have chosen well. This is Ohio State's time. This is your time.
>
> You are embarking on a spiritual journey. A time of self-examination and personal growth. Along the way, you will be connected to the people of Ohio State and to its traditions in ways deep and strong.
>
> What is this Ohio State spirit?
> You will hear it in the words of "Carmen Ohio."
> You will see it when we walk into Ohio Stadium.
> You will feel it crossing the Oval.
> You will know it when I hand you your diploma.
> You are Ohio State spirit.
> That spirit brought me home to Ohio State.

THE GEE RETURN AND TRANSITION

It was evident from the very outset of his second OSU presidency that Gee was deeply committed to the success and well-being of the Ohio State student body.

Although Gee only officially started on October 1, he delivered a major policy address to the Faculty Council on October 4. It was obvious to all who heard or read the speech that the new president had "hit the ground running," that the transition period had been a time for serious contemplation about the condition and future of the university. In his Faculty Council address, Gee outlined his six strategic goals for the university:

1. Forge one Ohio State University.
2. Put students first.
3. Focus on faculty success as never before.
4. Recast our research agenda.
5. Commit to our communities and revitalize our covenants with them.
6. Simplify university systems and structures.

In his speech, Gee elaborated on these objectives to give them content and meaning so that his university colleagues would better understand the agenda that would be driving many university decisions. He focused particularly on the first objective—one university—because it reflected a fundamental change in how the university saw itself and how it presented itself to the world outside the university. It was also likely to be the most difficult objective to achieve because of the university's size, comprehensiveness, complexity, patterns of operations, and culture. But it did become a core organizing and prioritizing theme in the second Gee presidency. In his address to the Faculty Council, Gee argued that in the time between his first and second presidencies, the university had moved from good to excellent. Now it was time to move from excellent to eminent. From excellence to eminence became a recurring theme.

In summary, the Gee transition was very successful. He connected well to the students, faculty, staff, and deans as well as to the broader Columbus and state communities. He laid out a vision for the university that built upon the excitement generated by his return to the university. Now it was time to build the leadership team that would move the university from excellence to eminence.

3

Building a Team

Gee had ambitious goals for his second administration. To achieve these, he believed he had to assemble the best talent and to create a university culture that enabled that talent to flourish (see chapter 4). His approach to attracting talent had a number of core principles. First, the talented individuals he wanted at Ohio State would come from a very diverse set of professional and occupational backgrounds, and not only from academia. The business community, the nonprofit world, the public sector, and other domains could all be important sources of talent. Second, the university president had to take an active role in assembling talent. One could not sit back and wait for people to come to you. One could not rely only upon traditional academic search committees to uncover qualified persons. And one could not rely too heavily on hired gun search firms to identify talent.

Gee believed that because he had been a university president for so many years and at five different institutions, he had a good sense of the external talent pool and, more importantly, a set of confidants and colleagues he could turn to for advice on hiring decisions. Gee thought that often the ideal candidate for a position was the person who was *not* seeking to move to Ohio State. For Gee, this meant that he would have to be personally involved in the recruitment process to convert a reluctant candidate into a genuine prospect. The final principle that drove Gee's thinking about recruitment was to not slot potential hires into narrow categories based on their current and former positions, but instead to ask how a person's skill set could contribute to the many tasks that needed to be done.

FIGURE 3.1. Provost Joe Alutto with Board of Trustee member Robert Schottenstein (center) and President Gee. Credit: The Ohio State University.

Thus, when Gee returned to Ohio State, he retained numerous Ohio State personnel such as Joe Alutto (provost; see Figure 3.1); Chris Culley (general counsel); Jay Kasey, who moved from being the chief operating officer of The Ohio State University Health System to senior vice president for Administration and Planning); Larry Llewellyn (human resources); Bobby Moser (agriculture; see Figure 3.2); Bill Shkurti, (business and finance; see Figure 3.4); Curt Steiner (university relations); Dick Stoddard (director of federal relations and special assistant to the president); and Caroline Whitacre (research; see Figure 3.3).

And he brought back people who had previously worked for him at Ohio State, such as Steve Gabbe, Jeff Kaplan, Kate Wolford, and Herb Asher. Throughout his second term he also recruited colleagues from other higher education institutions: Bruce McPheron from Penn State as vice president for agriculture; Joe Steinmetz from the University of Kansas as executive dean of the arts and sciences; Javaune Adams-Gaston (see Figures 3.5–3.8) from the University of Maryland as the vice president for student life; Peter Weiler from Penn State as vice president for development, and later Michael Eicher from Johns Hopkins to head development; Dolan Evanovich from the University of Connecticut to head enrollment services and planning; Jonathan Hook from Baylor to be the chief investment officer; and Brian Cummings from the University of Utah to head technology commercialization.

FIGURE 3.2. Gordon Gee and Bobby Moser (agriculture vice president) in a serious conversation. Credit: The Ohio State University.

FIGURE 3.3. Carol Whitacre (research vice president) and Gordon Gee. Credit: The Ohio State University.

FIGURE 3.4. David Frantz looking skeptically at finance vice president Bill Shkurti. Credit: The Ohio State University.

FIGURE 3.5. Geoff Chatas, Shkurti's successor as finance vice president; Kate Wolford; general counsel Chris Culley; and Katie Chatas. Credit: The Ohio State University.

FIGURE 3.6. Jeff Kaplan and Gordon Gee walking on the Oval. Credit: The Ohio State University.

FIGURE 3.7. Gordon Gee discussing government relations with Curt Steiner (left), director of federal relations Dick Stoddard, and counselor to the president Herb Asher. Credit: The Ohio State University.

FIGURE 3.8. Dr. Jauvanne Adams-Gaston, student affairs vice president, greets President Obama at the June 2013 spring commencement. Credit: The Ohio State University.

Chapter 3

Particularly noteworthy in Gee's recruiting from other academic institutions was bringing two former university presidents to Ohio State to serve in key positions. Gee convinced Andy Sorenson, former president of the University of South Carolina and the University of Alabama to head the development/advancement effort at Ohio State. Tragically Sorenson died suddenly and was later succeeded by Mike Eicher. Gee also got David Williams to come to Ohio State as dean of the college of engineering. Williams had been president of the University of Alabama, Huntsville.

The business community was also a major source of talent for Gee. He brought Geoff Chatas to Ohio State as senior vice president for business and finance and chief financial officer. Prior to coming to Ohio State, Chatas was the managing director for the Infrastructure Investments group at JP Morgan Asset Management. Tom Katzenmeyer (see Figure 3.9) came to Ohio State to be the senior vice president for university communications; previously he had been at The Limited (now L Brands) as head of investor relations. Gee's choice for dean of the Fisher College of Business was Christine Poon, formerly vice chairman and member of the board of Johnson & Johnson and worldwide chair of the Pharmaceuticals Group. Gee brought in Kathleen McCutcheon to be the vice president for human resources; McCutcheon had been with AIG. AJ Douglas followed McCutcheon as HR vice president; Douglas had been with the consulting firm Senn-Delaney, which had worked very closely with Ohio State on culture transformation initiatives (see chapter 4). The HR job title was later changed to senior vice president for talent, culture, and human resources, very much reflecting Gee's perspective on personnel.

From the public sector, Gee recruited Joyce Beatty to be senior vice president of outreach and engagement. Beatty had been a member of the Ohio House of Representatives, where she had been the House minority leader. She had also been a small business owner and active in various nonprofit and social service organizations. To head the College of Public Health, Gee worked to get William Martin, who had been at the Eunice Kennedy Shriver National Institute of Child Health and Human Development at the National Institutes of Health, where he was the associate director for disease prevention and health. Lonnie King was selected as dean of the College of Veterinary Medicine. Prior to that, he was at the Center for Disease Control's National Center for Zoonotic, Vector-Borne, and Enteric Diseases.

I could go on and on with many more examples of the focus on talent. Talented persons were everywhere, but one first had to identify them and then convince them to become Buckeyes. Not all of Gee's hires were successful, but they were all exciting choices when they were selected. Gee did not believe

FIGURE 3.9. Gordon Gee and Communications Vice President Tom Katzenmeyer. Credit: The Ohio State University.

in settling for second best. The above list of hires does not begin to capture the recruitment process and the role of the university president in bringing talent to Ohio State. Thus, the remainder of this chapter will be a set of mini-case studies of how certain key appointees came to Ohio State and Gordon Gee's role in achieving these outcomes. In interviews with many of these individuals—Steinmetz, Eicher, McPherson, Chatas, Adams-Gaston, Evanovich, and others, they all said that Gee was an unbelievably effective and persuasive recruiter. He brought passion and enthusiasm, and knowledge and insight to the endeavor. He knew which buttons to push and would not take no for an answer. Gee knew how to recruit not only the candidate but also the spouse and family. Almost everyone I interviewed said that they had never seen a university president as immersed and as successful in the recruiting process.

Probably the best example of Gee's active role in the talent acquisition process was the successful recruitment of Joe Steinmetz to be the Executive Dean of the College of Arts and Sciences. In Gee's first administration, there were five colleges of the arts and sciences, and efforts were made to consolidate these five colleges into one unified college of arts and sciences. These efforts were not successful the first time around, but in the second Gee administration this consolidation was accomplished (see chapter 7). One reason for the consolidation was to enhance the profile and role of the arts and sciences at Ohio State. To that end, Gee believed he needed a strong, able executive dean, and so a search process was begun. At the outset, it was a typical search process with an internal search committee composed of faculty, staff, and students and an external firm hired to help the search committee identify the best candidates. When the committee gave Gee its recommended finalists some months later, he examined the three recommended names and told the search committee that none of their finalists were acceptable to him. He asked the search committee whether these three names were really the best candidates out there. Some members of the search committee said no, but that other, more qualified candidates did not apply and/or were not interested in the Ohio State position. This response frustrated Gee. He asked whether the search committee was proactive in seeking out candidates. Or did the search committee just sit back passively and wait to see who had applied? Or did the search committee rely too heavily on the external search firm? Gee told the committee that the best candidate is often the person who does not want to move, who does not want to come to Ohio State. Then Gee asked who was the best candidate who had not applied and was told it was Joe Steinmetz, the dean of the College of Liberal Arts and Sciences at the University of Kansas. Gee then thanked the search committee for its work and began his own personal recruitment of Steinmetz. He first checked with colleagues internally and externally that Steinmetz was indeed the person for the Ohio State job, and the answer was an enthusiastic yes. Gee then contacted Steinmetz personally and said he wanted to talk to him about the Ohio State position. Without going into great detail here, the courtship began. It entailed many steps, including a "secret meeting" at an airport hotel in Indianapolis. Steinmetz himself commented to me that Gee's commitment and persistence amazed him and certainly made Steinmetz feel like he was the most important hire for Ohio State. The end result was Joe Steinmetz moved to Ohio State to become the executive dean of the Arts and

BUILDING A TEAM

FIGURE 3.10. (left) Dr. Steve Gabbe, head of the medical center, and Dr. Pat Gabbe; Dr. Joe Steinmetz, executive dean of the arts and sciences and later provost, and Sandy Steinmetz. Credit: The Ohio State University.

Sciences, did a fine job in that capacity, and later became the University Provost (see Figure 3.10). Later Steinmetz moved from Ohio State to become the chancellor of the University of Arkansas at Fayetteville. For Gee, this entire episode reinforced his already strong belief that the university president must be actively engaged in recruiting talent. You may not always be successful, and your "successes" may not always work out well. But the president has the responsibility to try.

As mentioned earlier in the chapter, Gee was successful in recruiting two former university presidents (Sorenson and Williams) to join him at Ohio State in vital but "lesser" roles. Here the key to Gee's success was his ability to articulate a vision that he knew would intrigue the two former presidents. These former presidents knew that Gee would empower them and would not micromanage them. Instead, he encouraged them to be expansive and ambitious in how they approached their new responsibilities.

Gee's recruitment of Geoff Chatas to be the senior vice president for business took a similar path. Gee defined the job as much more than being a numbers cruncher or book balancer. He was looking for someone who would be a central player in his core policy leadership team. And Gee also wanted a

CHAPTER 3

FIGURE 3.11. Development Vice President Mike Eicher (left), Gordon Gee, Jeff Kaplan, and Brandon Eicher. Credit: The Ohio State University.

chief financial officer who would be empowered to identify alternative revenue streams (see chapter 12) and generate strategies to seek them out. Gee created and described a position that he knew would excite Chatas and attract him to Ohio State.

Gee's recruitment of Mike Eicher had some unique features (see Figure 3.11). Before his Johns Hopkins stint, Eicher had been at UCLA. Gee new that Eicher enjoyed the pageantry and traditions of university life, so he made sure that Eicher visited Ohio State on a home football weekend, where Eicher was fully immersed in the hoopla surrounding the game. He sat in the president's box in Ohio Stadium, went down to the sidelines during the game, heard the OSU marching band in its pre-game performance, and traipsed the parking lots where the fans were tailgating. Eicher told me that this experience was one of a number of events that really won him over about Ohio State.

Gee's recruitment of Joyce Beatty to be the senior vice president for Outreach and Engagement was also a very personalized endeavor (see Figure 3.12). As mentioned earlier, Beatty had been the minority leader of the Ohio House

FIGURE 3.12. Outreach and Engagement Vice President Joyce Beatty standing between two OSU trustees, Alex Shumate (left) and Judge Algenon Marbley, in Ohio Stadium. Credit: The Ohio State University.

of Representatives and had an extensive background in the private and nonprofit sectors. She was also a highly visible member of the central Ohio civic and political community. To get her to come to Ohio State, Gee had to assure her about her portfolio, about her freedom to operate in the broader community, and about her direct access to Gee. He did all these things, and Beatty, somewhat to the surprise of many, came to the university. She served the university and Gee well by better linking the university to the community and by serving as a set of eyes and ears for Gee about community politics. Beatty left the university to run successfully for the US House of Representatives, a very courageous move, as discussed in chapter 11.

Similar to the Beatty recruitment, Gee was able to personally recruit Tom Katzenmeyer to join his university team as senior vice president for University Communications. Katzenmeyer had been at The Limited (now L Brands) for 14 years as head of investor relations. Before that he had been active in Democratic Party politics and had worked in the administration of Governor Richard Celeste. Prior to Katzenmeyer's arrival, Curt Steiner had been senior

Chapter 3

vice president for University Relations, which included both university communications and government affairs. When Katzenmeyer arrived, Steiner's portfolio was changed to Government Affairs. Thus, Gee had working for him and the university three people in Beatty, Steiner, and Katzenmeyer who were incredibly well connected to the broader civic, political, and business communities. Yet even with these three superb colleagues, Gee immersed himself in the external, off-campus politics of the university.

One reason Gee was such an effective recruiter of talent is that he made it exciting to work for him and for the university. This is reflected in the number of current and former OSU leaders who stayed on or came back to work for him. Foremost among these was Joe Alutto, who became Gee's executive vice president and provost in his second administration. Joe had held many positions, including interim president, business college dean, and others. Gee described Joe's willingness to serve as provost as absolutely critical to the success of his administration. Gee said that Joe provided the necessary discipline and focus as Gee himself was out there saying yes to too many requests. According to Gee, Joe made the trains run on time. He enabled Gee to be confident that many of the internal university issues were being addressed in a timely and competent fashion. Alutto's leadership allowed Gee to do many things he would not otherwise have been able to do.

Chris Culley also stayed on as vice president for Legal Affairs and General Counsel. But Culley was more than a lawyer. He was a problem solver who looked at issues from a legal and a broader perspective. He was very much a worrier (a good thing to Gee) who tried to anticipate three moves ahead. He was very much a part of the core leadership team and was heavily involved in the issues of the day.

Gee also brought back to Ohio State from Vanderbilt Steve Gabbe as the senior vice president for the Medical Center and Health Sciences (see chapter 15) and Jeff Kaplan as senior vice president and special assistant to the president. Gee described Kaplan as his utility infielder who took on assignments and responsibilities, whether this was running university development or leading university planning efforts or whatever. Like Steiner, Beatty, Katzenmeyer, and Asher, Kaplan was very well connected to key players in the Columbus community. But unlike these others, Kaplan always operated very quietly behind the scenes. He was a wonderful link for Gee to various external constituencies and always pursued Gee's and the university's agenda.

Gee also brought back to Ohio State from Brown Kate Wolford as assistant to the president and director of operations. Or, in other words, to run his life, his schedule and the office (see chapter 5). Wolford had gone with Gee to

Brown, but stayed at Brown when Gee went to Vanderbilt. Now she returned to help manage Gee's most valuable resource—his time. Gee also plucked from retirement Herb Asher, who had worked in his first administration as special assistant, counselor and advisor, both with respect to the internal politics of the university as well as external state and national politics. When Steiner departed the university, Asher took on the position of senior vice president for Government Affairs. Asher's main reason for "unretiring" was that it was fun to work for Gee. Gee made one feel good about the university, about public higher education, and about the collective enterprise that was Ohio State. Almost every senior administrator I interviewed echoed that sentiment; working for Ohio State was more than a job, mainly because Gordon Gee turned it into a mission and a calling.

One of the fun aspects of working for Gee was that he was always contacting his senior staff to ask them what was happening, not only in their own shops, but also throughout the university and the broader community. Gee was an incredibly active information seeker, especially on university politics and on the politics of the community, the state of Ohio, and Washington, DC. Colleagues such as Jeff Kaplan, Curt Steiner, Joyce Beatty, Chris Culley, Herb Asher, Tom Katzenmeyer, Dick Stoddard, and others would regularly hear from Gee requesting the latest scuttlebutt. It got to the point where one always wanted to have some tidbits of information ready to share with the president. For example, Dick Stoddard had held a number of university positions in academic departments and the office of research and also represented Ohio State on Capitol Hill and at the higher education professional associations in Washington, DC. He knew that Gee would routinely interrogate him with such open-ended questions such as "What's new?" "What are you hearing?" and "What's going on?" Stoddard decided that he would always be ready with information when Gee inquired.

This information seeking behavior on the part of Gee meant that his senior colleagues were in regular personal conversations with the president beyond all the formal meetings that occurred. One felt that Gee was very accessible, that one did not have to go through bureaucratic barriers to talk to the president. More importantly, Gee wanted to hear the good news *and* the bad news. And Gee never shot the messenger delivering bad news. This mindset facilitated the free flow of information essential to success.

Gee was also very active in the recruitment of faculty to the university, but here at the request of deans and department chairs. Deans and department chairs knew that if a call from the president or a visit to his office would help in the recruitment of faculty, Gee would say yes and his schedulers would

CHAPTER 3

make that happen in a timely fashion. Gee was also active in the recruitment of students, not simply by visiting high schools and holding a major session in the auditorium, but also through more personalized contact. If a parent or a legislator or anyone came up to Gee and said that they had a child who had been accepted to Ohio State and that they hoped the child would go to Ohio State, Gee would instantly volunteer to call the son or daughter and make the case for Ohio State. Parents were thrilled that a university president would do this, and the recipients of the calls—the students—were surprised and stunned and at the very least gave Ohio State a much closer look.

Thus, Gee believed that the university president must play a central role in the recruitment of talent. He also believed that he had a major responsibility to help retain the talented people who were already at Ohio State and who might be lured away by OSU's competitors. Gee tried to impress upon the provost, the deans, and the department chairs to constantly be re-recruiting existing talent and not simply wait to make counteroffers when other institutions were trying to steal them. (As a side note, after he left Ohio State to become the president of West Virginia University for the second time, Gee continued to demonstrate his recruiting skills by poaching faculty talent nationally [including numerous individuals from the Ohio State Medical Center] to become members of the West Virginia University community in Morgantown.)

The university president also had the responsibility to replace people who were not getting the job done. Gee could be tough in these matters, but in most cases he made sure that people losing their positions maintained their professional dignity and reputation. And in many instances, he helped the departing person find a new job elsewhere. An amusing story shows Gee's humanity in these sensitive personnel matters. When he returned to Ohio State, Gee encountered a person from his first administration who was still working at Ohio State. Gee said to me, "I thought I had fired him." And I replied, "No, you put him on special assignment. And ten years later he is still working at the university." Gee acknowledged that this was actually a very good outcome because there was a much better match between the person's skill set and the responsibilities of his current position than there was in his previous job.

In summary, Gee assembled an impressive leadership team that most often worked in a constructive and collegial fashion, but occasionally less so. Gee acknowledged in my interview with him that he should have devoted more time to ensuring that all members of the team were working well together, that they respected each other's contributions, and that they celebrated the accomplishments of their colleagues. This, in part, was what the focus on culture and culture change was designed to do, a topic discussed in the next chapter.

Finally, a personal note: In all my years at Ohio State, my familiarity with the presidents of many Ohio public institutions, and my lesser familiarity with the presidents of Big Ten universities, I have never observed a university president who took such an active and persistent role in recruiting and retaining talent as Gordon Gee. Talent was essential to achieving his goals for the university. And to be maximally successful, that talent needed to work in a supportive and inclusive environment.

4

Shaping a University Culture

In his first term as Ohio State's president, Gee frequently compared the university to Noah's Ark: there was two of everything. He complained about the redundancies, the inefficiencies, the silos, and the unhealthy internal competition, all of which undermined the collegial, collaborative, supportive environment that an institution needed to achieve success. When he returned for his second presidency, Gee used the term "One University" to label the culture and mindset he sought for Ohio State. At the outset, many of his colleagues did not know what "One University" really meant. And one colleague (Asher) teased Gordon that before there could be "one university," there first needed to be one medical center, for the OSU Medical Center was rife with internal conflict and unhealthy competition (see chapter 15).

On October 4, 2007, only a few days after his second term officially began, Gee addressed the Faculty Council to present his vision and aspirations for Ohio State. After discussing some of the impressive trends and developments at Ohio State, including enhanced student quality, impressive faculty successes, major research advances, and more, Gee than declared that Ohio State University had moved from good to excellent and it was now time to move from excellent to eminent. He then presented six strategic goals "that will continue the momentum at the university." And at the top of the list was a commitment to forge "one Ohio State University." Gee asserted that Ohio State was "the most massive intellectual platform in America gathered on one campus." As such, he wanted the university to think of itself comprehensively and "not a collection of colleges hitched to a heating plant, or a detachment of departments connected by corridors." Instead, Gee wanted the university to be more transinstitutional in its approach. For Gee, transinstitutional did not mean restructuring and/or abolishing the existing academic framework of colleges and departments. But it did mean "creating incentives that encourage the emergence of free-standing new structures that cut across boundaries and make departmental and college borders more permeable." The later development and implementation of the Discovery Themes (see chapter 11) is an example of this new perspective. Gee also stressed that the university must recognize faculty for their strengths, even if these strengths and contributions did not fit neatly within department and disciplinary boundaries. Gee argued that faculty members contribute in different ways to their research, teaching, and service responsibilities and that this mix will change for individual faculty members at different stages of their careers. Thus, the university needed to develop a reward system that recognized the value of transinstitutional contributions as well as the unique contributions and career paths of many faculty.

Thus, on October 4, the faculty heard the first element of "one Ohio State." They also heard President Gee articulate the five additional strategies (numbers 2 through 6) goals listed below:

1. **Forge One Ohio State University.** We are the most massive intellectual platform in America gathered on one campus. We unite a stellar liberal arts tradition with professional schools second to none and health sciences on the frontiers of medical discovery. We must capitalize on that platform by defining ourselves comprehensively.
2. **Put Students First.** Being student-centered is a fundamental priority for Ohio State. We must provide our students—undergraduate, graduate, and professional students alike—with unique and compelling educational experiences.
3. **Focus on Faculty Success.** We must do everything we can to retain, attract, and reward world-class teachers and researchers in all academic areas of the university. Likewise, we have great expectations that our faculty will contribute in remarkable ways to the success of their students, the community, the state, and beyond.
4. **Recast Our Research Agenda.** Our mission to create new knowledge is considered by many to be a sacred social compact. Ohio State must not fail to keep that compact. Accordingly, we must stimulate new discoveries on the frontier of research and innovation in all its forms and all across the institution.
5. **Commit to Our Communities.** We must revitalize our covenants with our communities and, understanding our responsibilities to Ohio's tax-

payers who want their assets to be used wisely, we must make a difference in the state and in the world.
6. **Simplify University Systems and Structure.** It is only through an uncompromising focus on performance, through transparency and accountability that Ohio State will earn the public trust and allow our faculty, staff, and students to thrive. We will, therefore, examine and modify our administrative practices, review our budget system, share resources, and streamline services.

Note that immediately after one university came putting students first. This was core to Gee's vision of a university and to his own commitment of his time and energy (see chapters 6, 13, 17, and 18). It was a reflection that the failure to address student life and the student experience in such areas as affordability, student success, student safety, and others would open up the university to significant external and internal criticism. And immediately after students first was faculty success. Again, the support of faculty was central to Gee's vision of a successful university. And a productive and committed faculty was clearly critical to the ability of the university to be a significant contributor to the well-being of Ohio and the nation.

Gee believed that a major intervention was required to address some of the dysfunctions of the university culture that impeded progress and created a less than optimal work environment. Thus, he hired the firm of Senn-Delaney to help the university achieve a high-performance culture. Two people from the firm were especially critical to this endeavor—Larry Senn and Andrea "AJ" Douglas. The plan was to have the very top leadership stratum of the university undergo a series of exercises and experiences to foster collegiality, teamwork, trust, an appreciation of the contributions of others, and a broader appreciation of the university writ large rather than one's own narrow area. This experience was then replicated for other leadership circles within the university. There were materials focusing on the broader question of culture-building, but also more specific topics such as how to have shorter, more productive meetings. Most of the participants felt that, at minimum, they came away from the Senn-Delaney experience with a greater appreciation of their colleagues and their roles within the university. In addition, many participants gained keen insights into what was necessary to move successfully toward "one university." Senn and Douglas did a superb job working with their Ohio State clients. Some years later, Douglas formally joined the Ohio State leadership team as the senior vice president for Culture, Talent, and Human Resources, and in this job she learned that it was easier to teach about culture change than to do it as a university vice president. Note that the title of her position changed with the inclusion of culture and talent, demonstrating how the mission of the former human resources office had been greatly reshaped and expanded. While the HR office in the past may have been focused on the routines and paperwork of personnel, now it was charged to think more expansively about how to build a more productive culture and how to better support the recruitment and retention activities of the university.

Gee himself went beyond the Senn-Delaney culture shaping and issued his own "Rules of Engagement," the full text of which is in Appendix A. At the top of the list were two closely interrelated statements: "We must hire and keep extraordinary people" and "The acid test of leadership is the ability to hire and keep extraordinary people." Gee then describes the characteristics of extraordinary people. First they must be smart, but that does not mean acting smart, demonstrating superiority over others. A smart person should be able to listen carefully and exercise common sense as well as good judgment and discernment. The smart person should also be able to tell the important from the unimportant and to express ideas in a clear and direct fashion. Gee stressed the importance of people who were able to get things done in a timely fashion and who understood that all decisions entailed risk and were willing to take that risk. Next Gee emphasized that extraordinary people are nice; they are respectful and courteous with the "proper touch of humility." They are not irritable, arrogant, or rude, and they shun academic politics. They take their colleagues seriously, but do not take themselves too seriously. And they are not status conscious, hung up on titles. Finally, the extraordinary person is one who has developed the "habit, courage, and ability to be straightforward."

One can see in this description of the extraordinary person and in Gee's other rules of engagement how central effective interpersonal relationships are to institutional success and how a toxic culture will bring misery to colleagues and grief to an institution's goals and objectives. In my personal interview with Gee, he expressed some regret that he was not more actively engaged in promoting a healthy culture and "enforcing" the rules of engagement. He acknowledged that when you hire highly talented and ambitious people, there would inevitably be frictions, sharp elbows, and the like, and a culture-shaping experience like Senn-Delaney and a written rules of engagement might not be sufficient to ensure good behavior. The president may have to step in on occasion to restore peace and tranquility.

It is difficult to quantify precisely how much the one university approach and concomitant culture shaping initiatives changed the university. But one can point to many examples where one university took hold. For one thing, the one university vocabulary became prominent so that as ideas and proposals developed, it became routine to ask how they would affect "one university." That is, the one university approach became a prism through which many university decisions and actions were evaluated. The one university approach was also reflected in the increased number of joint faculty appointments made across two or more academic units beyond the impact of the Discovery Themes. And the one university approach raised questions about the promotion and tenure process and its reform: how does one address non-traditional academic appointments, and how does one evaluate non-traditional career paths with non-traditional academic contributions? The move to the "advancement" model (see chapter 8) was undergirded by the notion that Ohio State look at university communications, alumni relations, and development/fundraising in a more comprehensive and university-centered way. Likewise, the subsequent strategic planning process begun in 2010 was informed by the one university approach in a number of ways, foremost being the belief that an effective strategy focuses more on the university as a whole and its success and survival rather than on more traditional concerns, such as specific academic programs or faculty salaries or new facilities.

Finally, the One Ohio State University Framework, a document focusing on the university's physical environment, was very much influenced by the one university goal. The intent of the framework was to be transinstitutional, ensuring that academic mission drives decisions about the physical environment and integrating strategic, physical, and financial planning. This framework will help guide specific facilities' decisions over a long span of time—even decades—as particular decisions could be placed in a broader context to determine whether they contribute to the larger vision guiding the university. Thus, Gee's initial emphasis on "One University" ultimately helped shape many processes, decisions, and outcomes at Ohio State. The question remains how sustainable is this. How strong will the commitment be from successive university leadership teams and future Boards of Trustees? Certainly, the Framework plan, for example, continues as a guidepost for future facilities' decisions if subsequent leadership teams opt to utilize the Framework Plan.

5

The Face of the University

Organizing the Calendar

Introduction

Gordon Gee believed that his most significant resource was his time, which he needed to use strategically and purposively. He saw himself as the major face of the university to audiences on campus, in Columbus, throughout Ohio, and in Washington, DC, and other national and international settings. In order to work successfully with all these audiences and in all those settings, his calendar had to be constructed to maximize the best uses of his time. The idea of "downtime" was alien to Gee He believed that the job of university president did not fit into a traditional 9 to 5, Monday through Friday schedule. Instead, it was a 24/7 job. Work-life balance would take care of itself. Gee's interpersonal skills, his passion for Ohio State University, his genuine regard for people, and his boundless energy and enthusiasm were incredible assets that needed to be utilized and exploited to the fullest. Thus, he created a team of wonderfully talented colleagues led by Kate Wolford to organize and build his calendar. We will highlight the activities of this team in the second part of the chapter. But first I want to give the reader a sense of what the Gee calendar looked like.

The Gee Calendar

The following is a typical day on campus in the life of Gordon Gee. The actual day was Thursday, October 20, 2011. And the calendar does not reflect that Gee

CHAPTER 5

was up hours earlier than his first appointment reading and exercising. It also does not include the note that October 20 was the birthday of Chris Culley and Tami Longaberger and that Gordon should call them at the numbers listed on the calendar.

TIME	ACTIVITY
7:30–8:30 am	Meeting with Alex Shumate at Pizzuti House (Shumate is a member of the OSU Board of Trustees, and Pizzuti House is the university residence.)
8:30 am	Depart for campus
9:00–10:00 am	Commercialization Structure meeting with Geoff Chatas (senior vice president for finance), Joe Alutto (provost), Gil Cloyd and Jeff Wadsworth (trustees) in 205 Bricker Hall (president's office)
10:00–10:30 am	Office time
10:30–11:00	Meeting with Egondu Onyejekwe in 205 Bricker Hall
11:00–11:15	Phone call with Bill Cheng
11:30–Noon	Walk around time at the Ohio Union (the student union)
Noon–12:30 pm	International Poverty Solutions Collaborative Conference—REMARKS at Ohio Union, Archie Griffin Ballroom
12:30–1:30 pm	Faculty lunch in 205 Bricker Hall
1:30–1:45 pm	Michelle Compston (scheduler) stopping by
1:45 pm	Depart for Fisher College of Business
2:00–2:45 pm	Chris Poon annual dean meeting in Dean Poon's office, 201 Fisher Hall
3:00–3:30 pm	Meeting with Joe Alutto and Jeff Kaplan (senior vice president) in 205 Bricker Hall
3:30–4:00 pm	Meeting with Jeff Kaplan and Tom Katzenmeyer (senior vice president) about Medical Center naming in 205 Bricker Hall
4:15 pm	Depart for Mendenhall Lab

TIME	ACTIVITY
4:30–5:15 pm	First Year Success Leadership series—REMARKS in 173 Mendenhall Lab
5:15–5:30	Stop by History of Art Lecture—George Skestos (former trustee) sponsor in 100 Mendenhall Lab
5:45–6:15	South Asian Studies Initiative reception—REMARKS in Hagerty Hall Auditorium
6:30–7:00 pm	Stop by Kids'nKamp Auction (Donna Foster request) at Ohio Stadium (the football stadium) Huntington Club
7:15–7:25 pm	Diversity Lecturer-Professor Jorge Castaneda—REMARKS at Ohio Union, Performance Hall

Note that this calendar day is at least a twelve-hour commitment, assuming that Gee arrived home shortly after the diversity lecture. Note also that Gee delivered remarks at four of the events on the schedule; fortunately, Gee had a superb briefing staff that we will discuss later. Note further that for the last five events on the calendar, Gee only stayed 45 minutes (the First Year Success Leadership series) or less. It was this ability to get in and out of multiple events in a relatively short span of time that enabled Gee to do so many events and say yes to so many groups and organizations that wanted a piece of his time. And this ability reflected his amazing interpersonal skills. Gee could work a room like the best of politicians seeking office. He would give each person in the room a very short period of time, but in that span the person felt that he or she had the undivided attention from the president. And if Gee already knew the person, it made the short visit even more personal because Gee seldom forgot a name or other biographical details about the person. When Gee said, "How wonderful to see you again Mr. Johnson," Mr. Johnson was often stunned and flattered that the university president had remembered his name, his family, his hometown, and other biographical details.

Note also that on October 20, Gee touched base with all of the university's major internal constituencies. He met with three trustees, had lunch with the faculty leadership, and met with many of the senior members of his own leadership team. Although there were no formal meetings with students only, Gee also interacted with a large number of students. His walk around time at the

Chapter 5

Ohio Union drew many students to him. And when students used their phones to let their peers know that President Gee was at the Union, he was quickly surrounded by enthusiastic students who wanted to talk with him and have their pictures taken with him. Indeed, it became a rite of passage that Ohio State students have their picture taken with the president. And at the five evening events there were additional opportunities to mingle with students as well as faculty and other members of the university community.

The use of "walk around time" was a great tactic for Gee to use on campus and off. He might walk over to the English Department and ask the staff whether the department chair was in. If so, Gee would walk in and chat for a few minutes. And if not, everyone in the English Department quickly heard that their president had stopped by. Sometimes if there were a longer break in his calendar, Gee would head downtown to the Statehouse (about two miles away) and just drop in to legislators' offices. If the members were not there, Gee would simply leave messages of best wishes and move on. The word quickly spread that there was actually a university president who came down to the legislature just to chat and say hello, and he did this when the higher education budget was NOT under consideration. It left an indelible impression on the lawmakers that Gee respected their enterprise and liked them as people. He was not an ivory tower president. (We'll say more about this in chapter 18.)

The schedule for October 20, 2011, was typical; most days were at least as packed with events and meetings. It took a village to support such an ambitious schedule: people to identify what events were most critical to the university's success, people to brief the president, people to organize special events when necessary, people to help transport the president from one meeting to another, people to make sure that the president kept on schedule. We will talk about the construction and organization of the president's calendar and who was responsible, but let me conclude this section by moving beyond the daily calendar to the scheduling of less routine events.

As president of Ohio's flagship university, Gee believed that he should personally bring Ohio State to all regions of Ohio. In his first term as OSU president, he would try to visit all 88 Ohio counties on a regular basis. While this was not feasible in his second term, he still believed that he should travel to all regions of the state. Sometimes this was accomplished through a set of one day or overnight trips to particular Ohio destinations. In other case it was done through state (summer) tours, typically multi-day events in which Gee and his entourage visited a cluster of counties in a particular region of the state.

The one-day trips were very carefully organized to maximize exposure to many audiences. For example, if Gee were traveling to Cleveland to meet with a major donor prospect, there would be a stop at the *Cleveland Plain Dealer* to talk with the editorial board or the higher education reporter or simply to visit friends who worked at the newspaper. There might also be a visit to a Cleveland area high school to tout the benefits of an Ohio State education and to recruit students from that school. There would also be a get-together with the local OSU alumni club and visits with Cleveland area public officials working in city, county, and state government. To Gee, the mayor of Cleveland, the county commissioners of Cuyahoga County (the home of Cleveland), and the legislative delegation from northeastern Ohio were all potential or actual university friends who should be cultivated and thanked for their support. If the schedule permitted, Gee would also try to stop by some local businesses run by OSU alumni and/or businesses and companies that had benefitted from university-based research and outreach. And when traveling to Cleveland by car, Gee would work en route. Typically, he would make many phone calls in the car, feeling very comfortable that the driver and other OSU staff in the car would hear his end of the telephone conversations. He would also dictate correspondence while in the car and, on the return trip to Columbus, he would write hand-written personal thank you notes or dictate thank you notes to be typed up back in the office to those people he had just visited hours earlier. When those thank you notes arrived within a few days of Gee's visits, the recipients were genuinely surprised and appreciative of that gesture.

Weekends were not free time for Gee. When he was in town and there were no scheduled university events such as a football game (a weekend-long activity), Gee instructed his staff, especially Tracy Stuck (see Figure 5.1), to build his weekend schedule around student events. Stuck did a superb job identifying student activities that Gee could simply drop in on and also creating opportunities for students to meet and interact with President Gee. Every Thursday Stuck would generate a list of student events happening off campus over the weekend. Stuck was a genius in identifying and creating events. For example, a student might be having a birthday party at his or her off-campus residence, and Stuck would arrange for Gee to stop by the party to the surprise and delight of the student and the guests in attendance. Sometimes while at the party, Gee would call the student's parents and let them know that the party was great and then put the stunned son or daughter on the phone to talk with mom and dad. Or Stuck would create an event such as a birthday party for OSU students whose birthday fell on a particular date. Stuck once built a party around the theme of "art" where the guests were all named Art and the decorations and refreshments reflected the "art" theme, including artichoke dip.

CHAPTER 5

FIGURE 5.1. Gordon Gee and Tracy Stuck. Credit: The Ohio State University.

In other instances, Stuck would provide Gee with information about students encountering difficulties and Gee would call or visit them. For example, a freshman student was suffering from a severe case of homesickness. While her RAs and friends helped her to adjust to college life, a call from Gee provided a boost to her morale. The fact that the university president cared about her convinced her that she belonged at Ohio State. As Gee himself often said, "You can make a big university small, but you can never make a small university big." Stuck told me that Gee gave her clear instructions that he wanted to meet a diverse representation of the Ohio State student body, that there were over 50,000 students in the campus area, and that he did not want to see the same faces at event after event. Stuck made sure that did not happen.

Gee always had student associates accompany him to these events and provide a protective entourage just in case. While Gee's presence probably promoted better student behavior at off-campus parties, there was always the possibility that students could misbehave or perform excessively, particularly in an era of social media and cell phones where everyone could be a photographer. Fortunately, these student-centered events went off without a hitch, reflecting careful planning by Tracy Stuck and her staff, and also good fortune.

THE FACE OF THE UNIVERSITY

As Tracy and I and others observed, students and student successes (as well as faculty successes) energized Gee. Whenever there were stressful and challenging situations, student interaction always reminded Gee what he and the university were about. When students and faculty were prospering, Gee was further energized.

Another student-centered event was graduation. When Ohio State was on the quarter system, the university had four commencement ceremonies annually, the largest being the spring commencement held in Ohio Stadium with 50,000 or more people in attendance and upwards of 10,000 graduates receiving their degrees. There were three smaller graduations held at the Schottenstein Center at the end of the summer, fall, and winter quarters. But no matter the size of the graduating class or the prominence of the commencement speaker, Gee always played a key role in the commencement ceremony (see Figure 5.2). Commencement to Gee was not simply a university ritual but also a celebration of student successes and university impacts. Gee would deliver extensive remarks at graduation. Some of these were humorous observations about student life and student culture as well as advice to the graduating class about their futures. Other comments took great pride in the achievements of the graduates overall as well as the accomplishments of specific students whose own stories were very compelling. Typically, Gee would mention five specific graduates and highlight their accomplishments. It might be the mother of three children who just completed her BA degree at the age of 44. Or it might be the military veteran whose schooling was interrupted by service to one's country and who returned to Ohio State to complete his/her degree. Or it might be the young man who was the first person in his extended family to graduate from college. Or it might be a young woman building on a family legacy by being the fifth generation of her family to graduate from Ohio State. All of these stories added to the celebratory and inspirational nature of the commencement ceremony and reminded the audience of the impact of an Ohio State education. And when Gee asked the graduating class to acknowledge the support and love they had received from friends and family in the audience, they stood and cheered enthusiastically. The commencement ceremony was a joyous and emotional occasion led by a university president who clearly took great pride and joy in the achievements of the graduating class.

After the commencement ceremony ended and students received their actual inscribed diploma right there (an impressive logistical feat given the size of the graduating class), Gee would make himself available for photographs with the members of the graduating class and their family and friends. He would spend hours doing this, and it provided one more (and perhaps last)

FIGURE 5.2. President Gee congratulates former trustee Tami Longaberger on receiving the Distinguished Service Award at commencement in 2011. Credit: The Ohio State University.

FIGURE 5.3. (from left) Carol Ries, director of special events and commencement, Ann Lawrence from the Board of Trustees Office, and Mary Basinger from the president's office. Credit: The Ohio State University.

THE FACE OF THE UNIVERSITY

FIGURE 5.4. Barbie Tootle in the center as her spouse Jim Tootle shakes hands with President Gee. Credit: The Ohio State University.

opportunity for students to get that cherished photo with the president. Board of Trustees member Cheryl Krueger said that it was particularly moving to see international students and their families having their pictures taken with Gee. Many of these family members had traveled thousands of miles from Asia, Africa, Europe, and elsewhere to attend the commencement ceremony. Krueger marveled at Gee high-fiving students, hugging family members, and sharing in their collective joy.

Successful commencements do not just happen. They require thorough planning and precise execution. The Office of Special Events and Commencement headed by Carol Ries handled the logistics of commencement superbly (see Figure 5.3).

And one staff member—Barbie Tootle—was primarily responsible for Gee's commencement script (see Figure 5.4). Barbie truly captured Gee's voice in her written comments and was a genius in incorporating student culture and foibles in the president's remarks. She sometimes would create a top ten list for commencement and for other special events, although one had to make sure that neither Barbie nor Gordon got carried away. Barbie also played a major role in the preparation of many of Gee's speeches and presentations, as did Melinda Church, director of executive communications, and Melinda Nelson

Chapter 5

from the Office of Academic Affairs, who were particularly skillful in helping to prepare academic addresses to such audiences as the University Senate and higher education professional associations. Yet Church and Nelson would also find the right words for nonacademic audiences.

Football weekends provided another opportunity to showcase the Ohio State student body as well as the research and public service contributions of the faculty and staff. For home football games, there would typically be a pregame buffet organized by Special Events and Carol Ries with a guest list of 200–300 Buckeye friends and supporters. The program for these pregame events would typically highlight a student group such as the men's or women's glee club or some student instrumental combo. Students would also serve as hosts greeting guests, getting name tags, and escorting guests to their seats. The cheerleaders would stop by to lead a few cheers, and a subset of the marching band would play a few traditional Buckeye songs to rev up the crowd. And the athletic director would stop by to give an analysis of the day's opponent, always exhorting the guests to cheer loudly when the game started. All of these activities left the guests with the sense that Ohio State was indeed a student-centered university. Finally, these pregame buffets featured some faculty research whether in medicine, the arts and sciences, education or whatever. As faculty members discussed their research, they would often incorporate into their presentations some of the students who had been assisting them on the research.

The guest lists for the pregame events were very strategically constructed, as were the decisions as to who would actually sit in the president's box during the football game (see Figures 5.5–5.8). Typically the pregame guests fell into categories such as major university donors, leading university citizens, prominent public officials, and significant community leaders from the business, nonprofit, and communication sectors.

The summer tours, sometimes referred to as state tours, were the most ambitious university effort to take Ohio State directly to the people of Ohio. Gee wanted to bring the banner of Ohio State personally to all regions of the state, be they urban, rural or suburban. He wanted Ohioans to believe that Ohio State was their university and one of the best ways to achieve that was to meet the people of Ohio in their own communities. Gee's aspirations were facilitated by the fact that Ohio State already had a presence in all 88 Ohio counties because of strong alumni clubs throughout the state and university alumni living in all corners of the state, many of them the doctors, lawyers, teachers, and business leaders in their home communities. Ohio State also had programs and facilities in many parts of the state. Certainly one of the most prominent was Ohio State Extension (formerly the Cooperative Extension Ser-

THE FACE OF THE UNIVERSITY

FIGURES 5.5, 5.6, 5.7, and 5.8. Public officials and former public officials were often guests in the presidential box at football games. In Figure 5.5, John and Annie Glenn join Gordon Gee. In Figure 5.6 are three former governors (from left) Bob Taft, George Voinovich, and Ted Strickland. In Figure 5.7, former Speaker of the US House of Representatives John Boehner enjoys a conversation with former Governor Ted Strickland as Tom Katzenmeyer looks on. In Figure 5.8, former congressman Pat Tiberi and his wife Denise join President Gee at the game; Curt Steiner is to the left. Credit: The Ohio State University.

vice) working in all of Ohio's counties to share university-based knowledge with the citizenry on such topics as farming, health and wellness, financial literacy, and so many others. Ohio State Extension was part of the College of Food, Agriculture and Environmental Sciences, formerly the College of Agriculture. Having the only comprehensive agriculture college in the state of Ohio gave Ohio State University a wonderful opportunity to work with and for the citizens of Ohio, especially since agriculture and agriculture-related business comprised the largest sector of the Ohio economy. Ohio State also had physical facilities located throughout Ohio, including regional campuses at Lima,

FIGURE 5.9. Sue Jones with one of the many vehicles she commandeered on travels throughout the state. Credit: The Ohio State University.

Mansfield, Marion, and Newark. The Agricultural Technical Institute and the Ohio Agriculture Research and Development Center were located in Wooster, while the university's Sea Grant Program had a major presence at Lake Erie on Gibraltar Island. In addition, Ohio State had numerous medical, engineering, and outreach activities off the main campus in Columbus. So President Gee going on state tours personally reinforced the reality that the university was already a partner to communities throughout the state. Finally, one other factor that enhanced the state tours were the county fairs held throughout Ohio, mostly in the summertime. The vast majority of these fairs had a major agriculture component with substantial participation by 4-H students. And 4-H was a youth program overseen by Ohio State Extension, but with impressive volunteer contributions from the local counties.

The summer tours were typically two days long and visited multiple cities and counties on the same tour. Usually five tours were held each summer. The tours were truly a team effort organized by Sue Jones (see Figure 5.9) in University Communications with the assistance of staff from many university offices. In one summer, the planning group was Becki Crowell from the University Foundation, Tracy Stuck from Student Life, Eric Reasoner from Enrollment Services, Colleen O'Brien and Jack Hershey from Government Affairs, Denny Hoobler from Athletics, Kathy Bickel from the Alumni Association,

THE FACE OF THE UNIVERSITY

FIGURE 5.10. Three staff members critical to the success of Gee's travels were (from left) Anna Stevenson handling security, Sondra Shook from the president's office, and Becki Crowell from University Advancement. Credit: The Ohio State University.

Ben Lewis from Outreach and Engagement, and Linda Montler from the Medical Center.

The breadth of the planning group reflected the scope of the university and the wide range of audiences that the summer tours hoped to reach. Sue Jones would examine President Gee's calendar and the schedule of previous summer tours and then try to select counties and regions where Ohio State had not visited very recently. Then the team would work together to identify the stops and construct a schedule of events for each stop (see Figure 5.10). As mentioned earlier, county fairs were in full swing during the summer and thus became a great place to visit; the Ohio State presence was already prominent at the county fairs given the participation of Extension and 4-H. But the fairs were also opportunities for public officials to attend along with their constituents. Thus, Gee would often meet with these public officials at the fair with the appropriate publicity and photographs surrounding the event. Other frequent events on the state tours were meetings with local area college and university presidents, interviews with the local radio and television stations and the local newspapers, and visits with business and civic leaders.

Chapter 5

In arranging these trips, Sue Jones tried to make them very economical, avoiding any appearance of luxury and extravagance. Jones and Gee and a staffer or two would travel in a car (driven by Jones), while the other staff members and students on the trip would ride a bus or van, often labeled the "fun bus." Overnight accommodations could be a dormitory, as they were when visiting Cedar Point, or a motel or a bed and breakfast or the home of a friend of the university. It was important that the university contingent come across as resembling the communities they were visiting, and this meant no showy displays of wealth or privilege.

Probably the most famous, most media-covered summer tour stop occurred in 2011. Between June and August of 2011, there were five summer tours. Each of those tours was a two-day affair with an overnight stay away from Columbus. According to OSU Communications, Gee traveled 2,795 miles, visited 47 of the 88 counties, and made 75 stops along the way. And at every stop there was extensive media coverage, be it a visit to the county fair, a community hospital, a local high school, or a meeting with public officials, local business leaders, or newspaper editorial boards. It was clear the local media outlets, particularly in smaller, more rural communities, treated the visit of the Ohio State University president as a newsworthy event.

Of the 75 stops made in the 2011 tours, the one that received the greatest attention was Gordon Gee's visit to the Little Sisters of the Poor in Oregon, Ohio. This story is a prime example of how remarks go viral in the age of social media and how easy it becomes to be embarrassed by such remarks. But it is also a lesson on how to apologize and make amends and convert an embarrassment into a wonderfully uplifting story.

The story began the year before when Gee publicly asserted that Ohio State was more deserving to be in the football Bowl Championship Series than other contenders such as TCU or Boise State. His argument was that Ohio State played a tougher schedule than these other contenders, who, Gee uttered, played "the Little Sisters of the Poor." Unbeknownst to Gee was that there was actually an order called the Little Sisters of the Poor and, moreover, that it was located in Oregon, Ohio. Shortly after his comments became public and had received some media attention, the receptionist in the Office of the President at Ohio State received a phone call from a very soft-spoken woman who requested, "Would you please tell President Gee that there is a Little Sisters of the Poor that has nothing to do with football?" When this message was delivered to Gee, he was mortified and wrote a letter to the Mother Superior apologizing, promising to visit the order, and making a contribution. Sister Cecilia indicated he would be most welcome to visit the order.

FIGURE 5.11. Gordon Gee and the Ohio State entourage visit the Little Sisters of the Poor Order and are greeted by Sister Cecilia. Credit: The Ohio State University.

FIGURE 5.12. Members of the Little Sisters of the Poor Order visit Ohio State and Join President Gee on the football field for the game against the University of Toledo. Credit: The Ohio State University.

Chapter 5

On August 17, 2011, Gordon Gee and his colleagues, including the students, cheerleaders, professors, staff, and others on the "fun bus" arrived at the Order. Gee was warmly welcomed by Sister Cecilia, who showed him around the facility and introduced him to many of the elderly residents (see Figure 5.11). After an hour of socializing, Mother Cecilia and Gee went to the podium for a quasi-press conference in which Gee said that his comments about the Order were among his ten worst gaffes. But he was thankful that something good had come out of it by bringing greater attention to the Order's mission to help the poor and elderly. Gee told the audience that he had invited members of the order to attend the Ohio State/University of Toledo football game the next month and be his guests in the president's box.

The warmth of the event was truly moving (see Figure 5.12). Sister Cecilia gave Gee a bow tie with the Little Sisters of the Poor emblem on one side and OSU on the other. It was a wonderful example, to use a cliché, of turning lemons into lemonade. But it was also an excellent example of how flippant, spontaneous comments can go viral and come back to haunt one, a point that will come up again later in the book.

The Mechanics

The first part of the chapter showed how seriously Gee and his team took his charge to utilize his time effectively and strategically. The responsibility for accomplishing this goal rested in a talented team led by Kate Wolford (see Figure 5.13). Wolford had worked for Gee in his first term at Ohio State and moved with him when he went to Brown. Kate stayed at Brown when Gee went to Vanderbilt but rejoined him when he returned to Ohio State, as assistant to the president and director of operations in the office of the president.

Wolford was superb leading the effort to build Gee's calendar guided by core strategic principles. Likewise, she was also very adept in ensuring that communications and messages from the president's office reflected Gee's and the university's priorities, values, and goals. She assembled a team, gave the team members clear directions and responsibilities, and empowered them to take ownership of their tasks. Indeed, prior to Gee's official October 1, 2007, start, Wolford had sent out a memo focusing on interface with the president's office and outlining many procedures and policies. This memo dealt with many important process matters such as requests for the president's time, briefings for presidential appearances, correspondence, travel, and many others.

FIGURE 5.13. Gordon Gee and Kate Wolford at a planning meeting. Credit: The Ohio State University.

Wolford also played an important role in working with the university's senior leadership team to help Gee set up the committee structure that would oversee university deliberations and decision-making. Wolford was very skillful in working with vice presidents and special assistants and others who were not fully happy with their committee responsibilities. The initial structure included a larger president's council that met monthly, chaired by Gee and which focused on messaging and information sharing. There was also a smaller Senior Management Council chaired by Provost Joe Alutto that met weekly and had more of a policy/issue focus. A third entity was the Executive Committee chaired by Gee that met biweekly and dealt with final policy discussions and decisions. Finally, there was a small, three-person group called Integrated Financial Planning, which worked on budget models and financial integration. It was chaired by Provost Alutto, with Bill Shkurti, the finance vice president, and Chip Souba, head of the medical center, initially being the other two members. This overall committee system was modified regularly with respect to structure and membership throughout Gee's second term, but the initial outline remained in place. Over time, other committees and working groups

Chapter 5

were created as the need arose; many of these were ad hoc and short-term, while others had a longer life. In the latter category was a so-called cultural cabinet that Gee met with occasionally, often over dinner. It was composed of campus people such as Sherri Geldin, head of the Wexner Arts Center; Ann Pendleton-Julian, director of the school of architecture; Karen Bell, Arts Initiative associate vice president; Tom Lennox, head of Pelotonia; Nancy Kramer, CEO of Resources Interactive; and others as appropriate. There were also periodic communications strategy meetings usually held at the university residence that focused on important topics of the day. These topics often entailed the intersection of university and external concerns, and the participants in these meetings were appropriate university officials and relevant external actors. The most frequent communication strategy meeting focused on higher education governance in Ohio and included Eric Fingerhut, the Chancellor of the Ohio Board of Regents, and his staff, and some of the senior leadership of the university—President Gee, Provost Alutto, SVP Curt Steiner (government affairs), SVP Geoff Chatas (finance), SVP Tom Katzenmeyer (communications), and counselor to the president Herb Asher. There were seven such meetings between October of 2008 and November of 2010. These meetings ended after the election of a new governor (John Kasich) in 2010 and his subsequent selection of a new chancellor—Jim Petro. These meetings were important because the state of Ohio under the leadership of Fingerhut and Governor Ted Strickland was in the process of creating the University System of Ohio. Ohio State worked diligently to ensure that this new organizational structure for higher education not harm Ohio State's distinctive status as Ohio's flagship, national research university.

Another regular, high-powered set of meetings was the quarterly gatherings between Columbus Mayor Michael Coleman and his leadership team with the university's senior leaders (see Figure 5.14). Organizing these meetings and constructing the agenda fell largely to Trudy Bartley, vice president in the office of government affairs who had chief responsibility for community relations with a special focus on the city of Columbus. While many of the university representatives who participated in the meetings with Chancellor Fingerhut also attended the discussions with Mayor Coleman, there were some notable additions because of the breadth of the issues that linked the city and the university. For example, Jay Kasey, senior vice president for administration and planning, and his colleagues would often attend when issues such as campus planning and campus area safety were on the agenda. During Gee's second term, the points of contact between the city and the university continued to grow across a wide range of issues, including economic development, campus

FIGURE 5.14. Mayor Coleman and President Gee enjoying an amusing moment. Credit: The Ohio State University.

area housing and code enforcement, university investment in distressed neighborhoods abutting the campus area, the removal of low head dams on the Olentangy River, urban and regional planning internships in city government, traffic and transportation issues, and so many more. The breadth and depth of city/university cooperation represented a sea change from what had existed forty years earlier. The university increasingly recognized what an advantage it was to be located in Columbus, a thriving, vibrant metropolis that had become by far the largest city in Ohio and the 15th largest in the nation (and now the 14th largest). And the city increasingly appreciated the university's contributions to economic growth and development, to health-care delivery, and to enhancing the quality of life for the residents of Columbus.

With respect to the actual scheduling of meetings, Wolford chose Becki Crowell to oversee the strategic use of Gee's time. All requests, internal and external, for appearances by Gee had to go through Becki, who would then work with a small group of colleagues to determine whether replying affirmatively to the request would advance the president's and the university's goals. If an invitation were accepted, Crowell would then follow up with her coworkers to ensure that the appropriate briefings were prepared for Gee and

CHAPTER 5

that the travel arrangements and other logistics were made. The instructions that Wolford provided for those preparing the briefings were detailed and comprehensive. One person who played a key role in getting Gee from one event to another was Tom Near. Tom was a driver, a delivery person, and a personal assistant. He did an incredible job getting Gee to events mostly on time, often finding vehicular shortcuts unbeknownst to most university personnel and often interpreting parking regulations and restrictions from a very permissive perspective.

Wolford assigned Carol Ries and her staff in Special Events and Commencement the responsibility to plan events that the president himself personally hosted, often at the university residence. Wolford said very directly, "Events should be fun, lively, and have a clear purpose." She also directed that where feasible students should serve as hosts and greeters at these events. She regularly reminded her colleagues that Gordon expected to see a diversity of guests at events "so invitations lists should be creative and full."

With respect to the president's travel, whether for fundraising or other purposes, Wolford wanted each trip to be reviewed by a small planning committee composed of one person from each of the major areas of the university, such as communications, development, government affairs, alumni, and others as appropriate. (Later in Gee's second term, the development, alumni, and communications activities were joined together under the rubric of advancement, a topic discussed in chapter 8.) On any trip, Gee wanted to take full advantage of Ohio State connections in the area. According to Wolford:

> Dr. Gee expects to take advantage of the Ohio State connections in any given City. This will include visiting alumni, trustees, donors, guidance counselors, families, farms, schools and universities, local attractions or anything else connected to Ohio State. There should always be a list of "stop-bys" in a city, should there be any extra time on the schedule. These may include offices of alumni or local businesses owned by alumni.

With all of the structures and processes in place producing an incredibly packed schedule, how would one know whether all this past activity and the upcoming flood of events were actually meeting Gee's goal of the strategic use of his time and advancing the university's agenda? Part of the answer to this question were regular meetings of various kinds, some to look prospectively at upcoming events and scheduling, and others to look back retrospectively and review how well activities had gone. In the latter category were the semi-annual "detention" meetings held on Saturday mornings at the university residence. Participants included some of the senior leaders of the university as well as members of the president's office staff such as Becki Crowell and Shea Bugala. Wolford, Crowell, and Bugala would prepare a summary of the events Gee participated in the previous six to seven months. This list was organized by target audiences and functional areas. For example, university events were classified into faculty, staff, and student categories as well as medical center, alumni, and development classifications. There was also a category of external and community events. During the meeting, the participants would discuss what went well and what did not and would make recommendations about priorities for the next six months. One question that was always asked is "Whom have we missed?" Another question was to whom should we pay more attention. Tracy Stuck suggested more interaction with the parents of students. Wolford, Crowell, and Asher urged more events with faculty, stating that one could never do too much with faculty. Melinda Nelson from the Office of Academic Affairs praised Gee's addresses to the faculty but raised two questions: How do we get better attendance at Gee's formal faculty speeches, and how do we connect better with the younger faculty who are not as active in university governance activities such as the University Senate? An important meeting that looked both to the past and to the future was the weekly calendar meeting. Becki Crowell provided the participants an updated calendar and a list of all the requests that had come in for the president's time since the last meeting. The committee members would then review how the events of the past week had gone and, more importantly, examine the new requests and address how well they fit into the president's strategic goals and objectives. If the committee had to say no to a specific invitation, the question became how to say no. Should we respond with an alternative date or recommend resending the invitation the following year with greater lead-time. Or should we ask the requester whether some other high-ranking university official such as Executive Vice President and Provost Joe Alutto might represent the university? One other purpose of the calendar meeting was to give Gee the opportunity to scan the upcoming events of the week to make sure he felt comfortable about the events and to also make sure that the logistical arrangements such as travel and briefings were in place.

Conclusion

The reader may be surprised by how much detail I have provided about the scheduling of President Gee. I did so because one of Gee's major contributions was to try to make Ohio State the institution of all Ohioans, no matter whether or where they attended college. He wanted Buckeyes to think of Ohio State as their institution, regardless of the fact that there are four-year public universities in all regions of the state and likewise a robust community college system. Gee understood that he was a personality, a character, a highly visible personage, and a media star who enjoyed much recognition and popularity because he was a cheerleader for Ohio State and for the State of Ohio. But this reputation does not just happen. And it was much more than wearing bow ties and telling funny jokes, although that certainly added to his quirky appeal. A reputation had to be built, sustained, and reinforced. And Gee himself needed to be heavily involved in this, maintaining an incredibly ambitious schedule that allowed him to touch many Ohioans on their own turf and not just in Columbus.

Gee was very successful in accomplishing this, in becoming a popular and effective spokesperson for the value of higher education and a champion for the state of Ohio and her people. He ensured that the university was a major player in policy initiatives at the local and state levels (see chapter 17). On campus, Gee was seen as a leader advancing Ohio State's interests at the state and national levels. He clearly took great pride in the achievements of faculty and staff and loved to share that pride with audiences everywhere. With respect to students, I have never seen a university president at any college or university in Ohio connect so well with his or her student body. Gee was an incredible resource in building the Ohio State brand, and that resource had to be exploited skillfully and fully. Fortunately, Gee had a talented team around him to accomplish this.

6

The Internal Constituencies

Introduction

Like most college and university presidents, Gordon Gee believed that progress in achieving university goals was enhanced when the internal constituencies of the university—the faculty, students, and staff—had confidence in the university administrations and its values and priorities. Gee also recognized how critical it was that the Board of Trustees supported the president and his administration and felt that they were in the loop as university priorities moved forward. It was key that the board knew about university developments—good or bad—before they became public. The board should never be surprised by first learning about an incident in the newspaper or on television or online.

Thus, the Gee calendar had another core strategic focus: Gee would meet and interact regularly with faculty, students, and staff and with the Board of Trustees. But here the interactions would go well beyond the informal breakfast and dinners and university events. Gee would also have regular, focused meetings with all of these constituencies every academic quarter (later semester). These meetings would focus on the more formal governance, representational, policy, and communications/advancement issues that each of these entities had. For example, the student body had three student-elected governing bodies—the Undergraduate Student Government (USG), the Council of Graduate Students (CGS), and the Inter-Professional Council (IPC). In addition, there was the student newspaper *The Lantern*, which had wide circulation on campus and online and often had superb coverage of campus issues.

CHAPTER 6

What made *The Lantern* even more noteworthy is that it accomplished this even as its editorial leadership turned over every year. With respect to staff, the University Staff Advisory Committee was the preeminent voice of staff concerns. Some staff (non-administrative) were members of unions that provided another voice for their interests.

Faculty Governance

With respect to the faculty, there were of course departments and department chairs, colleges and college deans, institute and center directors, and a myriad of committees and councils organized around various themes and functions and interests. But the core of faculty and university governance was the University Senate, which included faculty, students and administrators, but not staff representatives (although staff were designated by University Senate bylaws as members of some University Senate committees). The Senate was composed of 26 administrative members (e.g., vice presidents, deans) chosen primarily by the university president or designated in Senate rules and bylaws, 70 faculty members selected through elections held by the academic colleges, and 41 student members (26 undergraduates, 10 graduate students, and 5 professional students) appointed by the leadership of the respective student governments. The university president by bylaw served as the presiding officer of the Senate, and in his/her absence, the executive vice president and provost presided.

There was also a secretary of the University Senate, a tenured faculty member appointed by the president from three nominees submitted by the Senate Steering Committee to serve a three-year renewable term. In 2010, Gee appointed Tim Gerber as the new Senate secretary; Gerber was a faculty member in the School of Music (see Figure 6.1). The Senate secretary could be thought of as the chief administrative officer of the Senate. Gerber's duties in addition to record keeping, meeting announcements, and the like included serving as a resource for members of the university community on matters of university governance, promoting active participation in university governance by the various constituencies of the Senate, and serving as a voting member of the program and the rules committees and a non-voting member of the Senate steering committee, in effect the committee on committees for the Senate.

The Senate had a well-developed committee system where much of the policy work was done; all committees had faculty, student, and administrative members. There were three organizing committees—steering, rules, and program—that oversaw the processes and flow of business of the Senate. The

THE INTERNAL CONSTITUENCIES

FIGURE 6.1. Tim Gerber, former secretary of the University Senate and professor in the School of Music. Credit: The Ohio State University.

steering committee was the most significant committee, in part because of its composition and its responsibilities. Among the members of steering were the three student government presidents, the provost, the senior vice president for business and finance, and the Senate Secretary (non-voting). The steering committee had the responsibility to review the operation and effectiveness of the Senate and its committees and could initiate recommendations about the workings of the Senate. Moreover, the steering committee served as a channel of communication between the Senate, the president, and the Board of Trustees, and could serve as an advisory body to both the president and the board on important university matters.

The remaining committees of the Senate were the standing and special committees that were primarily organized around substantive subject matter areas. One key committee was the council on academic affairs, which dealt with the educational and academic policies of the university by initiating and reviewing proposed changes in university policies. Other important committees were the council on student affairs, the athletic council, the council on enrollment and student progress, the fiscal committee, the diversity committee, the committee on academic misconduct, and others. The key point here is that there was a well-delineated committee system prepared to handle important issues as they arose. And if need be, a special committee could be created within the University Senate framework to handle unusual issues.

Another important feature of the Senate was the faculty council, comprised of the faculty senators in the Senate. The faculty council provided a setting where faculty members could convene and address issues of concern without university administrators and students being involved in the conversations at that stage. The faculty council chose a chair and chair-elect from among its members. Finally, there was a small group of four faculty members of the Senate labeled the faculty leadership; these were the Senate secretary, the chair of the steering committee, and the chair and the chair-elect of the faculty council. This faculty leadership group met regularly (usually monthly) with the president and separately with the provost. These meetings provided an opportunity to share information and concerns and to address emerging and ongoing issues. The faculty leaders thus had the chance to bring issues directly to the president and provost. This in turn gave the president and the provost the opportunity to share these issues with their own administrative colleagues before these issues had spiraled out of hand.

I have devoted so much attention to the structure of the University Senate because Gordon Gee believed that a strong, well-functioning university governance system was beneficial to the university and good for his administration. Gee argued that when the Senate enjoyed credibility among the faculty and students, it became the legitimate place to channel disagreements and controversies into well-established processes. But if the Senate lacked credibility and support, then the resolution of contentious issues would be left to more ad hoc, more uncertain venues. Thus, Gee worked hard to ensure that the Senate maintained its well-deserved reputation as a site for meaningful campus deliberations on important university issues.

Fortunately for Gee and the university, Ohio State was blessed with well-functioning university governance structures. Credit for this goes to many people, including Senate Secretary Tim Gerber and his immediate predecessors Chris Zacher, Susan Fisher, and Gerry Reagan. Gerber built upon the accomplishments of prior secretaries to make the Senate an even more viable institution. Gerber was very focused on getting strong faculty to run for the Senate and worked closely with department chairs and others to encourage faculty to seek Senate office. Gerber also appreciated the importance of well-performing committees, which meant that strong faculty needed to be appointed to key committees. On some committees, appointees had to be senators, but on other committees there were opportunities for non-senator faculty from throughout the university to serve. Gerber recruited throughout the university to identify potential committee appointees with emphasis on enhancing Senate diversity with respect to gender, race, academic rank, and disciplinary affiliation. Gerber also did an excellent job enhancing the capabilities of the Senate office by providing timely information and analyses to Senate members and to the committees. In short, the Senate was a genuine asset to university governance. And the importance of a well-regarded University Senate became evident when Gee and the university addressed two critical issues: the consolidation of the five colleges of the arts and sciences and the move to a semester system from the existing quarter academic calendar. Gee had tried to achieve both of these objectives in his first presidential administration but was unsuccessful. This time around he was successful (see chapter 7), and, more importantly, the "losing" side on these issues felt that by and large the processes that generated these outcomes were fair and legitimate; hence, there was very little residual bitterness and divisiveness.

Student Groups

There was one cluster of issues that did not readily fit into the normal university processes and committee structures. There were a number of student groups and organizations, many from the progressive wing of the political spectrum, who were highly critical of particular university actions and policies and who were willing to express their dissatisfaction outside the normal governance channels. For example, great attention was focused on the manufacture of OSU apparel; student activists believed that the university was benefitting financially from the exploitation of workers in overseas factories where workers labored in deplorable conditions for subsistence wages. Other student groups focused on the university's environmental policies, especially as they related to energy use and efficiency and the university's carbon footprint. Other student groups were concerned about personal safety and crime, particularly in the off-campus neighborhoods populated heavily by students. A related concern was the quality of the housing in the campus area; many students believed that too many campus area landlords were offering rental properties that failed to meet health and safety standards. Finally, other student groups (as well as faculty and existing campus committees and offices) were upset with what they deemed to be inadequate minority representation in the student body and inadequate minority and female representation in the faculty and administrative cohorts of the university.

Chapter 6

These issues and others had the potentiality to generate student protests that might range from peaceful expressions of sentiment to the occupation of campus buildings. But these more extreme protests did not happen, in part because Gee insisted that his administrative leadership team address student concerns in a timely, respectful, and, where appropriate, responsive fashion. Gee believed that even when student complaints could not be resolved to everyone's satisfaction, the process by which these decisions were reached was itself highly crucial. Gee fully understood the maxim that if objectors cannot "get" you on the merits of their issues, they can still win over supporters if the process is flawed. Thus, Gee wanted to ensure that both process and substantive concerns were handled appropriately.

With respect to process, Gee urged his leadership team to work constructively with student groups, to be open and honest, share information, and be good listeners. He repeatedly reminded his staff that unhappy students might actually be justified in their views and urged his leadership team to look for points of common ground. He also wanted to ensure that official student organizations, especially the student governments, were brought in early in dealing with controversial matters. After all, it was the student governments that were the elected representatives of the student body. But Gee also recognized that there were other student organizations, some of them very informal and ad hoc, that needed to be at the table when serious issues arose. Gee was willing to meet with the most disgruntled of student groups with certain caveats. Civility was to be encouraged, and bad behavior was not to be rewarded. Existing legitimate student organizations were also to be at the table. Gee would never give critics any ammunition to say he was isolated from students and out of touch. And, of course, Gee's immense popularity with the overall student body (discussed earlier) helped in times of stress and made it difficult for anyone to claim that Gee was not connected to the student body. Gee would also happily meet one on one with individual student activists. One such relationship was with Patty Cunningham, who had been an undergraduate student at Ohio State, then earned her PhD at Ohio State, and then, known as Dr. Patty, led a number of social justice and leadership programs at Ohio State. Dr. Patty and Dr. Gee were a truly unique and inspirational odd couple.

Two members of Gee's senior staff were particularly critical in channeling potential protests into constructive dialog—Kate Wolford and Dr. Javaune Adams-Gaston. Both Wolford and Adams-Gaston maintained an open-door policy with student groups. Both reinforced Gee's message to his senior leadership team to listen to and be responsive to student concerns. Wolford and

Adams-Gaston did an excellent job establishing ground rules about how disagreements would be addressed and helped Gee to have productive meetings with disgruntled student groups. Gee disliked threats and ultimatums and tried to help protesting students understand what tactics and strategies would best facilitate achieving their goals. Gee never saw unhappy students as the enemy; instead, he viewed them as passionate young citizens with sincere grievances that merited serious attention. This meant that in most instances there was little conflict about the processes employed to address disagreements. And in many instances, the student activists could claim success, whether in modifying current policies or establishing mechanisms to continue the dialog on challenging issues.

Faculty and Staff Interactions

With respect to faculty concerns, the vast majority was channeled through the university governance processes because, as mentioned earlier, faculty governance and the University Senate were viewed as legitimate and meaningful at Ohio State. For example, the Faculty Compensation and Benefits Committee of the University Senate would address faculty compensation issues. But as much as Gee worked through the official faculty governance processes, he also took myriad actions to build his relationships with the university faculty. Gee was always open to meeting with faculty individually or in group settings. Every academic quarter, Gee tried to attend four to five departmental faculty meetings. He regularly had breakfasts, lunches, and dinners with clusters of faculty from throughout the university. He defended the faculty vigorously from external criticism. When testifying before legislative committees and queried about tenure and faculty workload, Gee would passionately defend tenure and the work ethic of professors with their teaching, research, and public service responsibilities. Gee would routinely send handwritten notes of congratulations to faculty who had just published a new book or received a good teaching award or won a new research grant. And he would send personal notes of condolences when tragedy occurred. Gee was renowned for surprising faculty members by showing up to their classes while they were teaching to award them an outstanding teaching "apple" award (see Figure 6.2). The faculty member was stunned, and his/her students were delighted to see their professor receive an award from the university president. And all faculty recipients of teaching, research, and public service awards were honored on the football field at halftime in front of 105,000 fans.

Chapter 6

FIGURE 6.2. President Gee surprises Professor Janet Box-Steffensmeier (right) by making an unscheduled visit to the political science department to congratulate her on receiving a distinguished faculty award. Credit: The Ohio State University.

Gee was also appreciative of the contributions of the staff. Some of the staff was classified civil service; others were unionized employees. Whatever their status, Gee recognized their accomplishments through special events similar to faculty activities and with regular meetings with the University Staff Advisory Committee (USAC). At commencement, Gee routinely recognized a category of staff who had made the student experience better, be it the academic advisors or the cafeteria workers or the maintenance staff that kept the university running. One important part of the culture that Gee was trying to foster was respect and appreciation for all those who contributed to the Ohio State experience. He was especially sensitive to the possibility that the contributions of the staff would be overlooked and undervalued by the faculty and high-level administrators.

Board of Trustees

Thus, in Gee's second term, the relationship between the president and the faculty, staff, and students was generally healthy and productive. But there was one other constituency with whom Gee needed to have a harmonious relationship and that, of course, was the Ohio State University Board of Trustees. Between Gee's first and second OSU presidencies, the board changed in significant ways. First, it was enlarged from nine to fifteen members, all still appointed by the governor of Ohio. Second, because the governor was constitutionally prohibited from appointing non-Ohioans to the board, the OSU Board decided (with the approval of the attorney general of Ohio) to select charter trustees to serve on the board. Charter trustees were prominent citizens residing in other states who brought particular skills to the board. Charter trustees would typically be OSU alumni and former residents of Ohio. As in Gee's first term, there were also two student trustees on the board, one being an undergraduate student and the other a graduate or professional student. When student members were added to the board in the 1990s by state law, the statute prohibited students from being voting members and left open the question of students being permitted to attend executive sessions of the board. However, the Ohio State Board of Trustees, unlike the boards at most of the other Ohio public universities, welcomed student trustees and granted them the right to vote on committees and to attend and participate in executive sessions.

Another major change between the first and second Gee administrations was the way the chair of the Board of Trustees was selected. The term of office of trustees is nine years, and in the first Gee presidency there were nine trustees, with the governor appointing one new trustee annually as the term of the most senior member expired. The board operated under a seniority system in which the member entering his or her ninth year on the board automatically became the chair, thus removing any jockeying about who would become chair. And the board stayed with this process even when the person becoming chair was not of the same political party as the governor or perhaps was no longer at the top of his or her game. When the board was expanded to fifteen members, the term of office for board members remained at nine years, which meant that not every member would have the opportunity to chair the board. At this point, the board changed its procedure to provide for election of the board chair. Moreover, the board decided that a chair could serve a second term, thus changing the dynamics of the board.

Yet another change between Gee's two terms was a board that reflected the greater geographical diversity of Ohio. It would only be a slight exaggeration to say that earlier boards were largely composed of successful businessmen from the central Ohio region who knew each other well prior to joining the board. But by the second Gee administration the board itself had recognized that a wider geographic representation would be beneficial for the board and for the

CHAPTER 6

university and thus began to encourage the governor that there be a sufficient number of members from southwest and northeast Ohio as well as other parts of the state. Thus, Gee in his second term worked with a board more broadly representative of the state and with a more diverse set of backgrounds.

A more profound difference between earlier and later boards was the greater willingness of the former to be more deferential to the university president and his administration, even though the board was the governing authority of the university. But the board that hired Gee in 2007 was a much more active and engaged entity for a number of reasons. One obvious factor was the presence of members who were not content to sit back and be passive observers of what was transpiring at the university. There were two prominent members who had been reappointed to the board, and they surely felt comfortable and confident in addressing university issues. The board members themselves had undergone training about the appropriate roles and responsibilities of trustees at a public flagship, land grant university. One person the board relied upon for guidance was Richard Chaitt, a nationally renowned expert on higher education and board governance. Chaitt helped the board understand its broader oversight responsibilities without getting bogged down in the weeds. He helped develop a stronger, more effective board committee system and continually kept the focus on university policy governance and away from micromanaging.

Thus, it was clear that when Gordon Gee returned to Ohio State, he came back to a Board of Trustees with whom he would have to devote greater time, energy, and focus. In his first term, Gee would often ask individual board members to work on particular, often significant tasks, and this would occupy their time, leaving Gee freer from board involvement. In an April 2010 *Columbus Monthly* article, Gee said somewhat flippantly to reporter Ray Paprocki:

> Early on, [my board] philosophy was essentially, bring them in for a football game, sing "Kumbaya" and send them on their way. Now... it's about making them partners so they don't micromanage—that is, you make them part of the process, then they won't try to run the university for you.... A college president has "two Passes"—two times to make a big decision without informing the board.

Gee's attempt to make the board members partners took many forms. Certainly the most basic approach was regular one-on-one interactions with board members, whether in person or over the phone. In addition, there was close collaboration between the president's office and the office of the Board of Trustees. The administrative head of the board was the secretary of the Board of Trustees,

FIGURES 6.3 AND 6.4. Bob Duncan in Figure 6.3 served the university in many capacities beyond board secretary. He was also a member of the Board of Trustees and former chair. He also served as vice president and general counsel to the university. His off-campus career was equally impressive, including a stint on the Ohio Supreme Court. David Frantz in Figure 6.4 is shown with the staff of the board office, from left: Suzanne Nagy, Theresa Drummond, Korenia Querry, and Ann Lawrence. Frantz was also a renowned professor in the Department of English and served the university well in many administrative settings. Credit: The Ohio State University.

whose official duties dealt with such matters as record keeping and minutes, meeting notices, and other technical matters. But the board secretary was also much more than a clerk; he was also a major conduit for communication and information transfer between the president and the board, especially the chair of the board. Different board secretaries would carry out this responsibility in more or less constructive ways, depending on their own views of university operations and their relationships with the board and the president. In his first term as president, Gee inherited Board Secretary Madison Scott, who really believed that he knew how the university should be run. Scott viewed himself as a traffic cop or perhaps roadblock in keeping the president and his administration from interacting too freely with board members. After deposing Scott, Gee vowed to never let a board secretary accumulate so much power again. And in the rest of his first term and his second presidency, Gee and the board and the university were blessed to have senior, distinguished secretaries such as Judge Robert Duncan (see Figure 6.3) and Professor David Frantz (see Figure 6.4) of the Department of English, and younger secretaries such as Dr. Blake Thompson and Professor David Horn, also from the Department of English.

When Ohio State was in the academic quarter system, the Board of Trustees met six times a year in two-day meetings in both executive and public sessions. The preparation for the meetings was extensive and time consuming. In Gee's second term, the board meetings became even more substantive and strategic,

Chapter 6

with a very carefully crafted agenda and a more strategic focus. There was a much clearer sense of what the takeaways should be from any meeting and ideally what the media should be writing about after the meetings were over. While there were still a number of public relations events at the public meetings, such as recognizing faculty, staff, and students for outstanding achievements, there were rich and often well-scripted discussions about university policies and priorities. In executive sessions, though no votes could be taken or official decisions made, university issues were discussed in a very frank and in-depth manner. Gee's senior staff had the responsibility of providing the supporting materials and documentation to the board and its committees. Key senior presidential staff members participated in the board's executive session as needed and appropriate. The board itself had its own committee structure organized around key functional areas of the university. For example, there was an academic affairs and student life committee; Provost Alutto and Senior Vice President for Student Life Adams-Gaston worked closely with this group. Likewise Senior Vice President Geoff Chatas and his staff aided the fiscal affairs committee admirably. The medical affairs committee worked closely with Steve Gabbe, senior vice president for health sciences, while the development and investments committee (later advancement) worked with Mike Eicher, senior vice president for advancement. I am oversimplifying the relationships between board committees and the senior leaders of the president's cabinet. Indeed, there were many issues on which it was many or all hands on deck. The key point was that board/university interactions were fulsome and ongoing.

In the ideal world, these board/university interactions would reflect a two-way flow of communications so that neither entity was taken by surprise by the actions of the other. And this is indeed the way it worked—in most cases. But there were certain situations in which the information flow was interrupted, incomplete, or inaccurate, which created stresses between the board and the president. At times, university vice presidents worked directly with individual board members without sharing this with their colleagues or even with the president and provost. Likewise, board members might contact specific vice presidents to get information on a particular topic and then not share that information with their board colleagues. These rare instances of a breakdown in collegial information sharing occasionally created consternation and distrust, which generally (but not always) was resolved without lasting consequences.

To ensure continuity and trustee involvement in the months between board meetings, both Gee and Provost Alutto each sent personal, biweekly confidential reports to all board members with Gee's memo copied only to Alutto and senior vice president Asher (although undoubtedly copies were quickly disseminated). The content of Gee's reports ranged from the routine, such as recommendations on new books about higher education and reports of his recent travels, to more significant updates on ongoing university issues, projects, and initiatives. And occasionally, there would be very detailed presentations on some critical challenge facing the university. Provost Alutto's reports typically dealt with important university priorities and processes. The aim of both Gee's and Alutto's reports was to keep trustees in the loop; they did not want the trustees to be taken by surprise by developments. The reports encouraged trustees to contact the president or the provost if they had any concerns about matters discussed in the report. I have enclosed in Appendix B an example of a Gee and an Alutto report. Between these reports, the regular formal and informal interaction between the board with Gee and with Alutto, and the six (now five) annual meetings of the entire Board of Trustees, the board members were very much kept in the loop. Overall, the relationship between the Board of Trustees and Gee and his cabinet was a healthy one, characterized by trust, confidence, and appropriate respect for the distinct roles of the university administration and the board—*with one major exception.*

Starting later in Gee's second term, the board became concerned about Gee's penchant to utter spontaneous, unfiltered comments that the board believed hurt the university's image. While the "Little Sisters of the Poor" quip mentioned in the last chapter turned out fine, there were other humorous comments that did not. In March of 2011, a press conference was held to discuss a problem in the Ohio State football program. Jim Tressel was still the coach at that time and was at the press conference. A very important trustee encouraged Gee to not attend the press conference and leave it to the athletic director to handle the situation. But Gee chose to go to the press conference, partly out of his high regard for Tressel. During the event, a reporter asked Gee if he had thought about firing Tressel, and Gee joked that he just hoped that the coach would not fire him. Everyone in the room laughed, recognizing that Gee's remark was a joke designed to defuse the tension in the room; Gee was in no way being serious about the football coach firing him. But in this age of social media, Gee's comment went viral so that people all over the United States heard that the president of Ohio State University was worried about being fired by the football coach. Some trustees were concerned that this comment would damage the reputation of Ohio State by portraying the university as a football factory where the president was subservient to the football coach. There were other Gee quips that upset the trustees. Some of them involved trash talking between the SEC and the Big Ten. Others involved the unsuccess-

Chapter 6

ful efforts to get the University of Notre Dame to join the Big Ten Conference. Referring to the failed negotiations, Gee said that the Notre Dame fathers were holy on Sunday and holy terrors the rest of the week. By early 2013, the trustees had had enough of Gee's spontaneous humor, and on March 11, 2013, in a letter signed by board chair Robert Schottenstein and board governance committee chair Alex Shumate, the board chastised Gee for his recurring comments. Some key sections of the letter read:

> Your passion for the university and your sense of humor are infectious and typically serve this university very well.
>
> However, on occasion your words that may be intended to bring a bit of levity to some significant issues have, in fact, had the opposite effect. There have been occasions on which your comments were insensitive and inappropriate and have offended others. As a result, instead of your words promoting and uniting us, they have sometimes embarrassed and divided us . . . those inappropriate comments, particularly about certain groups or classes of people as a whole, do not align with what we know you believe and with what we are and aspire to be as a university . . . Although we do not believe that you intended harm, such comments risk diminishing the effectiveness of our collective efforts and of your good work. Through the course of our recent discussions, we are convinced that you share our concerns and appreciate just how powerful your platform can be,
>
> It is our mutual understanding that any comments you make or actions you take that detract from our core values and message are not productive, do not serve the University well, and are not acceptable.
>
> Although none of us expects this to be the case, should future instances take place, they could constitute cause for even more punitive action, including dismissal, and the Board will have no choice but to take such action.

Many of Gee's colleagues and friends saw the letter as demeaning and insulting to Gee, describing the letter as overkill and overblown and political correctness run wild. But the letter reflected the board's collective view that Gee's spontaneity and sense of humor, which had once been an asset, was now too often a liability. When Gee announced his retirement three months later, ostensibly to spend more time with his family and grandchildren and to recharge his batteries after decades of high-pressure work as a university president, the campus community by and large took his announcement at face value and wished him well in his retirement. But Gee's friends off campus, especially in state government, were livid, seeing the letter and the board as pressuring Gee into retirement. The Ohio House and the Ohio Senate were so angry that they briefly considered intervening in the situation by adopting resolutions that would declare an expression of no confidence in the Board of Trustees and another resolution that would declare board positions to be vacant. Governor Kasich urged the legislature to not take such actions, as it would make a bad situation worse and hurt the university. But the governor also twice read the riot act to Board Chair Schottenstein for the board's shabby treatment of Gee. Within a few weeks of Gee's retirement, Governor Kasich, the speaker of the Ohio House of Representatives and the president of the Ohio Senate hosted a very well-attended reception at the Statehouse Atrium to honor their friend Gordon Gee. No such event was ever held on campus to honor Gee for his years of service to the university. But the trustees did establish the Center for Higher Education Enterprise in 2013 with Gee at the helm and funded by $1.5 million from the university and a private gift of the same amount. The center mission was to develop "multidisciplinary research programs and policy recommendations focused on finding creative and enterprising ways to improve student success outcomes for public higher education." When Gee left later that year to become the president of West Virginia University (for the second time), Professor Terrell Strayhorn was designated the director of the Center. It became clear that Strayhorn was mismanaging the center, its budget, and its personnel, and he was removed. Ultimately, Professor Josh Hawley, who became the interim director of the Center, recommended that it be shut down, as it was redundant to other entities at Ohio State doing similar work. The Center was closed in 2018.

Conclusion

In his second term as Ohio State president, Gee worked very effectively to build strong relationships with the internal constituencies of the university—the faculty, staff, and students, and also the Board of Trustees before the fallout arising from Gee's controversial public comments. These relationships established the foundation that enabled many important initiatives to move forward at Ohio State: the shift from quarters to semesters, the consolidation of the arts and sciences colleges, the move from a development to an advancement model, the building of the new James Hospital, the construction of the North Campus residential facilities, the adoption of new and creative revenue generating

CHAPTER 6

strategies, and so many more. I am not saying that these and other initiatives all proceeded smoothly without bumps and challenges. To the contrary, there were many hurdles that had to be overcome. But I am saying that an institution as large and complex as Ohio State has a limited appetite and capacity for major changes. But that capacity is enhanced when the institution and its key players have bought into the legitimacy of the mission and goals and processes that define the institution. And this legitimacy is in large part due to the skillful leadership of Gee in building partnerships of trust and cooperation with the internal constituencies.

7

Old Issues and New Outcomes
Semester Conversion and Arts and Sciences Consolidation

Introduction

During his first term as Ohio State president, Gee wanted to institute two very important structural changes in the university: move the university academic calendar from a quarter to a semester system and consolidate the Colleges of the Arts and Sciences into a better integrated, more coherent, and more powerful configuration. Both of these efforts were unsuccessful in the first Gee administration, but both were successfully accomplished the second time around. Thus, we will discuss what factors contributed to these outcomes and what differences changes in the academic calendar and a new ASC structure made for the university.

Semester Conversion

When Gee originally proposed a move to semesters in his first term, too little groundwork had been done to try to win over key constituencies, especially the faculty and the students. In the early 1990s, the quarter system was still very popular on many college campuses, and the Ohio State community wondered whether a change was really necessary. Almost immediately, many of the faculty, particularly those conducting off campus field research throughout the nation and the world objected. Professor Richard Gunther of the political sci-

CHAPTER 7

ence department made a very cogent argument. Under the nine-month quarter system (three quarters, each of three-month duration), if a faculty member had a course load of four or five classes, they could complete those responsibilities in six months by teaching two courses in two quarters or two courses in one quarter and three courses in another quarter. This would leave faculty members with two quarters or six months to devote to their research agenda. If the faculty members' research projects required extended off-campus travels, the quarter system could accomplish this quite readily. However, under the semester system, if the teaching load was four courses, it was very unlikely that faculty members could complete their teaching responsibilities in one semester. Instead, they would teach over two four-month semesters, leaving only a four-month block to focus on their research. And even for faculty members who could conduct their research on campus, in their office, and at the library, the quarter system gave them more uninterrupted time to focus on their research. Gunther and others rallied their faculty colleague to argue that a switch to semesters was an idea whose time had not yet come.

Many students, especially undergraduates, were also opposed to the semester switch, although some of their reasons were far less compelling than the faculty rationale. Many students liked the ten-week quarter system because, as many said, if one had a bad course or a bad instructor, it would all be over in a short ten-week span rather than in a fifteen-week semester. Students also believed that the quarter system gave them more flexibility and choice in their academic schedule. And undergraduates were also legitimately worried that a switch to semesters would be an obstacle to a timely graduation. In contrast, graduate and professional students were more supportive of a semester system. They realized that many of their academic endeavors did not fall neatly into a ten-week framework. But as the discussion about the possible conversion went on, it was the undergraduate voices that were the most prominent.

Thus, with the faculty and students not supportive of moving to semesters and with the university leadership having done an inadequate job of making the case for the switch, Gee wisely decided to not push the initiative. But when he returned to Ohio State in 2007, Gee was determined that the move to semesters would be accomplished. In the ten years that he had been gone from Ohio State, the semester system had emerged as the dominant academic calendar nationally as the quarter system waned in popularity. On campus, some colleges such as law and medicine had already moved away from the quarter system. For example, for law students taking the bar exam after graduation, the quarter system would have been a disaster. The quarter system ended in June, the bar exam was administered in July, and law students would have little time for preparation. In contrast, the semester system ended in April, leaving law students more time to get ready for the bar exam. While the college of law moved to semesters before the university did, other graduate and professional programs and students began to see the benefits of a semester conversion, in part because their peers at other colleges and universities were already working under a semester system and seemed to be thriving.

Many undergraduates were still skeptical about the move and here it became essential for the university administration to answer up front what the move would mean for students' academic careers. How would graduation requirements change, including the number of credits needed for graduation? When would the academic year begin and end? Under the quarter system at Ohio State, the typical beginning would be the third week of September and the end would be the middle of June. Students were told that the academic year would begin in mid- to late August and end in late April. Some students then worried that an August start would mean that they would not be able to work as late on their summer jobs and summer internships and thus be at a disadvantage. But here the university was ready with solid evidence that Ohio State students had been disadvantaged under the quarter system in seeking summer internship and jobs. All other things being equal, employers preferred students who would be available earlier rather than later. And for students entering their final year of college and getting serious about job hunting and placement, students at semester institutions had a one-month head start over students at quarter institutions.

The university also reassured students who were enrolled when the actual conversion occurred that they would not get caught up in any bureaucratic impediments that might delay their graduation or prevent them from completing their chosen program of study. The university made explicit commitments that students who were on track to graduate at a specific time under the quarter system would be able to do that under the semester system. If, for example, requirements changed or became more burdensome or if some required courses were no longer being taught, students caught up in these situations were guaranteed that accommodations would be made, that flexibility would be the operating principle, and that their time to graduation would not be lengthened.

As the conversion was being discussed in the university governance processes, there were additional reassurances and "sweeteners" offered to students (and faculty), and one of these was the development of the Maymester. The spring semester would end in April, the summer sessions would start in June, but the month of May was to be reserved for something (at the time) very

CHAPTER 7

unique and exciting—the Maymester. After much planning, the May session began in May 2013. It incentivized students to experience academic topics outside their core academic program. More importantly for many undergraduates the May session was free and students could earn three credit hours. Students who had been enrolled in the spring semester and had not yet graduated could take advantage of the May session at no cost. Many of the university's colleges and departments were very creative in developing May session experiences for undergraduates with 130 specialized courses and 40 study abroad programs developed to fit the May 2013 session calendar. Thus, the university leadership worked hard to win the support of the student body, and when the calendar conversion proposal reached the University Senate, undergraduate, graduate, and professional students all strongly supported the measure with the president of the Undergraduate Student Government praising the process and the substance of the proposal.

The faculty and the faculty leadership still remained to be won over, but as Professor Gunther told me, many things had changed since the demise of semester conversion in the first Gee presidency. Number one was Gee's own commitment to getting this done. He energetically lobbied faculty, asking for their support. The university was much better prepared to address the questions that faculty members had raised about how semester conversion would impact them. Faculty had questions about teaching loads, flexibility of scheduling, and reward systems, and the university administration demonstrated that it was taking these concerns seriously. Another development weighing in support of the move to semesters was the fact that many other universities had made the switch and that Ohio State was in an ever-shrinking group of universities still on the quarter system. There were also external political pressures on the university to move to semesters. Eric Fingerhut, Chancellor of the Board of Regents and architect of the University System of Ohio, let it be known that he wanted all of Ohio's universities and community colleges to be on the same semester system in order to foster student transfers and articulation agreements among the institutions. Gee shared this political pressure with the faculty and the faculty leaders and raised the possibility that there might be negative consequences for the university if it remained the lone institution on the quarter system. While some faculty leaders resented the external pressure, they recognized that it was a legitimate consideration in making the conversion decision. When the semester conversion proposal was finally voted on in the University Senate, faculty and student support was strong. Of course, the administrative voting members of the Senate voted overwhelmingly for semesters since they all worked directly for either the president and/or the provost.

FIGURE 7.1. Randy Smith and Carole Anderson have both served the university superbly in a variety of positions within the Office of Academic Affairs and elsewhere. Randy was routinely counted upon to take on the most challenging tasks such as the arts and sciences transition and the university's accreditation renewal. Carole was dean of the College of Nursing and later a vice provost in Academic Affairs. She also served as dean of the graduate school and dean of the College of Dentistry, among her many contributions. Credit: The Ohio State University.

Once the proposal was adopted, the next round of very hard work commenced. The university community did itself proud in the care and attention it gave to issues arising in the conversion to semesters. Every academic unit reviewed its overall set of requirements to harmonize them with the new semester system. Moreover, every unit reviewed the content of its curriculum to determine whether the switch to semesters provided a good opportunity for curricular reform. And, of course, every quarter course had to be reworked to mesh with the new semester system. This entire process was a massive undertaking for the academic community and was led by Randy Smith and the Office of Academic Affairs (see Figure 7.1). Smith did an incredible job keeping the process moving forward in a collegial and constructive fashion. As this fundamental revision of curriculum was being conducted, the university also adopted policies and procedures to ensure that students enrolled when the switch actually occurred would not encounter barriers to the completion of their academic programs and to their timely graduations. Again, the semester conversion process revealed a university committed to constructive change that strengthened the core academic component of the university.

Arts and Sciences Consolidation

Gordon Gee had long believed that great universities had at their core outstanding arts and sciences colleges. When he first arrived at Ohio State in 1990, he encountered an academic structure in which the arts and sciences were divided into five administratively autonomous colleges: Arts, Biological Sciences, Humanities, Mathematical and Physical Sciences, and Social and Behavioral Sciences. Each of these colleges had its own dean, its own budget authority, and its own backroom functions such as human resources, communications, and development. And even though one of these five deans was given the title of executive dean of the arts and sciences, he or she had very little formal authority with respect to budgeting and resource allocation across the colleges. Furthermore, the executive dean had little role in the promotion and tenure decisions of the five colleges. Gee thought this structure diminished the visibility and the reputation of the arts and sciences at Ohio State. He also believed it created unnecessary roadblocks to cross-disciplinary and non-traditional research collaborations. And he certainly believed that it was bureaucratically and fiscally inefficient with all the redundancies in backroom services in the five independent colleges. He knew that Ohio State had some truly distinguished, nationally recognized academic departments, scattered throughout the five colleges and especially in Social and Behavioral Sciences, and yet Ohio State's national reputation in the arts and sciences overall was not nearly as good as he thought it should be. He claimed that one reason Ohio State's arts and sciences were undervalued was the academic structure under which they were operating. The five-college structure also worked against Gee's "one university" guiding principle. Gee thought the five independent college structure was too complex and shifted attention away from the overarching "arts and sciences" to specific colleges and units therein. Thus, Gee encouraged the dialogue that was already ongoing at the university about the structure of the arts and sciences. And the questions were not just about financial inefficiencies and duplication. They were also about the fundamental role and stature of the arts and sciences at Ohio State University.

While Gee pondered these and related arts and sciences issues in his first term, nothing changed. After his departure in 1997, discussions about the future of the arts and sciences continued. In 2002 a report was issued recommending a new organizational structure. The actual shape of that structure was outlined in a 2003 white paper *Federation of the Colleges of Arts and Sciences at The Ohio State University*. This document established a formal Federation of the Colleges of Arts and Sciences and also an Office of the Executive Dean of the Colleges of Arts and Sciences. The goals for this new federation were similar to those discussed earlier: elevate the stature and visibility of the arts and sciences internally, nationally, and internationally; enhance the reputation and quality of all colleges . . . ; and enhance coherence, collaboration, and synergies. Eight additional goals were identified, and there was to be a formal review of this new administrative structure in four years in 2007. By good fortune 2007 was the year that Gordon Gee returned to Ohio State and the review of the existing structure of the arts and sciences was already on the agenda. That review was comprehensive and thorough and concluded that "the organizational and administrative structure adopted in 2003 is highly dysfunctional." The report pointed out that the executive dean was never given real financial authority or effective control of personnel policies. It said that progress toward achieving major goals was very uneven and much of the reason for that was the dysfunctional organizational structure. In effect, the 2003 "reforms" had to a large extent replicated the autonomous, ineffective structure in place during Gee's first presidency. The review committee submitted its final report in April 2008 and urged a redesign of the current dysfunctional structure, but was largely silent about what the ultimate configuration should look like, except that it not repeat the mistake of the "sixth college." By that, the review committee meant that the current system made a bad situation worse. The university had five colleges of the colleges of the arts and sciences and then created the federation college office, the sixth college, which often seemed to be in competition with the five colleges for resources and stature.

Thus, the issue of the restructuring of the arts and sciences was handed to Gee early in his second term, and he relished the opportunity. There was a mandate for change, but the details of that change were up for grabs. There were many competing interests arguing for very different outcomes. Some colleges feared losing budget authority to a strong central executive dean. Some were worried that if the five colleges were folded into one huge arts and sciences college, the burden on the executive dean and his or her staff would be enormous, especially in the areas of personnel and promotion and tenure decisions. Some faculty members welcomed strong central leadership; others feared that a strong central office would not be as sensitive to the unique perspectives of department and academic disciplines. Gee himself made it clear

Chapter 7

that he strongly supported a strong executive dean, yet he recognized the concerns of the faculty.

The ultimate reorganization that was adopted represented a compromise along multiple dimensions. The new executive dean of the new college was given budget authority to the chagrin of some of the existing deans of the existing five colleges. The five existing colleges were not eliminated. Instead, they were divided into three areas—Arts and Humanities, Biological and Mathematical and Physical Sciences, and Social and Behavioral Sciences—each with their own divisional dean. Personnel decisions including promotion and tenure would remain at the divisional level, which was very reassuring to faculty who worried that a central office could not fully appreciate the uniqueness of the scholarship and research methods of the five colleges. But the executive dean would have the responsibility to coordinate the promotion and tenure decisions as they were transmitted upward to the provost and the Office of Academic Affairs.

When Provost Alutto announced the organizational changes, he also recommended the interim leaders of the college and the three divisions. The selection of Joan Leitzel as interim executive dean and vice provost of the arts and sciences was a brilliant decision. Leitzel, through her long and distinguished service at Ohio State and her prominent leadership positions at other universities, provided reassurance to the faculty who knew her well that the college was in good hands. Alutto also reassured the faculty that there would still be academic departments with chairs and that the divisions would have deans. He stated that "the new federation will not be duplicating, competing with, or inhibiting the efforts of the individual colleges. . . . Rather, precisely because the executive dean will have control over all university resources generated for the arts and sciences, the federation will be poised to promote the academic excellence and visibility of the arts and sciences as never before" (*On Campus*, May 22, 2008).

Now the task was to find the permanent dean of the new college, a search detailed in chapter 3. The search committee recommended three names; Gee thought that none of the three were of the stature and competence to be dean of the new college. Gee believed that the new structure was important, but he also believed that strong leadership was required to make the structure successful. Gee was looking for someone with vision, decision-making skills, and toughness and found Joe Steinmetz, who became the first executive dean of the reorganized arts and sciences. Steinmetz subsequently became the university provost and then moved to become chancellor of the University of Arkansas. Steinmetz got the college off to a good start, but his successor David Manderscheid was not as skillful in leading the federation. Making Manderscheid's task even more difficult were the financial challenges facing the arts and sciences discussed below.

It is difficult to assess how well the arts and sciences consolidation achieved the goals that Gee and Alutto had for it. Certainly, there was an increase in joint academic appointments and cross-disciplinary activity in both teaching and research. More generally, it helped create an environment where collaborative research and service was valued. And some savings were achieved by eliminating duplicative operations. The voice of the arts and sciences did become more prominent in university deliberations during Steinmetz's deanship, but that presence weakened with his successor.

Thus, it is not at all clear that the arts and sciences have achieved higher visibility and recognition. Nor is it clear that the arts and sciences are a higher priority within the university than they had been. In the post-Gee, post-Alutto, and partially post-Steinmetz era, new dean David Manderscheid encountered a set of budgetary and enrollment crises for which he was not well prepared. Manderscheid was not very adept in advocating for the arts and science with the upper levels of university administration, nor was he particularly effective in making reallocation decisions within the arts and sciences. One of the challenges for the arts and sciences at Ohio State is a budgetary model in which colleges earn dollars through course enrollments. One trend at Ohio State is that more and more freshmen are entering Ohio State having already earned one year of college academic credit while still in high school. And most of this coursework has been in the general education requirements, courses disproportionately taught by the arts and sciences departments. Hence enrollments in these courses have declined, and that has resulted in budgetary shortfalls in the departments. Moreover, non-arts and sciences colleges were changing their requirements or offering their own courses in certain areas that mimicked arts and sciences courses. And some would argue that the heavy university emphasis on STEM—science, technology, engineering and mathematics—hurts some of the arts and sciences departments. Likewise, the broader societal emphasis on getting one's first job after graduation and the related (and in my opinion mistaken) view that majoring in the arts and sciences is not a good path to obtain a job after graduation are resulting in fewer majors and lower course enrollments in many arts and science departments. Many departments, such as English, history, and political science, have witnessed substantial declines in their number of regular faculty members, which makes it more difficult to staff courses, which further hurts efforts to boost enrollments. Dean Manderscheid left Ohio State to become the provost of the University of Tennessee at Knox-

CHAPTER 7

ville. Janet Box-Steffensmeier served superbly as the interim dean but indicated that she would not be a candidate for the permanent position. In 2019, Gretchen Ritter from Cornell became the executive dean. She is fully aware of the challenges facing the arts and sciences at Ohio State.

Thus, all of the efforts made over the years to enhance the place and prestige of the arts and sciences at Ohio State are being overwhelmed by multiple factors, many of which the arts and sciences departments and the dean cannot control. But there is much they can do, including a greater emphasis on career counseling and internships in their programs, more creativity in offering courses that would attract more students, and greater creativity in how instruction is delivered. But without strong leadership within arts and sciences and without university leadership that prioritizes arts and sciences as core to a university, the fate of arts and sciences at Ohio State may be dim, and all of the earlier emphasis on the structure and organization of the arts and sciences may in hindsight seem to be a fruitless enterprise.

8

From Development to Advancement

Introduction

Shortly after Gordon Gee returned to Ohio State after a ten-year sojourn at Brown and Vanderbilt, he asked the OSU development office to provide him a list of the top 30 major donor prospects. It took the development office weeks to produce that list. By the time Gee received the list, he had already personally contacted 28 of the 30 names on the list. In effect, the top prospects had not changed in the ten years that Gee was gone. Even though Ohio State had added almost 100,000 new graduates in that period, and even though many of the existing alumni base had moved a decade further along in their careers, life experiences, earnings potential, and perhaps retirement, there were few signs that new major donor prospects were being cultivated. Nor was there much evidence that younger alumni were being groomed to become significant donors to the university down the road.

This situation really frustrated Gee. He knew that he had some outstanding development officers, yet he believed that the overall system was malfunctioning. For Gee, long-term cultivation of friends and alumni was critical. Friendraising preceded fundraising. For Gee, the solicitation of donations from friends and alumni of the university should be a longer-term relational activity and not simply a short-term transactional one. Having been at Ohio State and two other public universities—University of Colorado and West Virginia University—and two private universities—Brown and Vanderbilt—Gee had seen firsthand the major differences between public and private universities in their approaches to philanthropic fundraising. The private schools started early

Chapter 8

maintaining relationships and inculcating a habit of philanthropy from their young graduates. This cultivation was not simply the responsibility of the university president and the development vice president. It was also the responsibility of all the vice presidents, the deans, the department chairs, and other leaders of the university. They followed these young graduates throughout their life span, continuing to build deeper relationships with them. In contrast, for many public institutions and especially for their undergraduate alumni, little effort was made to stay in contact and build relationships with them after graduation. For many university leaders, especially those with an arts and sciences background, private fundraising was not as high on their radar screens as it should have been; it simply was not in their job description or part of their skill sets. Others too quickly accepted the idea that public universities received public funds and that therefore the private universities should have first rights to private giving. In some instances, asking for private donations was seen as demeaning and inappropriate.

For Gee, this inattention to private fundraising at public institutions was wrongheaded. He saw that public universities would be increasingly challenged financially to support their mission. State budgets across the country were under heavy pressure from a whole host of worthy public services such as primary and secondary education, health care, and rehabilitation and corrections. Moreover, state budgets were always subject to the whims of economic downturns. And whereas in the past public universities had the freedom to raise tuition in order to compensate for the inadequacy of state support, that source of revenue was also being squeezed as the affordability of public higher education became a prominent issue and many states put constraints on tuition hikes. Thus, Gee was committed to finding alternative revenue streams to support university priorities. Some of these were nontraditional, as discussed in chapter 12. But Gee also said that the university had to do a much better job in some traditional development areas—annual giving, major donor giving, endowment growth, unrestricted giving, alumni donations, and others.

To that end, he charged his colleagues to establish for Ohio State a new advancement model that would integrate university development, university communications, and the Ohio State University Alumni Association, an independent 501(c)(3) entity. A historical note is appropriate here before we discuss the establishment of the advancement model. When Gee returned in 2007, Ohio State had an office of university relations headed by Curt Steiner, senior vice president for university relations. This office had responsibility for internal communications, marketing communications, media relations, research communications, WOSU Public Media, and government relations. Gee decided in

2008 to reorganize these functional areas and brought in Tom Katzenmeyer from The Limited to be the university's senior vice president for communications, while Curt Steiner was made the senior vice president for government affairs. Under this structure, it was university communications, and not government affairs, that was formally incorporated under the advancement model.

The goal of the advancement approach was not simply to raise more philanthropic dollars. Instead, it was more critical at the outset for the university to do a much better job connecting with its multiple constituencies. The university needed to share with its friends why it was a worthwhile investment. What was the university doing on campus to foster student access and student success? How was the university contributing to the life of the community and the economy of the state and nation? How well was the medical center working on and off campus to improve health outcomes for Ohioans? How were the research activities of the faculty and staff benefitting not only the academic disciplines they represented but also the broader citizenry? Under the advancement model, the stories of the successes of Ohio State were to be told more effectively to audiences internal and external to the university.

Gee understood how the civic and social environments within which universities operated were changing dramatically and not necessarily for the better. Therefore, if universities did not tell their own stories, less sympathetic entities might do it for them—or perhaps to them. Gee wanted external audiences to feel in their hearts that Ohio State was their university. If alumni, parents of students, donors, public officials, and everyday citizens with no formal ties to the university believed that Ohio State mattered to them and to their communities, then other goals such as fundraising, enhanced academic reputation, and student recruitment would be facilitated. Beyond that, if universities could connect to their various publics in a deep and sustained way, they would be much better positioned to head off or overcome some of the political and social challenges likely to confront them in the future.

Thus, the university's approach to fundraising would now move from a more traditional development model to the new advancement model. Implementation of the advancement model required a change in mindset at the university in both the development and communications functions, and it also required a buy-in from the OSU Alumni Association. Since the senior vice presidents for development and communication reported directly to the president, Gee could guarantee that they would be partners in building the advancement model, even if there was some grumbling within the development and communications bureaucracies. But the Alumni Association was an independent organization. After some stumbles, Gee finally recruited Andy Sorenson, former

CHAPTER 8

FIGURE 8.1. The sudden death of Andy Sorenson was a terrible shock to his family, friends, and colleagues. Credit: The Ohio State University.

president of the University of South Carolina and the University of Alabama to be the senior vice president for advancement and lead the effort to embed the advancement model into the fabric of the university (see Figure 8.1). Sorenson, a wise and thoughtful leader, was making great progress. When he died suddenly in April 2011, the implementation of the advancement approach was dealt a setback, and the university lost a superb citizen and colleague. Ultimately, Michael Eicher was hired to bring the advancement model to fruition and to lead the next major university fundraising campaign.

The Alumni Association and the Advancement Model

Bringing the Alumni Association on board was a more difficult task. As mentioned earlier, it was a freestanding, independent entity with its own Board of Directors, its own staff, its own business model and business operations, its own network of alumni clubs throughout the United States and the world, and its own membership list. This is not to say that the Alumni Association acted independently of university interests and priorities. To the contrary, under the leadership of Dan Heinlen and Archie Griffin, the Alumni Association had worked skillfully to advance university priorities. For example, the Association had an Alumni Advocates program that worked very closely with the university's office of government affairs to help advance the university's agenda in Washington, DC, and in state government. For all members of Congress from Ohio and every member of the Ohio General Assembly, alumni were selected to be points of contact with these public officials. The alumni advocate might be a longtime friend or a relative or a major donor or a business associate of the public official and would have great access to help deliver the university's message. This program worked superbly for many years and continues to do so. Another example of university/Alumni Association cooperation involved the president's travels. In most instances when President Gee traveled off campus, one of his stops and presentations would be at the local alumni club, once again suggesting the good working relationships that existed.

Despite this history of cooperation, the integration of the Alumni Association into the advancement framework entailed negotiations that at times were tense. The Association was headed by Archie Griffin, one of the most iconic and beloved Buckeyes and not simply because of his football exploits as a two-time Heisman Trophy winner (see Figure 8.2). He and Gee had a wonderful friendship, often teasing each other about being the only two-time Heisman Trophy winner and the only two-time university president. Griffin's loyalty and commitment to Ohio State were deep and genuine. He was a leader who always tried to do the right thing and resolve issues in a constructive and upbeat way. And the proposed advancement model had some skeptics among the Alumni Association Board of Directors and among some of the 500,000 plus living members of the Alumni Association. Critics worried that the advancement model was simply a way to raise more money from alumni and that incorporating the Alumni Association under the advancement umbrella would diminish the association and lessen the importance of alumni and alumni clubs in the life of the university. There were challenging negotiations between the university and the Alumni Association, but under the skillful and sensitive leadership of Griffin and Gee, issues were resolved and concerns were ameliorated. The core issues that needed to be resolved centered on governance and structure. Would the Alumni Association Board of Directors and its president and chief executive officer still exist? If so, how would future Alumni Association heads be selected? Would the Alumni Association president be a member of the university senior leadership team, and to whom would he or she report? Would the alumni association have access to university funding as it pursued university advancement goals? And what

CHAPTER 8

FIGURE 8.2. The universally admired Archie Griffin (center) was the president and CEO of the Ohio State University Alumni Association. Credit: The Ohio State University.

would happen to the staff of the alumni association as it was integrated tightly into the university?

The memorandum of agreement between the Ohio State University Alumni Association and The Ohio State University that was adopted in 2009 addressed these and many other issues. There would still be an Alumni Association Board of Directors and a president and CEO of the Alumni Association, who would also be part of the president's senior management team with the title of senior vice president for alumni affairs. When the position of Alumni Association president became vacant, the memorandum was more general in tone than prescriptive or directive. It read:

> It is the desire and the intent of the OSU Board of Trustees and the Board of OSUAA that both parties will be able to select the same individual to fill the role of Senior Vice President for Alumni Relations for OSU and the President/CEO of OSUAA . . . In electing the President/CEO

of OSUAA, the Board of Directors shall give appropriate deference to the determination of the University President, consistent with exercising fiduciary duty to the corporation.

The memorandum further stated that with respect to funding:

OSUAA, through the Senior Vice President for Alumni Relations, will participate in the university's annual budget process to obtain support for alumni programming determined to serve strategic advancement goals. Funds allocated by the University for alumni programming will be administered through a University budget for OSUAA's alumni relations.

Finally, with respect to the alumni association staff, the document read:

The President/CEO of OSUAA, who serves at the pleasure of the OSUAA Board and may also serve as the Senior Vice President for Alumni Relations, will remain responsible for all management rights relative to the OSU staff and ongoing business of the Alumni Association, in line with University policies and procedures.

It is clear that the language quoted above represents a carefully constructed compromise to protect the interests of both the university and the alumni association. And even as the memorandum was modified in subsequent years, these provisions were kept largely intact. Throughout the memorandum, there were pledges of cooperation and joint activities.

There was also some fleshing out of advancement strategies that would be jointly developed by the Association and the university in such areas as career services, alumni networking, regional engagement, lifelong learning, and volunteer recruitment and coordination. Note that these areas all involve engaging with alumni; none of them specifically mentions fundraising. This represents a commitment to staying in touch with alumni, to providing added value to their earned degrees, and to taking a longer-term relationship-building approach to the alumni base. This is the essence of an advancement model and brings to life Gee's firm belief that friendraising precedes fundraising, that relationship building must come before direct solicitation of contributions.

Even as the Alumni Association Board of Directors was kept, its composition was changed slightly to give the university president two appointments. In his first selections, Gee chose Jeff Kaplan and Herb Asher, two appointments designed to reassure the alumni association and its leadership of Gee's deep

Chapter 8

respect for the organization. Kaplan and Archie Griffin had been friends for decades dating back to Griffin's college football career. And Asher had worked closely with the alumni association's Advocates program in his role as government relations chief at the university. Asher was also good friends with Griffin and his immediate predecessor Dan Heinlen. More importantly, Gee would meet in executive session with the Board of Directors at its quarterly meetings. These were lively and fun sessions in which no topic was off limits. These sessions helped build confidence that the advancement model as it related to the Alumni Association was off to a good start.

The Impact of the Advancement Model

The implementation of the advancement model was a success on many fronts. When Gee left Ohio State and was succeeded by Michael Drake, the university's commitment to advancement remained firm. And when Griffin retired from the university, the somewhat complicated process to find his successor worked well and resulted in a leader committed to further building the advancement model—Jim Smith. The university and the Alumni Association changed the dues paying structure of the alumni association so that anyone who contributed at least $75 a year to *any* unit or program of the university automatically became a sustaining member of the Association. Smith and his colleagues at the Longaberger Alumni House worked creatively and successfully to make Association membership more valuable, developing paths by which alumni could stay engaged with the university and with their fellow Buckeyes. If one wanted to stay in touch with people and campus events, one could receive the superbly enhanced Ohio State Alumni print magazine, have access to University Libraries, share opinions on various websites and social media platforms, find fellow class members, keep one's university email for life, and get involved in alumni clubs and societies. If career concerns were important to alumni, they could network with or mentor fellow Buckeyes and get help from the Alumni Association for their own resume writing. And if alumni wanted to give back to the university, the Alumni Association would help them recruit future Buckeyes, learn about volunteer activities, participate in community service by working through alumni clubs and societies, advocate for Ohio State to public officials, and financially contribute to Ohio State. Smith and his staff were constantly seeking new ways for the university to engage with its alumni and friends and make cultivation a core activity of the university. Smith regularly shared information about the many activities promoted by the Alumni

Association in areas such as life-long learning experiences for alumni, opportunities for alumni to advocate on behalf of Ohio State, and regional (outside of Ohio) engagement.

In addition to the Alumni Association, many colleges and departments throughout the university began to appreciate the rationale for the advancement model and adopted appropriate tactics and strategies to advance Ohio State. Many colleges, including Arts and Sciences, established programs to enhance career and professional services for their graduates. Colleges took their programs on the road, sending distinguished faculty to meet with alumni clubs and other groups off-site. Departments and colleges revitalized their alumni advisory boards or created them if none had existed. It is these kinds of initiatives multiplied a thousand times over that will make the advancement model work and yield a larger number of friends and alumni of the university willing, even eager, to support their alma mater. This will be a long-term endeavor, which must constantly be sustained.

But even in the short term, there is solid evidence that the advancement approach is working with respect to engaging donors and raising money. During the last two years of Gee's second administration, annual giving hit record levels from a record number of donors. And this pattern continued in the Drake administration, especially in fiscal years 2016 and 2017 when record totals of $457 million and $532 million were raised. While total dollars and numbers of donors are relatively straightforward metrics for assessing the success of a fundraising campaign, they are not sufficient to measure the overall success of the advancement approach in such areas as building public support for the university. Much discussion, some of it passionate and fierce, surrounded the selection of indicators to measure the success of the advancement model. Public opinion surveys conducted with different constituencies were proposed to measure awareness of the university, approval/disapproval ratings of Ohio State, and feelings of connectedness toward the university. For these and other indicators, the university could set goals and then measure them annually to see where the university stood and how well it was progressing. And again, note that these indicators are not about dollars; they are about people's feelings toward Ohio State, about how much they value the institution.

The "But for Ohio State . . ." Capital Campaign

Even as the advancement model was successfully being developed under Gee's leadership, there was also a more traditional and extremely significant activity

CHAPTER 8

FIGURE 8.3. The kickoff of the "But for Ohio State Campaign" with Leslie Wexner, Abigail Wexner, and Gordon Gee standing among a throng of students. Credit: The Ohio State University.

unfolding, also under Gee's leadership—a $2.5 billion capital campaign labeled the "But for Ohio State Campaign" (see Figure 8.3). One of the major reasons trustees wanted Gee to return to Ohio State was to lead the university's next major capital campaign. The previous campaign had occurred in Gee's first presidency and it was very successful. But since Gee's departure, there had not been another distinct major campaign. There had been major efforts growing annual giving, but the times were not right for the next major fundraising campaign. A fundraising campaign in Kirwan's presidency, Gee One's immediate successor, seemed premature; it was too soon to go back to the same donors who had just contributed. Major capital campaigns are special events requiring years of planning and usually do not occur one right after another. It was a different situation with Kirwan's successor, Karen Holbrook. Here the trustees simply believed that President Holbrook did not have the skills and savvy to undertake a major fundraising campaign. Moreover, the overall development apparatus had fallen into some disrepair during her presidency. Thus, the trustees were looking to the president who succeeded Holbrook to lead the next campaign, and that was Gordon Gee.

FROM DEVELOPMENT TO ADVANCEMENT

Planning for the campaign began shortly after Gee returned in fall 2007 and continued well into 2012. This is considered the quiet phase of the campaign that precedes the public announcement of the campaign. The quiet phase is when all the campaign preparations and logistics have to be completed. A campaign structure needs to be built with various committees populated by major players who are friends of the university. The internal staff of development had to be rebuilt. Identifying major donors and donors at all income levels had to be done along with deciding on the strategy and tactics for connecting with the donor prospects. The university had to identify the top priorities for which dollars were being raised. The university also had to make four more key decisions before the campaign could be publicly announced: What is the overall goal of the campaign in total dollars? What will be the duration (in years) of the campaign? What will be the name and/or the tagline of the campaign? And who will be the faces of the campaign in addition to President Gee? And as these questions were being answered and the campaign team was coming into place, the actual fundraising had already begun. In most major philanthropic campaigns, in order to assure success, organizations want to have a third to half of the overall goal in hand when the announcement is made, and Ohio State easily achieved that.

The initial announced goal for the campaign was $2.5 billion, later raised to $2.7 billion, and when the counting finally stopped in the Drake administration, the total exceeded $3 billion. The duration of the campaign was to be seven years, but if one counts years starting from the day of the public announcement, it actually was a shorter campaign. Finally, the name of the campaign—"But for Ohio State" initially puzzled some observers, but it turned out to be an excellent choice. It was inspired by Les Wexner, longtime donor, board member, and alumnus of Ohio State. Wexner would tell stories about how had it not been for Ohio State, he would not have achieved so much in his career and life. His favorite way of expressing this sentiment was the simple phrase "But for Ohio State." "But for Ohio State" became the campaign theme, and it was brilliant because almost everyone had a "But for Ohio State" story to tell. Wexner contributed leadership, advice, and credibility to the campaign. And he gave Ohio State the largest single gift it had ever received—$100 million for the medical center, which soon became The Ohio State University Wexner Medical Center.

Gee of course devoted an incredible amount of time and energy to the campaign. He was on the road frequently, in Ohio and throughout the nation, meeting not only with major donor prospects, but also with friends and alumni

Chapter 8

whose generosity might be more financially constrained. Often Gee was sent in to "close the deal" after development staff had brought the potential donor close to an actual gift. Gee loved making donors feel that Ohio State was their institution as well as his.

Gee also was adamant that all units of the university do a first-rate job of stewardship: acknowledging the receipt of gifts in a very timely fashion, recognizing donors for their contributions, and letting donors know how their gifts were used. If, for example, donors contributed to student scholarship funds, they would likely be hearing from students who benefitted from their generosity. Gee himself was a wonderful steward, and even though he of course focused on major donors, he was continually thanking donors at all levels of contributions through letters, personal notes, phone calls, and so on.

When the public phase of the campaign began in 2012, it had five core goals: placing students first; elevating faculty and the academic enterprise; creating modern learning environments; emboldening the university's research agenda; and generating high impact innovation. As the core of the university, students and faculty were mentioned first. Ohio State needed to attract the best students, provide them outstanding academic experiences, and ensure an environment in which they could live and learn successfully. For faculty, the campaign emphasized recruiting rising academic stars while retaining and supporting our veteran talent. In this goal and in the "emboldening our research agenda" goal, interdisciplinary approaches were emphasized along with a focus on solving real-world problems. Also important here was the notion of faculty being able to patent their research when appropriate and being able to share in the benefits of commercialization when it occurred. The other two goals of "creating modern learning environments" and "driving high impact innovation" were fundamentally about change and about Ohio State being a leader of change, whether that be in modern campus design, new teaching methodologies, or breakthrough inventions and new technologies to address core problems and enhance the quality of life. These goals were stated this way to create a sense of excitement about what was possible and a belief that Ohio State had the road map and the talent to make great strides toward these goals.

Conclusion

When Andy Sorenson died suddenly in 2011 while leading the university toward the implementation of the advancement model, Gee named Jeff Kaplan to be (among his many titles) the senior vice president for advancement. In

February 2012, Kaplan sent an excellent advancement update to the university community. He began his message with the assertion that our aim is to make Ohio State one of the preeminent public universities in the world and that to accomplish this, we must enhance our reputation and deepen our relationships with key stakeholders. He further stated that "Every faculty and staff member has an important role in achieving our goal." Thus, even as the transition to the advancement model was appropriately being led from the top, its ultimate success would depend upon on how well it became ingrained in the fabric of the institution. Kaplan explained that the advancement work would be organized around three core activities: awareness, engagement, and giving. For awareness and engagement, he wrote the following:

> **Awareness:** Telling the story of Ohio State's excellence throughout the full range of our activities including academic programs, research, outreach, athletics, and so on. We will do this to enhance the connection people feel to the University and to increase our opportunities to recruit top talent, attract innovative research partners, and collaborate with national leaders.
>
> **Engagement:** Deepening the relationships between Ohio State and students, faculty, staff, alumni, and friends who can be ambassadors for the institution around the world and contribute their time, energy, and talents to our ongoing efforts to improve the University.

He ended his message asserting that Ohio State must have a clear, coherent voice. He succinctly explained what the advancement model could and should accomplish:

> We must make it easy for our constituents to learn more about what we are doing, create compelling and exciting opportunities for them to get involved and pursue *their* [my emphasis] interests, and provide clear reasons why we need their financial support and advocacy. As a public institution, Ohio State must strive for its constituents to be a meaningful part of the university's life and success. Advancement is a key to making it so.

It will be fascinating to look back 30, 40, and 50 years from now to see how well Ohio State achieved and expanded the advancement paradigm as articulated by Kaplan. How well did the university communicate with its many constituencies? To what extent did these constituencies believe that Ohio State

CHAPTER 8

was important and valuable to them and to the broader society? And how well did Ohio State survive and thrive financially *and otherwise* in a future era in which higher education was expected to be challenged by external and internal forces as never before? The underlying notion of the advancement model was to position Ohio State to be an institution that successfully navigated threatening currents because it was held in high esteem by so many key constituencies. One path in that navigation was insuring a solid financial foundation, but even more fundamental was having external voices in all sectors of society being willing to speak up and validate the significance of The Ohio State University.

9

From Redevelopment to Revitalization

On Campus and Off

Introduction

In this chapter and the next, we will discuss some of the major initiatives to improve the physical environment of both the campus and certain off-campus neighborhoods. With respect to the off-campus neighborhoods, our time perspective will both precede and extend beyond the second Gee administration of 2007 to 2013. We instead will focus on the time span from the first Gee presidency through his successors into the second Gee presidency and beyond to his successors. We examine this expanded time period for multiple reasons. First, redevelopment is an ongoing process that typically occurs over a lengthy time span not bounded by particular university administrations. Indeed, we will see that many of the specific development decisions made in the first (and second) Gee administrations continue to have long-term impacts on Ohio State and on Columbus neighborhoods. Second, it was in Gee's first administration that Campus Partners was established and it was late in Gee's second administration that major decisions were made that guaranteed the continuing improvement of the East of High Street corridor following Gee's departure in 2013. In 1995, Gee and the Board of Trustees with the support of Columbus Mayor Greg Lashutka created Campus Partners to fight against the continuing decline and decay of the university district. Even before that, in January 1994, Gee and Lashutka took the lead along with university community organizations to establish the University Area Improvement Task Force to address the

Chapter 9

decline in the campus area. This partnership between Lashutka and Gee was noteworthy since they had had sharp disagreements about the location of a new multi-purpose arena in Columbus. The fact that they were able to get past their differences is a tribute to their leadership and to their sense of community commitment.

Campus Partners became the catalyst for the first and the subsequent revitalization efforts in the campus area including the initial South Campus Gateway, the ambitious Weinland Park neighborhood revitalization, and the later east of High Street corridor. After detailing the Campus Partners successes, we turn to another community initiative PACT—Partners Achieving Community Transformation—a major joint city/university project focused on the Near East Side of Columbus. Finally we will return to the Ohio State campus itself to discuss an initiative very high on Gee's priority list—the University Arts District. In chapter 10, we will discuss the North Campus Residential District, another very high priority for Gee, as well the construction of three signature university buildings—the substantially renovated Thompson Library, the new Ohio Union, and the new intramural and recreation facility RPAC.

Lessons Learned

As the redevelopment projects unfolded, the university learned a number of lessons and underwent a significant transformation in its mindset. First, even though the university saw itself as a national research institution and as Ohio's flagship university, it began to realize that its geographic setting in Columbus, the state's capital city and by far its largest and most prosperous city, meant that Ohio State also had an urban responsibility. Moreover, because of the many areas of academic expertise in urban affairs such as geography, city and regional planning, sociology, social work, urban economics, urban education, and so many more, and because the eastern boundary of the campus flowed directly into some of the most distressed neighborhoods in Columbus, the university had to tackle some very difficult urban woes. The second lesson was the recognition by the city and the university that they needed to become much better partners to address urban challenges. The creation of Campus Partners in 1995 represented a major commitment between the city and the university. And when Gee left the university in 1997 and Lashutka completed his last mayoral term in 2000, the partnership blossomed under Mayor Michael Coleman and President Brit Kirwan, continued during the Holbrook administration, and became more energized when Gee returned in 2007 and built an even closer relationship with Coleman and his administration

A third lesson learned was the realization that to accomplish transformational urban redevelopment projects, the university could not rely on traditional academic committees and commissions and processes to get the job done. Instead, one had to have a full-time organization—Campus Partners—devoted to the mission as its prime responsibility. Such entities needed to be staffed, funded, and supported by the university leadership and by the Board of Trustees. But they also had to have enough independence and flexibility to undertake complex tasks such as property acquisition and the formation of city-university working agreements. A fourth lesson emerged from the previous three: For urban redevelopment to succeed, the commitment to this goal must reach deep into the bureaucracies of the city and the university. A commitment from leaders such as the mayor and the university president is necessary, but it is not sufficient to generate the ongoing, day-to-day cooperation necessary to complete projects. If, for example, the legal office, the finance office, and the planning office at the university and their counterparts in city government are not all on board, any initiative is likely doomed to failure. Campus Partners played a vital role in building teams of collaborators. A final lesson learned was that for urban redevelopment to be successful, there must be substantial buy-in, even ownership, by the local neighborhood organizations. One goal of Campus Partners was to build capacity and continuity in important neighborhood groups such as the University District Organization through a variety of means, including the provision of staff and financial support.

Campus Partners and Its Impact

A university president seldom has the opportunity to witness firsthand the long-term benefits of decisions and policies adopted many years earlier. But Gordon Gee had that experience with respect to Campus Partners when he returned to Ohio State in 2007. As mentioned earlier, Campus Partners was created in 1995 as a 501(c)(3) corporation "independent" of the university. As such it could do things in areas such as land swaps and land purchases that the university could not easily accomplish. Originally, Campus Partners had an eleven-member board, six appointed by Ohio State, and five at large representing residents, students, and the city, through the director of the Department of Development. Initially the board included three Ohio State trustees, and Cam-

Chapter 9

pus Partners itself was staffed by university employees. From the very beginning, Campus Partners saw itself as a transformational enterprise, a catalyst for subsequent projects and progress. It was careful to include the stakeholders who had a vital interest in its success. It understood that its long-term mission was to improve the quality and character of the campus neighborhood even if in the short term its goal was to simply "stop the bleeding." And it aspired to become self-sufficient over time. Finally, Campus Partners was blessed by outstanding leadership in Terry Foegeler, Doug Aschenbach, and Amanda Hoffsis, and with superb staff support, especially from Steve Sterrett, the long-serving community relations director of Campus Partners and an outstanding chronicler of Campus Partners' history and accomplishments.

As mentioned before, the primary reason for creating Campus Partners was the rapid decline of the campus area east of High Street. Crime, gangs, and drug dealing had become common. Housing values and housing quality were plummeting as the number of owner-occupied dwellings in the university district declined and the number of properties bought up by often-unethical absentee landlords grew. Many landlords did not maintain their properties since they believed they had a captive audience. Many Ohio State students wanted to live on their own outside the residence halls, often in rental housing that would accommodate ten or more students. And students themselves would occasionally trash their own neighborhoods, sometimes in riots celebrating fall football victories or warm spring evenings. The campus area became a magnet for attracting other transient, younger people to the neighborhood. It did not take much to trash a neighborhood, especially by temporary residents who had no commitment to the area and did not respect those trying to improve the neighborhood. The campus area became so seedy and rundown that the university gave visitors coming to campus automobile directions that avoided the neighborhood entirely. In the year before the creation of Campus Partners, OSU student Stephanie Hummer was brutally murdered in the campus area, adding another tragic sign of the decline of the university district. Both Lashutka and Gee realized that the situation had to be turned around lest the university and the city suffer irreparable damage to their ability to attract students, talented young professionals, and investment to Columbus.

The first major project of Campus Partners was the South Campus Gateway, a 500,000 square foot mixed-use development that included retail establishments, office space, apartments, and a parking garage. The project replaced a number of rundown establishments on the east side of High Street and was the first step in a long-term effort to make the High Street boundary of campus a more attractive place for people to visit, to shop, to dine, to enjoy entertainment, *and* to live. In his second term as president, Gee was instrumental in making decisions about finance, investments, and priorities that resulted in continued improvements to the High Street corridor years after his departure in 2013. At the same time that South Campus Gateway was under development, the city and the university were working closely on other urban issues such as public safety, sanitation, code enforcement, and others. When South Campus Gateway finally opened in 2005, it set a higher standard for campus area redevelopment and facilitated other private investments on High Street and in the campus area. The symbolic importance of the South Gateway project should not be underestimated. It demonstrated that the city and the university could succeed on major projects and inspired renewed efforts to address the ills of the campus area.

When the Board of Trustees created Campus Partners as a nonprofit redevelopment corporation in 1995 they set aside $25 million out of the university endowment for real estate acquisition and other revitalization efforts. In 1997, the trustees accepted a longer-term revitalization plan produced by Campus Partners and then authorized the release of $15 million of the $25 million dollars and earmarked it for the South Campus Gateway project. The trustees also authorized operating support for Campus Partners through June 30, 2000.

The trustees were impressed by the initial planning successes of Campus Partners and in July 2000 authorized continued funding. At the same time, they requested the development of a five-year business plan for Campus Partners, which was an indicator that the board was in it for the long haul. The board appropriated $650,000 annually for the next three years, provided $3 million more from the university's endowment for the purchase of property for the Gateway project, and also authorized $7.6 million for Campus Partners to purchase real estate and corporate stock to support long-range plans beyond the Gateway project.

It was to the Trustees' credit that they understood there could be no quick fixes to the problems plaguing the University District. And it was to the credit of the university and the Campus Partners leadership teams that they fully shared with the trustees the successes and the setbacks in undertaking this ambitious initiative. From that point on, the financial underpinning of Campus Partners was on solid ground, with the expectation that Campus Partners would do more to generate its own funding through residential rentals, commercial leases, and parking garage revenues, all part of the Gateway project. Moreover, Campus Partners would become more aggressive in seeking grants from foundations and other nonprofit entities as well as actively seek support from the federal, state, county, and local governments.

CHAPTER 9

Weinland Park

While the South Campus Gateway project was moving forward, there was growing awareness of a more serious neighborhood crisis—Weinland Park—that illustrated the worst of urban decay. Weinland Park was home to about 5,000 residents and was located immediately southeast of Ohio State. Most of the residents were African American; very few were students or university employees. More than half the population fell below the poverty level. The median household income (about $16,000) was less than half of Columbus as a whole (about $38,000). It had the highest concentration of Section 8 government-subsidized housing units in the city. These units were privately owned and operated and were in terrible shape. There was a 50 percent turnover rate annually in these units that contributed substantially to the mobility rate of 85 percent among students at Weinland Park Elementary School. Mobility refers to whether and how often a student changes schools within a school year. A high mobility rate is not a good thing, and 85 percent at Weinland Park meant that almost every student attended at least two schools in one academic year. Community Research Partners had conducted a broader study of mobility rates in Columbus public schools and found that in economically poor neighborhoods and schools like Weinland Park, it was not uncommon for students to attend two, three, and even four schools within one academic year. The economic and social factors that led to families changing residences and schools frequently were additional indicators of a distressed neighborhood. Weinland Park had every blight one could imagine in a declining urban neighborhood, and it became clear that if that decline was not reversed, it would spill over directly into adjacent parts of the university district that were in a very transitional stage. Ultimately a major initiative was designed to tackle the Weinland Park challenge; the university, the OSU College of Education, and Campus Partners were all important players in this undertaking along with the city of Columbus.

In the original Campus Partners revitalization document in 1996, there was recognition that Weinland Park and its problems would eventually spill over into student campus neighborhoods, but there were no specific recommendations about how to address this situation. By 2000, however, there was widespread recognition that Weinland Park was a crisis, that campus area revitalization could not succeed unless the problems of Weinland Park were dealt with head on. There were some initiatives prior to 2000, but they had limited impact, in part because of the highly transient nature of the population and the severity of the problems. In 1997, the Campus Collaborative, an Ohio

State consortium of departments and colleges that worked closely with Campus Partners, received a three-year federal Community Outreach Partnership Center grant to focus on Weinland Park. Faculty and staff from the OSU College of Education and Human Ecology and from Ohio State University Extension (formerly the Cooperative Extension Service) worked with neighborhood residents and agencies on such problems as economic development, family living skills, and education. It may be that the most significant benefit of this cooperation was to help set the stage for more successful interactions some years down the road.

Steve Sterrett believes that the "breakthrough" moment for Weinland Park came when Campus Partners with the support of Ohio State was able to purchase a portfolio of Section 8 housing, much of it in Weinland Park. Without going into all the complex details of what followed, Campus Partners convened a large and diverse group of interested parties to consider what should happen to these properties. A plan was developed that called for major renovation of the housing and better management and supportive services for the residents. Campus Partners then transferred its purchase agreement to Ohio Capital Corporation for Housing, and it began the implementation of the plan for renovation and new management in 2004. The quality of the housing improved, public safety programs were adopted, and the initial results showed lowered crime rates, increased occupancy and renewal rates, and higher school attendance.

With this initial sign of progress, other entities stepped up to participate in the Weinland Park revival, and Weinland Park attracted more public and private investments. Campus Partners itself got involved in a second transformational project in Weinland Park when it was able to purchase a twenty-acre Brownfield site (formerly Columbus Coated Fabrics) in bankruptcy court. The necessary demolition and environmental remediation was done with the property now ready for development. Wagenbrenner Development then came in and built hundreds of market-rate units on that site, contributing to a mixed income neighborhood that did not force out the current residents.

Another major addition to Weinland Park came when the OSU College of Education and Human Ecology in partnership with Columbus City Schools and the city's Department of Recreation and Parks built a new elementary school that opened in 2007. The university built the Schoenbaum Family Center, co-located with the school, which also opened in 2007. The Schoenbaum Center is essentially an early education laboratory studying child development among diverse populations. It was the first of its kind to be built by a university in a distressed neighborhood. Meanwhile, the city's Department of Recreation and Parks upgraded the city park adjacent to the school and family center. Yet

Chapter 9

another commitment by the city and the university was the construction of a police substation, "a neighborhood policing center" on East 11th Avenue. The center opened in 2008 and is located on the border between Weinland Park and the predominantly student neighborhoods to its west.

One final project merits attention: the building of a major new Kroger supermarket on 7th Avenue and High St. The old Kroger was a dilapidated store with a number of unpleasant nicknames. It appeared that Kroger would be leaving the area, which would leave the distressed neighborhood and its residents with limited options for grocery shopping, an all too common phenomenon in urban America. But Campus Partner entered into discussion with The Kroger Company about a new store. And, importantly, Gordon Gee got directly involved, working with Marnette Perry, a very senior official of the Kroger Company and a friend to higher education, especially Ohio University and Ohio State, to enlist her help in ensuring that the neighborhood had a first-rate Kroger, and indeed it does.

Weinland Park is still a work in progress. But the trajectory is upward, and many indicators are very promising. For example, residential turnover in 2003 in Section 8 units was about 50 percent; less than ten years later it was about 20 percent. Crime is down, community investment is up. Education, life skills, and employment training and services are making a difference. I personally believe that the university's and Campus Partner's involvement in Weinland Park is one of the most meaningful community outreach and engagement activities. An entire neighborhood is being transformed. Columbus has witnessed many neighborhood transformations, but usually that is accompanied by gentrification where old residents are forced out and replaced by more prosperous people. In Weinland Park, the beneficiaries of the changes are by and large the residents themselves. They are gaining the benefits of higher quality housing, better educational opportunities, enhanced safety, improved employment and job training programs, and much more. Residents who had been living under horrible and dangerous conditions now have more promising futures.

The success of Weinland Park is amazing given the magnitude of the challenges. Although it was a small neighborhood with only 5,000 residents, it had every dysfunction imaginable. For these problems to be remedied, many public, private, and nonprofit entities had to be on board. The neighbors and neighborhood associations had to be active partners. The commitment to the complex project had to be long-term, and the pieces all had to come together in a timely fashion.

The work that Campus Partners, the university, the city, and so many other allies accomplished was recognized by a number of national organizations.

In 2008 Ohio State was chosen as a regional winner of the Outreach Scholarship W. K. Kellogg Foundation Engagement Award, which honors outstanding outreach partnerships undertaken by four-year public universities. Ohio State was praised for building unique partnerships that have contributed to the revitalization of the Weinland Park neighborhood. The previous year the university received another recognition for its outreach with community partners, one of those projects being the partnership between Weinland Park and the Schoenbaum Family Center at Weinland Park. In 2019, the American Planning Association recognized Campus Partners with its prestigious National Planning Excellence Award for its revitalization efforts in the University District. Both Terry Foegeler and Doug Aschenbach were present to accept the award. The press release accompanying the event summarized well the accomplishments of Campus Partners: it "leveraged more than $150 million in investment including renovation and development of roughly 1,000 housing units of Section 8, affordable, and market-rate housing; the redevelopment of south campus with South Campus Gateway; a new police station; new public elementary school; and Ohio State's new early childhood learning center." I have not done justice to the complexity and difficulty of the decisions, actions, and transactions that led to the success in Weinland Park. For more details, see two papers by Steve Sterrett. One is an unpublished summary, dated October 30, 2007, titled "Accomplishments in the University District: Status of priority implementation measures." The second is an article published in the *Journal of Higher Education Outreach and Engagement* (Volume 13, Number 3) in 2009 titled "Planning and Partnership for the Renewal of Urban Neighborhoods." Finally, two people need to be recognized for their key contributions in planning and executing numerous campus and campus area initiatives: Keith Myers, who joined Ohio State in 2013 as vice president for Planning, Architecture and Real Estate (PARE), and Amanda Hoffsis, assistant vice president of PARE and now the president of Campus Partners. They have assembled outstanding teams to move projects forward in a timely and competent fashion and have been extremely effective in working with partners in the public, private, and nonprofit sectors.

The High Street Corridor and 15th and High

While the completion of the South Campus Gateway in 2005 was the first major Campus Partners' initiative to focus on the eastern boundary of campus, the attention to High Street did not end there. Major changes on the east side of High continued after 2008, an outcome hoped for when Campus Partners was created and after South Campus Gateway was completed. Late in Gee's second term, financial commitments were made to stimulate further High Street redevelopment, which will unfold in the Drake administration and beyond. There is particular emphasis on the intersection of 15th Avenue and High Street (on the east side of High) to create a new gateway/entrance to the campus. This intersection will be the site of a signature building anchoring 15th and High, and the intersection itself may be named University Square. WOSU Public Media will be moving its operations to a new facility on High Street. Pearl Alley, which runs parallel to High Street east of High will be upgraded and serve as a retail hub. These developments were made possible when Campus Partners negotiated successfully with Edwards Communities, a major Columbus real estate developer, to gain control of the properties in the area. High Street from campus to the Short North through the Arena District and all the way to downtown has become an urban success story. Some critics will say that there has been too much gentrification. Others will say that High Street has lost some of its rough and tumble urban charm. But most observers will agree that High Street is different: it is more prosperous and has become a destination point for entertainment, shopping, and living. All one has to do is talk to alums who haven't been on High Street for two decades or so. They do not recognize the place. Some mourn the loss of their old hangouts, no matter how sleazy (the hangouts, not the alumni) they were; they evoked memories of youthful exuberance.

PACT

Like Weinland Park, PACT is another example of the university's commitment to a distressed neighborhood, this time the Near East Side east of downtown. PACT—Partners Achieving Community Transformation—is a nonprofit partnership between the university, the city, and the Columbus Metropolitan Housing Authority. Its goals are very straightforward—to help the residents of an area that is economically distressed but does have many tangible and intangible resources to build a strong community characterized by affordable housing, improved health care and education, and enhanced employment opportunities. The initiative has been blessed with extraordinary leadership from both Dawn Tyler Lee (see Figure 9.1) and Trudy Bartley as consecutive executive directors of PACT. Both Lee and Bartley had served as assistant vice president at Ohio State with a focus on local government and community affairs.

FIGURE 9.1. PACT leader Dawn Tyler Lee with Columbus Mayor Michael Coleman. Credit: The Ohio State University.

PACT was created in 2010 in the second Gee administration as an initiative where the university could impact a Columbus neighborhood where OSU already had a major presence. The decision to maintain and expand OSU Hospital East in the heart of the PACT neighborhood was a major statement about the university's commitment to the area. The presence of what was once called the Black Studies Community Extension Center was another sign of commitment, although there were some serious concerns by the residents and community activists about the quality of the facility and the programming that was conducted therein.

The university initially pledged $10 million to PACT to support its administrative structure and overhead as well as some programming projects with the expectation that PACT would receive additional support from the other partners and compete successfully for federal, state, and foundation support, which it did. Lee and Bartley both had incredibly complex and difficult jobs and performed them superbly. They had to work with and between the three partners and the bureaucracies of each of the partners. They also had to work

Chapter 9

with the many community groups and individual neighborhood activists, as well as report to a PACT board of directors. Many of the neighborhood organizations and some members of the board were skeptical about the commitment of the three partners. They had heard promises before, especially from the city, that were not fulfilled. They were worried that the university, relatively new to the neighborhood, would come into the area with the condescending attitude "We're from the university and we're here to help you." And the reputation of CMHA was mixed, depending on whom you talked to about which housing projects.

Dawn Tyler Lee got PACT up and running, and Trudy Bartley helped it gain momentum and achieve greater focus. PACT had a number of successes in its early stage. There was the creation of the Health Sciences Academies, an effort by Columbus City Schools, Ohio State, and PACT to make the public schools in the PACT service area destinations of choice. The Near East Side Neighborhood Leadership Academy was a PACT initiative supported by the United Way of Central Ohio to develop neighborhood leadership and grass roots solutions to community problems. The Exterior Repair Program expanded on an earlier pilot project to improve the exterior of homes in the PACT geographical area. A Parent University was established to help parents become better at raising their children. PNC Bank and the Franklin County Commissioners through the Franklin County Department of Jobs and Family Services supported the Parent University. The Ohio State University Home Ownership Program was initially an effort to increase the level of home ownership in the University District that started in 1998. It provided down payment assistance to encourage people to buy homes in the target area. In 2017, the target area was expanded to include the Near East Side. These and other programs and projects demonstrated the seriousness of the university's efforts in the Near East Side and the success of PACT in attracting financial support from disparate external entities. PACT also established a long-range plan with major input from the stakeholders in the community. After extensive discussions, meetings, and public hearings, the resulting PACT Blueprint for Community Investment detailed improvements for the Mount Vernon Business District, Mount Vernon East, Poindexter Village, East Long St., Taylor Avenue, and other adjacent areas. Bartley repeated what had been the guiding principles from the very beginning: "to work so that all residents have access to safe and affordable housing, quality health care and education and employment opportunities."

The Arts and the Arts District

THE ARTS

Gordon Gee was a fan of the arts on campus. He routinely bragged about the university's outstanding, nationally prominent Department of Dance. He loved the School of Music and the student performers there, especially the Ohio State University Marching Band and the men's and women's glee clubs. He was an enthusiastic supporter of the Wexner Center for the Arts headed by Sherri Geldin, who Gee had hired in 1993. Gee was delighted that Geldin was still in charge when he returned in 2007 because he believed that she had done more than anyone at the university to bring visibility and prominence to Ohio State University in the contemporary arts scene. Geldin was a creative genius and an amazing organizer. She worked so effectively in so many different worlds—the university, the arts, and the business world—and was a schmoozer par excellence who enlisted disparate audiences to share her passion for the arts. She took over the Wexner Center when it was four years old and still in its infancy, and built a nationally renowned institution that changed the face of the arts on campus, in Columbus, and in communities across the country.

Geldin and her team staged many notable exhibitions throughout her tenure, yet many of these artists would not be known to the casual patron of the arts. Her programming genuinely pushed the boundaries of the arts and gave lesser-known artists opportunities to expand their presence. She also had exhibitions of established artists. In Gee's second term, the William Wegman, the Andy Warhol, and the Annie Leibowitz exhibitions brought excitement to the campus and national visibility to the university. Shortly after Gee stepped down, Geldin staged a spectacular showing of paintings and sculptures from the collection of the Wexner family titled "Transformations: Modern Masters from the Wexner Family Collection."

Two other programs at the Wexner Center brought visibility to it and the university—the Wexner Prize and the Wexner Center Artist Residency Award. Both of these initiatives were inspired by Les Wexner and financially supported by the Wexner family. Wexner recognized that the Wexner Center did not and would not have a permanent collection. He also knew that the gallery space in the facility was less than optimal, thus it was critical for the Center to make its reputation through the exhibitions it mounted and the special events such

CHAPTER 9

FIGURE 9.2. Director Spike Lee being presented the Wexner Prize. With him on stage (from left to right) are Abilgail Wexner, Gordon Gee, and Sherri Geldin, the head of the Wexner Center for the Arts. Credit: The Ohio State University.

as the awarding of prizes and the recognition that that could generate. Geldin and Wexner and their staffs were a wonderful team to advance the Center. The Wexner Center Artist Residency award supported artists from the visual arts, performing arts, and film. During their stay on campus, they worked with students and faculty across the university. The award has been given to artists from all over the world. And the recipients have gone on to earn other recognitions such as the MacArthur Foundation Fellowship, National Medal of Arts Awards, Tony Awards, Oscar nominations, and Cannes Film Festival Awards. The Wexner Prize is "given to contemporary artists whose work has been consistently original, influential, and challenging to convention." The prize is funded by the Wexner Center Foundation through a gift from Les and Abigail Wexner. The first recipient in Gee's first term was director Peter Brook (1992) followed by choreographer Merce Cunningham (1993), composer John Cage (1993), visual artist Bruce Nauman (1994), choreographer and filmmaker Yvonne Rainer (1995), and filmmaker Martin Scorcese (1996). The prize was awarded less frequently by Gee's second term, but the recipients were filmmaker Spike Lee (2008; see Figure 9.2) and photographer Annie Liebowitz (2012). Clearly, Geldin and her team at the "Wex" heightened Ohio State's vis-

FIGURE 9.3. Karen Bell at her retirement reception being photographed with Jo McCulty, senior photographer at University Marketing and, along with Kevin Fitzsimons, the source of most of the photographs in this book Credit: The Ohio State University.

ibility and prestige in the world of contemporary art throughout the nation and internationally.

Another significant development in the arts was Gee's appointment of Karen Bell, former dean of the College of the Arts, as the university's first associate vice president for arts outreach (see Figure 9.3). Her charge as associate vice president was to "expand Ohio State's community arts presence and broaden the university's national visibility as a leader in arts outreach and community arts engagement." Before taking on this assignment, Bell had been instrumental in launching the OSU Urban Arts Space in part of the old Lazarus building in downtown Columbus.

The opening of the Billy Ireland Cartoon Library and Museum (see Figure 9.4) in a remodeled Sullivant Hall was another exciting achievement for the cartoon library holds the world's most comprehensive collection of cartoon and comic materials. Founding curator Lucy Caswell did a spectacular job in obtaining, sorting, and cataloging materials that quickly became available to the scholarly community and broader public. So many renowned cartoonists are included in the collection such as Charles Schulz, Milt Caniff, and Billy

CHAPTER 9

FIGURE 9.4. The entranceway and lobby of the Billy Ireland Cartoon Library & Museum. Credit: The Ohio State University.

Ireland. One of the fun activities for the casual visitor to campus is to discover the Cartoon Library, wander through the collection, and discover some of one's favorite comic book heroes from yesteryear. The galleries and collections enable scholars from throughout the world to study the relationship of cartoons to significant events in history as well as the routines of everyday life. The library has an extensive outreach program with exhibitions, lectures, seminars, conferences, and panel discussions as well as extensive material accessible online.

The partnership between the Royal Shakespeare Company and Ohio State University was another high-profile arts initiative during the second Gee presidency. The goal was to make Ohio State a key player to foster appreciation for the works of Shakespeare through teaching, research, and performance. Once again, Les and Abigail Wexner were financial supporters early on, leading to the partnership with the Royal Shakespeare Company (see Figure 9.5). The Shakespeare initiative included many programs and activities. For example, in 2010, the Royal Shakespeare programs launched Standup for Shakespeare, a youth education program in Columbus. In 2011, former RSC actor Kelly Hunter introduced the Hunter Heartbeat Method in which Shakespeare was used as a therapeutic intervention for children with autism. This project continued over

FIGURE 9.5. The generosity of Les and Abigail Wexner to the arts at Ohio State has taken many forms, here support for the Royal Shakespeare Company. Credit: The Ohio State University.

the next three years. Throughout the partnership, central Ohio teachers and OSU graduate students had the opportunity to be trained by the RSC in the teaching and appreciation of Shakespeare, culminating in a weeklong visit to Stratford-upon-Avon. In 2013, CAPA and Ohio State presented a production of *Julius Caesar* that was set in Africa and featured an all-Black cast. The partnership with the RSC was a wonderful success and reflected well upon all those in the College of the Arts and Sciences, especially the Department of English, which worked so skillfully, especially David Frantz who labored so effectively behind the scenes (no pun intended) to keep the project on track.

THE ARTS DISTRICT

There were many exciting, first-rate events occurring in the arts during Gee's second term, but there was one major concern that Gee had: the physical facilities and spaces for the arts were in many cases not up to the standard for the

Chapter 9

quality of the programs they housed. Even though there had been major renovations of Hopkins Hall in 2011 and Sullivant Hall in 2013, there still remained spaces, be they theaters, auditoria, performance spaces, concert venues, or simply classrooms that were often dilapidated, technologically primitive, and scattered throughout the campus. There was no overarching notion of an arts district on the campus even though the Wexner Center, Sullivant Hall, Weigel Hall, Mershon Auditorium, Hopkins Hall, and the School of Music were all in close proximity to each other, though far removed from the theaters that supported the Department of Theater. Under Gee's leadership the university began the process of creating a world-class arts district located on the campus side of the 15th and High intersection. Thus, with the development of the east side of High and the Art District to the west of High, the university would have a world-class front door to the community.

The Arts District will focus on the area of campus from 15th to 18th Avenue and two blocks into campus from High Street. It will include facilities to promote interaction across the arts disciplines and new homes for the School of Music and the Department of Theater. Most important, it will be a strong statement about the importance of the arts at Ohio State at a time when there is so much emphasis in higher education and at Ohio State on the STEM disciplines, on economic development, and on tech commercialization. Too many observers see the arts as a luxury, as something frivolous without much practical use. Ideally a coherent arts district as well as skillful messaging will help more people appreciate the economic impact of the arts as well as appreciate art itself. To have a world-class arts and performance district on a prime campus location will be a signature statement about the arts at Ohio State University.

10

Signature Buildings, the North Campus Residential District, and the Two-Year Residency Rule

Introduction

Gordon Gee always believed that well-designed physical facilities played an important role in building community and camaraderie among students. In Gee's first term, three major projects were under consideration—the renovation of the William Oxley Thompson Memorial Library, a new student union, and a new recreational facility for the campus community to support intramural sports and general health and wellness activities. The library renovation had been on the agenda for a long time but kept getting delayed as the library gradually became more rundown and depressing. The need for a new Ohio Union was growing, but it suffered a setback in 1995 when a student referendum defeated a proposal for a new union that would be financed by student fees. And the major recreational and intramural facility on campus—Larkins Hall—was unable to meet the needs of a campus community increasingly concerned with health and wellness issues. Larkins was overcrowded, dilapidated, and obsolete in many respects. The library was a core academic initiative, while the student union and the intramural facility served more of a cocurricular function. But all three were important to Gee in his first term in providing a better campus environment for students. And a state-of-the-art student union and a first-rate recreational facility became part of universities' recruitment tactics across the country as they engaged in an arms race to build outstanding facilities to impress prospective recruits.

CHAPTER 10

The New Ohio Union

The old Ohio Union had become increasingly obsolete and unable to accommodate the growing need for students and student organizations to have well-designed spaces for meetings, programming, and events. Student organizations were growing exponentially and becoming more diverse in response to students expanding involvement in civic, social, and political causes. In 2000, Bill Hall was named the new vice president for Student Affairs, and he restructured his office such that the Ohio Union and Student Activities were merged into one department, and Tracy Stuck, who had been director of Student Activities, became the director of the Ohio Union. This was a key appointment when it came time to construct a new union. Stuck was incredibly creative in helping plan the physical features of the new Ohio Union. And because of her previous role in student activities, she was fully aware of the programming needs that the new facility would have to address. When the facility was completed, it was one of the finest student unions in the country. Stuck did a superb job of ensuring that elements of the old student union were woven into the new building. In addition, she played a key role incorporating the traditions and spirit of Ohio State into the new building. Trustee Les Wexner has often complained that Ohio State does a poor job of branding and capturing the core themes of Ohio State when it constructs and opens a new facility. But, according to Wexner, there was major exception to his complaint—the new Ohio Union. He said that whoever was responsible for the branding of the new union was a creative genius. That person was Tracy Stuck.

In 2004, the Board of Trustees approved the plan to demolish the old union and construct a new building on the same (expanded) site. From that point on, there was a planning process to help identify the elements of the new building with substantial student input. With that, the actual construction began, and the new union opened at the start of spring quarter in 2010 (see Figure 10.1). The new union was widely praised for its beauty, its functionality, and its blending of traditional and modern. The core of the building is the Great Hall, which captures the essence of Ohio State (see Figures 10.2–10.3). There are large event spaces such as the Archie Griffin Ballroom, which can be configured for different-sized events and have state-of-the-art video and sound capabilities. There are many other rooms of larger and smaller sizes that can house student meetings, events, and programs. There are also ample food facilities, including Sloopy's Diner. There are open spaces where students can mingle, offices for the Student Affairs bureaucracy, and so many other welcoming features. A flash mob video organized by Tracy Stuck and choreographed by

SIGNATURE BUILDINGS

FIGURE 10.1. The ribbon cutting ceremony for the new Ohio Union. Some of the participants were Curt Moody (left in overcoat), head of Moody Nolan, which built the Union. Moving to the right in the photo are Ben Anthony, Undergraduate Student Government (USG) president Martha Garland, vice provost for undergraduate studies; USG Vice President Jordan Davis; Gordon Gee; and Tracy Stuck Credit: The Ohio State University.

Jordan Davis, readily available on YouTube called "Ohio Union flash mob" dated 5/3/2010, will give the reader some sense of the beauty and expanse of the Ohio Union and provide a cameo of President Gee's participation in the flash mob.

Two years after its opening, the Ohio Union was the site of an unusual political event in the 2012 campaign for president of the United States. President Obama was a frequent visitor to the Ohio State campus in highly publicized events. He kicked off his 2012 re-election campaign on the West Campus. He had a major campaign rally on the heart of the Oval. He also gave the spring commencement address, although that was after his re-election. But there was one additional appearance that was a total surprise to most people. One day, the Obama campaign contacted me and Tom Katzenmeyer, senior vice president for communications, indicating that the president would like to make a surprise visit to campus the following day. We were astonished. Events like this never happen. How would Secret Service react with respect to security

FIGURES 10.2 AND 10.3. The exterior façade of the Ohio Union and the interior Great Hall of the Union. Credit: The Ohio State University.

SIGNATURE BUILDINGS

FIGURE 10.4. President Obama at Sloopy's diner in the Ohio Union. Credit: The Ohio State University.

arrangements? We were sworn to secrecy. The president was publicly scheduled to visit Capital University in Columbus the next day, but first there would be the unannounced stop at Ohio State. The presidential motorcade pulled up outside the Ohio Union on High Street. The President got out of his limousine and walked into the Ohio Union. Many students could not believe their eyes, but very quickly cell phones and text messages spread the word that the president was at the Ohio Union, and the crowd began to grow. The president walked through the Great Hall down to Sloopy's Diner, ordered some food, and went over to a booth where some students were sitting and joined their conversation (see Figure 10.4).

Needless to say, the students and the patrons of Sloopy's were stunned. Shortly thereafter, the president left Sloopy's, shook some students' hands, posed for some photos, and proceeded to leave the Ohio Union as he came in—back on High Street in the presidential motorcade. As a political science professor, I reminded students and the campus community how spoiled they were. Multiple presidential visits to the same campus in the same election cycle just do not happen that often (see Figures 10.5–10.6). And surprise, unannounced visits are almost unheard of. The Ohio Union and Ohio State were featured prominently in that day's news cycle. There is YouTube video of Obama's union stop; see "President Obama Makes Surprise Visit" 8/21/12.

FIGURE 10.5. President Obama at the spring commencement in 2013 having just received an honorary degree from Board of Trustees Chair Robert Schottenstein and having just been hooded by Board of Trustees Secretary David Horn. Credit: The Ohio State University.

FIGURE 10.6. President Barack Obama and First Lady Michelle Obama on one of their campaign visits to the Ohio State campus. Credit: The Ohio State University.

FIGURE 10.7. The futuristic appearance of RPAC. Credit: The Ohio State University.

Recreation and Physical Activity Center (RPAC)

RPAC was built to replace the outdated and inadequate Larkins Hall. It also was built so that Ohio State could claim to have recreation and intramural facilities as good as any in the country. Construction started in 2003 and was completed in January 2007 just before Gee's return at a cost of $140 million. A major funding stream for the project was user fees, which for students was a mandatory fee, and for faculty and staff was optional, depending on whether they want to utilize the facilities or not.

RPAC is a spectacular facility. It includes the McCorkle Aquatic Pavilion, a superb facility for intercollegiate swimming and diving championships. It also includes The Tom W. Davis Special Events Gym for athletic programs as well as special events. RPAC has squash courts, basketball courts, an indoor track, extensive cardio and weight-lifting equipment, saunas, lockers and showers, healthy snack bars, the Student Wellness Center, and much more. It truly is a world-class facility and a bragging point for the university (see Figure 10.7).

CHAPTER 10

William Oxley Thompson Memorial Library Renovation

The Thompson Library, the heart of the Ohio State library system, has always been a magnificent structure. But it was appalling what the university had done to it over the years. It was expanded in 1951 and 1997 and renovated to gain more office space. The Grand Reading Room had been carved up into many undistinguished smaller spaces. The library had lost the dignity and presence that a major university library should have. There had been plans to do a major renovation of the library as far back as the 1990s, but there was always some other project that leapt to the top of the priority list and delayed the enhancement of the Thompson Library. Finally, the major $109 million renovation began in January 2007 and was completed in the summer of 2009. The library was reopened to the public on September 24, 2009. The renovation was breathtaking. The Grand Reading Room was restored, as was the library's original east façade (see Figures 10.8–10.9). Many art pieces were restored; a replica of the Winged Victory of Samothrace was commissioned and installed in the Grand Reading Room. Metal engravings were placed throughout the library illustrating various written and graphic notation systems. The renovation opened the heart of the library to more natural light. The 11th floor of the library became a cozy, comfortable reading room with attic-like garrets that faced in all directions. The technology and the workstations in the library were state of the art. An exhibition space became part of the first floor to showcase some of the library's collections. And on the lower level, there was actually a food facility, a somewhat radical notion for Ohio State, which in the past had treated food and drink in a library as the work of the devil. The library became an incredible source of pride for the entire campus community. OSU students would routinely take their friends from other campuses to see their library, a renovation that won numerous architecture and design awards.

The Residence Halls: South Campus

Thus, when Gee returned to Ohio State, there were three new signature buildings completed or almost completed on campus—the renovated Thompson Library, the new Ohio Union, and the new RPAC. All of these buildings were widely seen as reinforcing the national stature of Ohio State. But in Gee's mind, there were still some major gaps that needed to be filled such as the arts facilities mentioned in the last chapter and a thorough upgrade of the residence hall system to make it more appropriate for the ever more talented student

FIGURES 10.8 AND 10.9. The view from the Oval of the library with the statue of William Oxley Thompson in the center. And the interior view of the magnificently restored Grand Reading Room. Credit: The Ohio State University.

body. Many of the residence halls on South Campus were among some of the most beautiful buildings on campus. But they were old and in great need of renovations, particular with respect to HVAC. When the university moved to a semester calendar and classes began in late August rather than late September, the lack of air-conditioning in these residence halls as well as some other issues could no longer be ignored. With the strong support of Dr. Javaune Adams-Gaston, the vice president for Student Affairs, Gee put the South Campus renovations high on his priority list and got the project done in a timely fashion.

The Residence Halls: North Campus

The residence halls on the North Campus were in far worse shape than those on the South Campus. They were an architectural nightmare in rundown condition and certainly not designed with the intent of building community. Thus, Gee decided he wanted to rebuild the entire North Campus housing and not tinker with renovations here and there. On this project, Gee had the support of Adams-Gaston, but other administrators on campus were reluctant to take on a project of such enormity. They worried that this project would take resources from initiatives that they ranked more highly, and they questioned whether a residential district and its proposed benefits were really necessary. Some members of the Board of Trustees raised similar questions, but Gee won the day, in part because of related issues that were coming to the fore.

The completed North Campus residential district truly transformed the northern part of campus (see Figure 10.10). The buildings themselves were much more attractive. The green spaces were much more inviting for social interactions among the residents. Each residence hall in the complex was designed to have meeting spaces and social venues to encourage student interaction. There was widespread agreement and acclaim that the end product of the North Campus renovation was outstanding and provided a wonderful place for Ohio State students to thrive.

Two-Year Residency Rule

As the North Campus renovations were being discussed, Gee decided to push for a two-year residency requirement for undergraduate students. Up to this point, students were required to live in the residence halls for only one year. Gee, again supported by Adams-Gaston, argued that the evidence was com-

SIGNATURE BUILDINGS

FIGURE 10.10. The North Campus Residential District. Credit: The Ohio State University.

pelling that a two-year residency requirement helped promote better student academic outcomes such as higher retention rates and faster progress toward graduation. Studies from campuses across the nation confirmed these patterns. And at Ohio State itself, data from the 2005 student cohort showed that students who lived on campus for two years had a six-year graduation rate of 88.2 percent compared to 76.5 percent for students who did not, and a two-year retention rate of 95.7 percent versus 88.6 percent for those who did not. Moreover, students who lived on campus longer had a higher participation rate in campus activities and were more involved in the life of the university.

Gee had another motivation for the two-year residency rule. He believed that such a requirement would help build more of a sense of community among the student body and also foster greater attachment to the campus community. Part of this belief came from his experience at private universities such as Brown and Vanderbilt where on-campus living was much more prevalent. But it also came from Gee's knowledge of how and when freshmen at Ohio State made decisions about their sophomore year housing. A very common pattern among Ohio State freshmen who would be living off campus in their sophomore year would be to start looking for housing by December of their first quarter at Ohio State. And many students would be looking for off-campus

Chapter 10

houses that could accommodate ten or more students. But if one were looking for that kind of housing or any residence that entailed multiple roommates, it was likely one would be looking with fellow students one had just met at Ohio State, such as floormates or even more likely friends at Ohio State from back in high school days. That is, the one-year residency rule had the unintended consequence of reducing the likelihood that OSU students would get to meet and know and live with new friends. This troubled Gee because he wanted college to be a more broadening experience that included meeting and getting to know fellow students from more varied backgrounds.

The move to a two-year residency requirement was met by opposition from three groups—students in general, the fraternity and sorority system, and some campus-area landlords. It was to be expected that the landlords would be unhappy since they would be losing a large number of potential tenants. After all, under the one-year requirement, only about 35 percent of the freshmen returned to the residence halls for their second year. Now all freshmen would be required to live on campus for a second year. But some landlords made the mistake of threatening Gee and the university. They said that if they could not fill their units with students, they might be forced for financial reasons to rent to less desirable tenants with unsubtle references to gang members, drug users, poor people, and the like. They said that would be unfortunate for the redevelopment of the campus area, but what could they do: they were small businessmen who had a business to run.

Gee, Adams-Gaston, and the city of Columbus were ready with an immediate response to this threat. Such landlords should then expect unbelievably strict code enforcement in all aspects of housing including plumbing, wiring, sanitation, sidewalks, and more. Every violation would be met with the maximum penalty. And the inspections would be ongoing and continual since the university would help defray some of the city's cost with this new inspection regime. Gee then suggested to the landlords that they might consider a different response. They might improve their properties and try to attract students back to the University District, for it was the case that there were thousands of undergraduate and graduate and professional students who had left the campus area because of concerns about quality and safety. Gee pointed out that as the university worked to improve the campus neighborhood, that should be beneficial to the landlords. And if the landlords actively cooperated in rebuilding the campus area, they would surely reap the benefits. But if they did not want to cooperate, Gee recommended that they sell their properties to responsible owners who would be good neighbors. Bad landlords would be fighting a losing battle with the city and the university; good landlords could be partners in progress and profit. The bad landlords by and large backed down and ceased their threats.

Another group that objected to the two-year requirement was the fraternity and sorority system, which argued that its business model assumed and required some number of sophomores living in the Greek houses to meet their financial needs. The university was somewhat sympathetic to this argument and provided some relief by allowing some sophomores to reside in fraternity and sorority houses if those chapters welcomed university programming comparable to that provided in the residence halls. This compromise was quickly agreed to.

The final group that objected to the two-year rule was the students themselves, many of whom argued that living off campus with many roommates and preparing one's own meals was a lot cheaper than the university's room and board rates. The students were largely correct, so the university reassured them that for students on financial aid, the aid packages would factor in the cost of living on campus. But the university went much further and proposed a new program called STEP—the Second-Year Transformational Program. STEP was designed to promote student success and development and to encourage students to become more deeply involved in activities that addressed their academic interests and aspirations. While there were many aspects to STEP, in its simplest form it enabled eligible students to receive a fellowship of up to $2,000 to pursue a STEP Signature Project under faculty supervision. The project could take many different forms, including research, travel, community service, creative and artistic endeavors, leadership initiatives, and many more. The key point is that at the same time the two-year residency requirement was being implemented, likely increasing costs for some students, the university also adopted an academic enrichment program—STEP—for which students could receive up to $2,000 after completing a very reasonable application process. STEP would result in more students working with faculty members outside the formal classroom setting. The combination of the two-year residency requirement, the renovation of the North Campus residence halls, and the adoption of STEP all worked together to promote Gee's goal of a more engaged campus community for students.

Conclusion

As discussed in this and the previous chapter, the physical characteristics of the campus underwent major transformation in the second Gee administra-

Chapter 10

tion. And new plans are being developed and/or implemented in the Drake administration, including the redesign and opening of Mirror Lake, the construction of a new dental school, and a major Innovation District proposed for West campus. Many older projects continued moving ahead, including the rerouting of Cannon Drive, which, among other benefits, will provide more acreage for development in the vicinity of the medical center, the continuing upgrades to Ohio Stadium, and the new facilities being built on the athletic campus (between Kenny Road and Olentangy River Road on the west and east respectively and between Ackerman Road and Lane Avenue on the north and south respectively). Among the more recent additions to the athletic campus were the Crane Sports Medicine Center and the Covelli Center.

There is one signature building I did not mention in this chapter that Gee was intimately involved in—the new James Hospital. We will discuss that in chapter 15 when we talk about the medical center. But we should note here that the most substantial building program at the university, at least with respect to dollars, has been and continues to be at the medical center with decisions by the Board of Trustees to build numerous medical facilities on campus and throughout Franklin County.

11
Other Initiatives and Actions

Introduction

In this chapter, we will consider various topics that might be labeled under the broader rubric of planning, be it broad-based university-wide planning or planning focused on more specific, narrower initiatives. A few topics that are included in this chapter may not at first glance be seen as planning per se. But all of the topics are linked in that they were designed to promote a more successful and secure future for Ohio State University.

Strategic Planning

Strategic planning and other forms of planning were a much higher priority in Gee's second presidency than in his first, in part because the Board of Trustees and Gee were both much more committed to the enterprise. Both the board and the president recognized that universities now existed in more volatile and perilous environments. The failure to plan for what the university aspired to be and how it was going to get there might result in an institution simply reacting to external and internal forces, an institution simply muddling through and lagging behind its competition. Many of the trustees saw that in their own world of business; those companies that did not plan for the future would most likely not have a prosperous future.

In September 2010, there was an initial meeting about strategic planning with the Board of Trustees and the senior leadership of the university focused

Chapter 11

on the key characteristics, principles, and caveats inherent in successful academic strategic planning. It was essential that the university leadership—trustees and campus-based—be fully aware of and in harmony about their roles and responsibilities and be proactive in monitoring the ever-changing external environment, while at the same time not lose sight of what was happening on campus. It was no longer sufficient to casually have one's fingers on the pulse of the environment; instead a much more in-depth understanding of the challenges was required. Thus, academic strategic planning had to recognize the market conditions and the strong competition from existing entities in the higher education domain as well as the challenges posed by new competitors that planned to enter the higher education space. And, as important as market conditions were, one could not ignore political and social changes that were also challenging universities. Ultimately, strategic planning had to concentrate on the fate and future of the institution. And in order to do this, it had to utilize a variety of approaches to develop strategy, always trying to ensure that the underlying process was fair, participatory, and tolerant of differences and disagreement. The university leadership, especially Gee, fully understood that opponents of change might first focus on the substance of change proposals. But if they could not win that argument, they would then turn to the accusations that the process was unfair. The university leadership also believed that strategic planning should emphasize decisions; it was not about proposals and plans that simply collected dust on shelves and never informed the actions and decisions of the institution.

There was also a greater focus on metrics and measurement, both of the internal performance of the university as well as of relevant characteristics of the external environment. The measurement strategy would itself be multimethod, with some measurements being more qualitative in content and others being more quantitative. Moreover, it was important that the metrics had an explicit longitudinal component to them so that the university could better assess the impact of changes over time. There was also the fundamental understanding that academic planning was an ongoing activity that needed to continually monitor changes in the internal and external environments and be prepared for midcourse corrections to plans if need be.

The academic strategic plan adopted by the Board of Trustees identified overall goals such as external assessments (such as by *U.S. News & World Report*) rating Ohio State as a top ten public university. The strategic plan also outlined resource and spending plans to achieve a top ten ranking: increase student access, attract and retain world-class faculty, and build highly ranked academic programs. On the resource side, the academic plan called for internal expense reductions, cost savings through process improvements, and then budget reallocation of these savings. It also called for new continuing revenues from traditional sources *and* new continuing money from nontraditional sources such as monetization of assets, more aggressive licensing plans, and other strategies (see chapter 12). On the spending side, additional dollars were needed to hire new faculty and pay for other programs such as STEP and additional student financial aid. In June 2014, interim university president Joe Alutto gave the trustees a report documenting how well goals of the strategic plan were met in 2012, 2013, and 2014. This report reflected the desire of the trustees to stay on top of decisions they had made earlier. Some more senior trustees had been highly critical in past years of the university's strategic planning. Now they were active partners in the process and needed to make sure that they were carrying out their responsibilities to oversee the university leadership and its actions. This focus on strategic planning at the top of the university set the stage for more serious strategic planning throughout the academic side of the university, reaching down to colleges and departments and other academic units. While such planning had always been done, it now became clear that these planning documents were being taken more seriously by leadership and had consequences for resource allocation and personnel decisions.

Throughout this period, the trustees were also doing more to enhance their own trustee leadership skills. They brought in Richard Chaitt, a renowned national expert on university and trustee governance, to work with the board as it redefined its roles and responsibilities in the ever more complex higher education environment. The board wanted to be more involved in "running the university," but the trustees did not want to be micromanagers. They wanted to engage in appropriate board oversight of the university administration, but they did not want the university leadership team constantly worrying about board intrusiveness. Chaitt did a superb job helping the board find that "sweet spot" between oversight versus control, between inquiry versus meddling. And, more importantly, Chaitt helped reinforce the idea that strategic planning and longer-range thinking were indeed central to the responsibilities of the trustees.

The Framework Plan

In 2008, another planning initiative began that in 2010 culminated in the One Ohio State Framework (Framework 1.0) report. A Framework 2.0 report was issued in 2017 that updated the earlier report. With respect to the 2010

Chapter 11

report, Gee wrote in his cover letter to the document that "we have engaged in a comprehensive effort to redefine how we think about our physical world. In our new integrated model, we holistically consider strategic, financial, and physical planning issues, ensuring that our academic mission drives our physical world." Gee thanked the hundreds of people who contributed to the plan, giving particular credit to "Ron Ratner, our lead trustee on the project, Jeff Kaplan, senior vice president and special assistant to the president, Julie Anstine from the office of administration and planning, Ricardo Dumont and his colleagues from Sasaki Associates, and Gerald McCue, former dean of the faculty of Design at Harvard University." All of these individuals devoted tremendous time and energy to this project, even when this was not their primary day job. For example, trustee Ron Ratner was chief development officer and executive vice president at Forest City enterprises in Cleveland, yet he still found the time to contribute his development expertise to Framework 1.0. Julie Anstine already had a full plate of responsibilities in her role as special assistant to the senior vice president for administration and planning, and to that plate was added managing the One Ohio State Framework project as well as additional responsibilities in the university's move to integrated planning.

The framework document integrated strategic, financial, and physical space planning with the initial focus being on space utilization. The first steps entailed developing a campus of strong neighborhoods located within four quadrants defined by two intersecting axes: an east-west axis that started at 15th and High and ran west through the Oval and the Thompson Library to the Olentangy River, and on to West Campus with Neil Avenue as the north-south axis and serving as the university's academic main street. Within these four quadrants, the plan envisaged creative ideas to utilize and reinvigorate those spaces.

Motivating the initial framework planning was a set of master plan principles. One key principle was a heavy emphasis on transinstitutional (interdisciplinary) linkages; this was seen as core to Ohio State's mission. With respect to campus culture, there was a strong emphasis on becoming a more nimble and strategic university rather than a reactive institution and also becoming a better steward of resources. As to the character of Ohio State, the focus was on a navigable, vibrant, and supportive campus with sufficient open accessible spaces where members of the university community could connect with each other and enjoy common experiences. When it came to implementing these aspirations, five principles were highlighted:

1. Prioritizing needs as One University

2. Ensuring financial achievability
3. Taking advantage of outside resources
4. Defining a clear, transparent, direct, and informed decision-making process
5. Establishing a timeline that encourages flexibility

This initial Framework Plan finished in 2010 became a guidepost by which university leaders and the trustees could assess decisions and choices that they would be called upon to make in future years. By 2017, there was a revised Framework 2.0 Final Plan that provided a more detailed roadmap for the cluster of interrelated issues that would face the university. For example, in talking about renovating or constructing new facilities, the discussion would more rigorously incorporate questions about their location, their cost and funding sources, and their overall contribution to the university's mission and aspirations. Thus, the strategic planning discussed in the previous section and the Framework Plan demonstrate how Ohio State had committed itself to a more rigorous, thoughtful, and intentional process as it pursued campus transformation.

At the same time that all this planning was going on, President Gee asked Provost Alutto and Vice Provost for Academic Planning Mike Boehm to undertake an effort to add more rigor, awareness, and discipline to the capital construction decision-making process at Ohio State. Although Ohio State routinely produced multi-year prioritized capital construction documents, these were often ignored or were not very useful because they did not provide sufficient information about funding sources, timelines, and tradeoffs. Indeed, the weakness of these documents made it easy for university leaders such as trustees and senior administrators to try to inject new projects onto a list without those projects ever having been truly analyzed for their impact on other projects and their prospects for completion. In earlier decades, the much-needed renovation of the Thompson Library kept being delayed and bumped down the list as advocates were successful in pushing their own preferred projects.

Thus, Alutto and Boehm decided to construct a more integrated planning model to bring discipline and meaningful prioritizing to the university's capital construction decision-making process. Boehm eventually produced a ten-year schematic that had a list of projects, their priority standing, their funding streams, and their timelines. One could look at that list and grasp very quickly what resources would be needed to move particular projects forward within certain timelines. One could also see how the insertion of a new project that had not gone through the normal internal vetting process would impact other projects on the list. This ten-year model had the obvious benefit of giving decision makers the big picture. It also made it difficult for decision makers to say that they did not realize the consequences for other projects when they inserted their favored projects into the capital planning process. It was clear that one aim of the Alutto/Boehm work was to impose more discipline on senior university leaders and the Board of Trustees to not too cavalierly upset university planning unless a compelling case could be made with respect to priorities and the needed resources.

Discovery Themes

Gee believed that Ohio State, as one of the nation's largest and most comprehensive land grant research universities, had a special obligation and capability to address critical problems that confronted not only the state of Ohio, but also the nation and the world. Thus, early in his second term, the academic leadership of the university participated in an off-campus retreat to begin the process of identifying key issues and problems that Ohio State's research talent might address. J. F. Rischard and his influential book *High Noon: Twenty Global Problems, Twenty Years to Solve Them* played an important part in shaping ideas at the retreat. After extensive discussion, three broad discovery themes were identified—health and wellness, food production and security, and energy and the environment. The list was later expanded to include humanities and the arts. These discovery themes were areas in which Ohio State had major strengths, both disciplinary and interdisciplinary, with existing research programs making important contributions to solving problems in their domains. Moreover, because of Ohio State's scope and the quality of its academic programs, most of them located in close proximity to each other on the Columbus campus, Gee thought that Ohio State would enjoy a comparative and competitive advantage over other institutions in addressing these complex Discovery Theme problems IF Ohio State could align its resources and talents to work for common purposes. For example, health and wellness would not simply be the domain of the College of Medicine and the College of Nursing. Instead, it would also include many of the social science departments that focused on human behavior and institutions such as psychology, sociology, and political science, and the Glenn College of Public Affairs and the College of Public Health, which focused more on the policy aspects of health and wellness concerns, and the Fisher College of Business and the Moritz College of Law.

Indeed, one of the attractions of the Discovery Themes to Gee was that they would help break down the academic silos, the arbitrary disciplinary boundaries that often impeded scholars from different academic backgrounds but with similar research interests from working collaboratively to achieve solutions to problems. This transinstitutional approach was aided by the creation of faculty advisory boards for each theme, each of which consisted of members from different departments, colleges, and disciplines. Moreover, many of the faculty to be hired for the Discovery Themes were to have joint appointments, further advancing an interdisciplinary approach. The initial goal was to hire 500 new faculty over a ten-year period, with about half of these new hires working within their own areas and the other half working in the intersection of all three themes. Some of the new positions were to be funded by proceeds from the parking lease deal (see chapter 12). From that initial 2008 retreat, the Discovery Themes initiative was officially launched in 2012, and under the leadership of Gee and Provost Alutto got off to a good start and has continued to evolve in the subsequent administration of President Drake and Provost McPheron.

The Internationalization of Ohio State

Ohio State has long had a significant international presence in its research and public service activities as well as a substantial role in teaching large numbers of international students at the undergraduate, graduate, and professional levels. Years ago, faculty in the College of Agriculture (now FAES) were very active in India's Green Revolution, which did so much to alleviate hunger and enhance food security in the nation. Rattan Lal, a faculty member in the college, continues to this day to receive international awards and recognition for his contributions to the world community. Faculty from throughout the university are engaged in research overseas, whether it be political scientists studying civic attitudes and democratization with European colleagues, or economists and finance professors working with international monetary organizations. These kinds of examples can be multiplied many times over. And with respect to teaching, Ohio State has one of the largest enrollments of international students in the United States, in part because of the size of Ohio State, but also because of the outstanding graduate and professional programs that attract students to Ohio State, and in many cases lead foreign governments to support their students studying at Ohio State.

Chapter 11

Thus, Ohio State has indeed had a substantial international footprint. But the university leadership, especially Gee and Alutto, felt the need to bring more discipline, strategic thinking, and resources to its international activities. The President's and Provost's Council on Strategic Internationalization in 2009 studied the university's globalization progress and concluded that more needed to be done along many fronts, including increasing the percentage of international faculty and students, stimulating scholarship on major global issues (an emphasis of the Discovery Themes), fostering collaboration between OSU alumni and Ohio businesses operating in the international sphere, developing an international physical presence, and increasing the international experience such as study abroad for the Ohio State student body.

To provide leadership for these aspirations, Gee recruited William Brustein from the University of Illinois to become the vice president for Global Strategies and International Affairs at Ohio State. Brustein got to work immediately on a number of initiatives. One of the first was the establishment of physical Ohio State offices—called Global Gateways—in a number of major international cities chosen very strategically to enhance Ohio State's international profile. The first office opened in Shanghai in February 2010; the next office opened in Mumbai in 2014. A third office opened later in Sao Paulo. These offices served many purposes. They were places where Ohio State faculty could meet with their counterparts in the host country. Or the offices might serve as a convening place assisted by Ohio State staff for Ohio businesses to meet with representative of the host country's business and political leadership. Or it provided a place for Ohio State to offer programming about the university, whether for the purpose of recruiting students from the host country or simply to heighten Ohio State's visibility overseas. And these offices could also host alumni club meetings, as the university did indeed have many alumni residing in China, India, and Brazil

Under Brustein's leadership, there was also a review of Ohio State's five area studies centers to ensure that their activities meshed well with the university's renewed focus on globalization. And Brustein recognized that the Mershon Center for International Security Studies was not getting the recognition and support that it merited and that the university was missing opportunities to utilize Mershon to enhance the university's international profile. Gee, Alutto, and Brustein also wanted Ohio State students to have expanded opportunities for enhanced international awareness. whether it was through strengthening the global components of the curriculum on the Columbus campus or by providing more opportunities for Columbus-based students to have a study abroad experience. Brustein not only wanted to increase the enrollment of international students on the Columbus campus; he also wanted to ensure that those international students coming to the Columbus campus had a good academic and social experience. This was especially a concern for the undergraduate international students, many of whom had never experienced American culture and who might have greater difficulty getting integrated in the life of the university. These concerns also existed for graduate and professional students but were not as worrisome, in part because the graduate and professional students were more likely to be enrolling in programs with greater structure, better orientation, and mentors from their home country.

The number of international students at all levels (undergraduate, graduate, and professional) has grown substantially between 1996, near the end of Gee's first term, to 2013, the end of Gee's second term. In 1996 there were 3,790 international students; by 2013, the number was 6,039, an increase of 59 percent. But the overall share of the university's total enrollment attributable to international students was still under ten percent, although higher among graduate and professional students. And in some graduate programs, particularly in the sciences and engineering, the percentage of international students exceeds 50 percent of the enrollment in those programs. These students are essential to these graduate programs, whether working as RAs or TAs or working on faculty projects supported by grants or on their own projects for which they obtained external funding. In many ways, graduate students are an inexpensive source of labor even as they are also students seeking a degree. This is both a reflection of the quality and attractiveness of these programs and the dearth of American and Ohio students who opt to earn advanced degrees in science and engineering. I mention these numbers because in previous decades in Ohio, the state legislature would periodically raise questions about the enrollment of international students. Are they taking spots at the expense of Ohio students? Is the state funding too many students, especially graduate students, who then return home after completing their degree? These questions have diminished in recent years, especially as it relates to Ohio State. For example, the percentage of international students in an incoming freshman class typically ranges from 10 to 12 percent. At other universities where enrollments are declining, there is the temptation to open the floodgates to international students for budgetary, financial reasons without little thought as to how well the institution can provide for these students. At the graduate and professional levels, the percentage of international students at Ohio State is much higher. Overall, the top two countries sending students to Ohio State are China and India, where the first two Global Gateways were established.

Chapter 11

Overall, the opportunities for international experiences have grown for Ohio State students. The STEP program mentioned in the previous chapter facilitates off-campus travel. The curricular revisions, including the effort to add an international component to courses that had not done so previously, expands the opportunity for international awareness. The many student organizations on campus that have an international component, whether that be cultural, political, or social, also give students the chance to learn more about other nations. And the two-year residency requirement will by definition increase the odds that native students will have a greater chance to meet international students, who tend to stay in the residence halls longer than American students.

The Office of University Compliance and Integrity

Higher education is increasingly operating in an environment characterized by greater external scrutiny from governments at all levels as well as from the media and other entities concerned about how well higher education follows the laws, carries out its responsibilities, and serves the interest of the broader public. Scandals, especially in high visibility divisions of the university such as the athletic department or the medical center or the research operations or academic leadership, bring much negative publicity and possible financial penalties, and clearly undermine the lofty brand that universities seek to establish and maintain. Public universities have higher expectations placed on them than private universities. There are a host of statutes in many states dealing with public records, open meetings, conflict of interest, and many others that apply to public institutions, but not to their private counterparts.

Thus, in an era in which the formal and informal obligations on universities have grown, the regulatory environment has gotten far more complicated, and the external factors monitoring and investigating the behaviors of universities and their leaders have gotten far more aggressive, Gee and the Board of Trustees became much more concerned about potential risks facing a complex and comprehensive university such as Ohio State. Compliance and integrity issues could arise anywhere in the university. But with a major medical center, decentralized, faculty-driven research programs, a huge athletic department with national visibility, and over 60,000 students, Ohio State University was certainly vulnerable should anything go seriously wrong in these parts of the university, As the board and the president conducted their risk assessments, they realized that the mechanisms that Ohio State had in place to protect the university's integrity and reputation were insufficient and inadequate. Thus the university decided to hire Gates Garrity-Rokous as the new vice president and chief compliance officer and tasked him with the responsibility to establish the Office of University Compliance and Integrity.

Garrity-Rokous was a superb hire. He saw his mission as educating the university about compliance and integrity issues and not just handing down edicts about what was and was not allowed. He wanted to empower university leaders at all levels and university employees to take some ownership in identifying potential illegal and unethical behavior and to head it off before it occurred. He assembled an excellent staff and produced useful and understandable instructional materials to heighten the appreciation and awareness of ethical concerns among the campus community at large. He and his staff were always available to meet with individuals or groups who needed some guidance and feedback on ethical concerns that they had. For people who were worried or afraid to report what they thought was an ethical violation, an anonymous hotline was established. As all this was happening, there was also a review of the substance of existing university policies with respect to their clarity and relevance since assessing compliance is far more difficult if the policies in place are ambiguous and inconsistent. And there was also an examination of how policies became policies in the first place and how they differed from recommendations and other less formal categories.

The wisdom of establishing this office was immediately self-evident simply by looking at various issues that emerged at Ohio State and at universities throughout the nation. Ohio State was often criticized and sometimes sued by media outlets because of how slowly it responded to media requests for public documents or how incompletely it provided these materials through redactions and other ploys. The Office of Compliance and Integrity helped university personnel come to a better and more responsive understanding of how they should treat public records requests. Likewise, the Office helped many university leaders better understand when and under what conditions they could avoid a public meeting and go into executive session. And the Office was instrumental in helping university personnel avoid violations of Ohio's ethics laws with respect to conflicts of interest and the receipt of inappropriate gifts. One university leader who came to Ohio State from a private institution in the South could not believe that the State of Ohio's ethics laws prevented him from accepting benefits from vendors who sought to do business with Ohio State. He was quickly disabused of that notion, although he still thought that Ohio's ethics laws needed be changed to allow such behaviors. One only has to read the national higher education headlines dealing with admissions scams, academic scandals, financial misdeeds, sexual assault crimes, and others to appreciate how vital it is to have a first-rate office of compliance and integrity. Such an office may not be able to head off bad behavior, but it does provide a roadmap of how to proceed when scandals erupt.

Garrity-Rokous and his team provided university employees a very simple way to determine whether they should be worried about compliance or integrity issues. They wrote:

> Please use the guiding questions below to help you identify compliance or integrity issues. If the answer to any of these questions is NO, then there is probably a compliance or integrity issue.
>
> 1. Are these actions legal?
> 2. Do these actions comply with university policy?
> 3. Do these actions seem fair and honest?

These questions strike me as setting an appropriately high standard for evaluating actions. Even if one cannot assess the legality of actions or whether they comply with university policy, the third question allows the "sniff test" or the "smell test" to kick in. That is, if something just does not seem right, that should be a sign that there might be a problem. And if the answer to any or all of these questions is NO, the document then provides a list of steps that the worried employee should take.

Miscellaneous Changes in Various Colleges

THE JOHN GLENN COLLEGE OF PUBLIC AFFAIRS

The university originally established the John Glenn Institute for Public Service and Public Policy, and I had the privilege of serving as its first director. The Institute established a number of internship programs for students on campus and in Washington, DC, and a living-learning center in the residence halls. It also took over the management training programs from the School of Public Policy and Management, at that time part of the College of Business. These training programs were primarily for public servants who were seeking skills enhancement so that they might carry out their responsibilities even more effectively. But these training programs were not academic coursework.

OTHER INITIATIVES AND ACTIONS

Indeed, the Glenn Institute did not offer courses for academic credit nor did it have tenure-track Ohio State faculty as part of its regular staff. With respect to public administration and public policy, it was the School of Public Policy and Management in the Fisher College of Business that offered academic degrees in this area, at the graduate level only and particularly the MPA degree (Masters of Public Administration). There were no undergraduate degrees offered. Joe Alutto, then the dean of the College of Business, was focusing on the MBA (Masters of Business Administration) as well as his undergraduate program, and the MPA program did not fit well into his strategic plans for the college. It seemed clear that the Glenn Institute would be the logical intellectual home for the School of Public Policy and Management, but the Office of Academic Affairs nixed that since at Ohio State, institutes are not permitted to offer degree programs.

Thus began a lengthy process to find the right academic home for the School of Public Policy and Management. In 2005, the John Glenn Institute initiated a formal proposal to merge with the School of Public Policy and Management to create the John Glenn School of Public Affairs. The Glenn School of Public Affairs formally began on July 1, 2006. It was an entity that combined the degree-granting authority of the School of Public Policy and Management and its academic research and outreach responsibilities with the Glenn Institute's public service training, outreach, student internship, and research support programs. From this point on moving into the second Gee presidency, the process began to elevate the Glenn School to the John Glenn College of Public Affairs. Faculty positions were added, degree programs were expanded to the undergraduate level, the most significant development being the creation of an undergraduate major in public affairs. Finally, on January 29, 2015, the Board of Trustees approved the creation of the John Glenn College of Public Affairs. Today, under the leadership of dean Trevor Brown, the John Glenn College is expanding its programmatic linkages to other academic units throughout the university and has become an even more active participant in public policy discussions at the state and national levels. Although Gee was no longer at Ohio State to enjoy this moment, it was a source of great pride to him since he was instrumental in the original discussion with Senator Glenn about locating his archives at Ohio State. During these discussions, Gee raised the possibility with Senator Glenn about a more substantial relationship with Ohio State. This notion was skillfully advanced by President Kirwan, which led to the creation of the John Glenn Institute. And from there, the rest is history.

CHAPTER 11

THE COLLEGE OF EDUCATION AND HUMAN ECOLOGY

In 2006, the last year of the Holbrook administration, the faculty and staff of both the College of Education and the College of Human Ecology voted overwhelmingly to merge as the College of Education and Human Ecology. Both colleges had had a century-long history under various configurations at Ohio State and over time had become highly rated in the external community. After the merger vote in 2006, the new college worked mightily during the second Gee administration to make the merged entity more responsive to its various constituencies and to its revised mission. Thus in 2012, the faculty of the College of Education and Human Ecology decided to restructure their academic programs into three areas: the Department of Educational Studies, the Department of Human Sciences, and the Department of Teaching and Learning. The new college has already demonstrated its enhanced ability to address challenges in teacher preparation, student learning, and community involvement.

THE COLLEGE OF PUBLIC HEALTH

Public health as an academic enterprise had a long and distinguished history at Ohio State dating back more than 100 years. In 1995, during Gee's first term, it became the School of Public Health within the College of Medicine. In 2003, it became a freestanding school, and finally in 2007, in Gee's second term, it became the College of Public Health. The move to a freestanding College of Public Health reflected how critical public health issues had become and how many of these issues required a transinstitutional approach rather than a singular medicine approach.

Gee's appointment of William Martin to be the Dean of the College emphasized how broad the reach of public health concerns could be and how complex the problems were. Martin had been at the National Institute of Health, where he served as associate director for disease prevention and health. Prior to that, Martin had been an associate director of the National Institutes of Health's National Institute of Environmental Health Sciences. It was clear that the college would have both a global and a local focus and would play a key role as it tackled key health issues through interdisciplinary research and teaching.

OTHER INITIATIVES AND ACTIONS

Sustainability

By the time Gordon Gee returned to Ohio State in 2007, the term "sustainability" had become a much-used shorthand device to refer to a wide-ranging variety of topics, issues, and concerns on campus and also in the broader society. Sustainability meant different things to different people and referred to different topics for different observers. But whatever the referent, sustainability was a good thing, whether it dealt with natural resources and energy, or food and food production, or the treatment of workers in potentially exploitative industries, or in the everyday habits of consumers in a mass society. Thus, on the Ohio State campus, individual faculty members became concerned about the inefficient use of electricity as evidenced by lights that were burning all hours of the day. Other faculty were worried about how wastefully university facilities were heated or cooled, depending on the season. A University Senate committee COPE, the Committee on the Physical Environment, was more concerned about the big picture surrounding sustainability in whatever area and linked those concerns to how efficiently or inefficiently the university spent its stretched dollars and how well it met the needs of its faculty, staff, and students. Student groups became increasingly concerned about energy, more often from an environmental perspective. What was the impact of the university's energy sources on a clean environment and also the impact on workers who helped produce the various sources of energy, with coal being public enemy number one to the students? Students also became more concerned about food, its sources, how it was grown, and the environmental impacts of these farming and commodity practices. Students also began to examine health-related issues, and some activist groups began to raise challenges to GMOs. Additional issues arose with respect to university-branded merchandise, particularly dealing with the treatment of overseas labor that manufactured Buckeye garb and paraphernalia. Many faculty became more interested in how sustainability could be incorporated into the academic curriculum. Many registered student organizations began to incorporate sustainability activities into their organization. For example, many Greek chapters would routinely conduct neighborhood cleanup drives. Other student organizations might focus on providing meals for the homeless. The list goes on and on.

Even though many of the activities mentioned above seem very different from one another, it became clear that there were some common underlying dimensions such as doing good by helping people or the environment, utilizing

Chapter 11

resources more efficiently to save money and put less stress on the environment, educating the campus community about what it could and should do to promote sustainability, and challenging individual leaders and institutional practices that were seen as impediments to sustainability. Gee saw that sustainability could very quickly become the rallying cry for all kinds of groups calling for all kinds of actions, reasonable or not and mutually consistent or not. Thus, he thought that there needed to be a campus-wide umbrella organization to help shape the various proposals, requests, and demands as they came forward, and also to anticipate what actions needed to be taken proactively. Hence Gee created a new President's Council on Sustainability chaired by his key assistant Kate Wolford. Wolford had the responsibility of trying to bring order and focus to the many sustainability activities on campus. Wolford also met with every group, constituency, or individual who had proposals or demands for greater sustainability. She was particularly adept at working with activist student groups who often thought that anyone in university administration was automatically untrustworthy. As Wolford began to get her arms around sustainability, Gee realized that it needed to become more ingrained in the academic and administrative leadership of the university. Hence academic departments and colleges as well as university administrative offices were tasked to identify their roles and responsibilities in the sustainability discussion. Finally, Gee also established the Office of Energy and the Environment, recognizing that this office would incorporate the research interests of many faculty and would also be a likely source of cost savings and enhanced performance for the university.

By the time Gee left in 2013, it was clear that a more formal organizational oversight structure was needed to monitor and to advance the many ideas and proposals that were being put forward under the rubric of sustainability. Thus, the President's and the Provost's Council on Sustainability (PPCS) was created, composed of members from the administrative units of the university with the greatest interest and stake in sustainability, leaders of student governments, and faculty representatives with expertise and research and teaching interests in sustainability. As its own mission states, PPCS provides strategic advisement on the integration of sustainable practices, programs, and projects throughout the university. The Council meets periodically "to guide campus planning and program development, working with a network of university committees, offices, and departments."

If PPCS is the high-level overseer of sustainability matters on campus, it is the Sustainability Institute that is much more involved in the day-to-day, hands-on sustainability initiatives and programs. The Sustainability Institute was created from a merger of the Office of Energy and Environment with the

Sustainable and Resilient Economy program. Kate Bartter is the executive director of the institute, which itself is composed of more than 600 faculty and research scientists who are doing the research, the teaching and curricular development, and the outreach and engagement to advance goals of sustainability throughout campus, Ohio communities, and beyond. Bartter has been a leader in various capacities since she came to Ohio State in 2007 from state government, where she served as chief of policy for Governor Bob Taft. Her state government experiences certainly prepared her well for dealing with all the campus entities with an interest in sustainability. She has done a wonderful job navigating the personalities and egos, the programs and policies, and the barriers and bureaucracies to help advance sustainability at Ohio State.

The Ohio State University Airport and the Center for Aviation Studies

Ohio State University Airport, referred to as Don Scott Field, is one of a small number of university airports in the nation, and one of only three owned by tier-1 research institutions. It was built during World War II after the US Navy leased Port Columbus (today John Glenn International) to train its own pilots, which resulted in the university no longer having a facility for its own aviation activities. The loss of Port Columbus and the concomitant threat to the university's own aviation program led to a proposal to build OSU's own airport. The trustees agreed to this, and Ohio State went ahead to purchase 385 acres in northern Franklin County on which it began to build runways, hangars, and airport fencing. When a very prominent, admired, and well-liked alumnus, Don Scott, enlisted in the Army Air Corps in 1941, and subsequently died in a training mission crash over England in 1943, the university leadership named the OSU Airport Don Scott Field. It began as a flight training facility for military and civilian pilots, but in the years and decades after World War II, the airport grew to be an outstanding general aviation facility that was among the busiest airports in Ohio as measured by takeoffs and landings. It became a great resource for the business community, especially for business leaders with business interests in the northern and northwestern part of the county, an area of rapid growth and development. It even became a wonderful way for out-of-town fans to fly to Columbus in the fall for football games and not have to worry about scheduled airlines. Even more importantly, the airport became central to Ohio State's academic programs in aviation, a point elaborated on shortly.

Chapter 11

With the initial successes of OSU Airport, one would have thought that subsequent development and growth would be a no-brainer. But that was not to be the case. Every time the university proposed some expansion of Don Scott, neighbors, particularly in the Worthington area, would protest, citing noise pollution and other inconveniences. Occasionally, a university president (e.g., Ed Jennings) would get so frustrated by this NIMBY attitude that he would threaten to shut down the airport and sell the land to residential and commercial developers. Even though this was not a serious threat, it served to energize other neighbors of the airport who believed that development was a far greater threat to the northwest area with its awful traffic problems and sprawling growth, problems that would be greatly exacerbated should the university ever sell this prime land for development. There were also other staged (not real) threats to the airport's future. When the university faced budget cuts and financial shortfalls, one response was to review university land assets such as the OSU Golf Course and the OSU Airport with the notion of selling them to address budgetary shortfalls. This was never a real possibility, but it served to demonstrate how severe the budget crisis was and helped to create some pressure to come up with solutions.

In 2005, the then Dean of the College of Engineering recommended to a subcommittee of the Board of Trustees some proposals for modest development for the OSU Airport. It deferred any recommendations for runway extension and hangar construction, in part because of concern over community opposition. Indeed, running through his proposal were worries about neighborhood complaints even as his report included potentially controversial proposals, which would be considered at some time in the future. It was clear that this proposal was a kind of holding action that would enable some progress in utilizing the airport, but which in no way fully took advantage of the resource that the airport represented.

When Gordon Gee returned to Ohio State in 2007, one of his key hires (as mentioned in chapter 2) was David Williams as Dean of the College of Engineering. Williams had been president of the University of Alabama at Huntsville, where he was a leader in aeronautical and aerospace challenges and opportunities. Gee looked to Williams to try to move the needle forward on making Ohio State a leader in aviation studies and utilizing the airport for research, teaching, and entrepreneurial purposes. Ohio State in the past had long had a School of Aviation, which was transferred to the College of Engineering in 1956. In 1963 the School of Aviation became the Department of Aviation, and in 2011 under the leadership of Williams and with the strong support of Gee, the Department became the Center for Aviation Studies. Dean

OTHER INITIATIVES AND ACTIONS

Williams has been the key player in moving airport growth and expansion plans forward, even in the face of some local opposition. He fully appreciated the fact that the College of Engineering was one of a very few colleges in the nation to have its own airport. He intended to take full advantage of this.

The Center for Aviation Studies is the home of education, research, outreach, and business development as it relates to aviation at Ohio State. It sees the airport as vital to its mission. Obviously pilot training is one such activity. But the Center notes that for every pilot of an aircraft, there are 40 other aviation specialists involved in successful flights, including airport management, cargo aviation, air traffic control, government and regulatory oversight, and many more. The Center along with colleagues from throughout the university is very much involved in research dealing with, among others, unmanned aerial systems, air traffic management systems, general aviation safety, and much more. After Gee's departure in 2013, the university under the leadership of Dean Williams embarked on an ambitious plan for the OSU Airport, likely to be completed in 2019 during the Drake administration. It certainly seems to be the case that the future of aviation studies and the OSU Airport are once again on the rise at Ohio State.

Strategic Enrollment Planning

Gee hired M. Dolan Evanovich to be the vice president for Strategic Enrollment Planning in 2009. Evanovich succeeded Martha Garland, who had served very ably as vice president for enrollment services and dean of undergraduate education. Evanovich's mission was to take enrollment planning to the next level, and he indeed achieved that. He oversaw many important offices and functions: the Office of Undergraduate Admissions and First Year Experience, Student Financial Aid, Economic Access Initiative, Student Services Center, the University Registrar, Graduate and Professional Admissions, Enrollment Services Analysis and Reporting, and Marketing and Strategic Communication. He hired outstanding leaders in these areas, and he and his team very skillfully built on the successes of their predecessors. Although his portfolio was broad, the central focus was undergraduate students. And during his time at Ohio State, all of the indicators about undergraduate student quality, accomplishments, and success kept on trending upward as did the indicators about the attractiveness of Ohio State as a destination of choice for students from Ohio and throughout the United States. His annual enrollment reports were models of clarity, content, relevancy, readability, and brevity—characteristics

Chapter 11

that many university documents could benefit from. I have provided one such report in Appendix C. Unfortunately, Evanovich was recruited away from Ohio State in 2016 by Syracuse University to be the senior vice president for Enrollment and the Student Experience there.

Outreach and Engagement

From Gee's perspective, outreach and engagement have always been central to the role of a public, land grant university. In his first term, he and his colleagues such as Dick Stoddard were very much involved with the Kellogg Commission and its focus on land grant universities. In his first term, Gee took the lead in changing the name of the Cooperative Extension Service, a well-established title in federal and state government, to Ohio State Extension. When citizens called the extension office, he wanted them to know that they had called Ohio State. In his second term the advancement model was adopted and integrated into university operations. One key component of the advancement model was reaching out to the university's many constituencies; outreach and engagement were essential to stay connected to the university's many friends. Moreover, the responsibility for outreach and engagement did not simply reside in the central administration's leadership. Instead, it had to be an activity distributed throughout the university where all department, colleges, centers, offices, etc. took some ownership of the outreach/engagement function.

When Gee hired Joyce Beatty to be the senior vice president for Outreach and Engagement, he knew he had gotten someone who could work with so many different audiences—business and labor, political and civic, Black and white, gay and straight, small business and big business, profit and nonprofit, public and private, and so on. Using the parlance of election campaigns, Beatty was truly a crossover candidate many times over. The passion, knowledge, and sincerity she brought to her responsibilities made her a superb representative of the university and a wonderful source of intelligence, insight, and gossip for Gordon Gee.

When Beatty left the university to run for Congress, these assets helped her to victory. It was a very courageous decision on her part to retire from a high-level, high-visibility university position to run for the US House. First, she had to run in a three-way Democratic primary, where all of the candidates were women. One of her opponents was Mary Jo Kilroy, the white former incumbent who had held the seat and a longtime player in Democratic Party politics.

OTHER INITIATIVES AND ACTIONS

Her other opponent was Priscilla Tyson, a member of Columbus City Council, and like Beatty, African American. Thus, there were two Black candidates and one white. The white candidate had previously held the congressional seat. Beatty was seen as a clear underdog.

But she did have some strong assets. She was seen as far more likable than her opponents, especially the former congresswoman. And she was seen as a more reasonable person with whom one might talk issues and negotiate policies. And she did have some strong supporters, including Columbus Mayor Michael Coleman and, albeit quietly and more behind the scenes, OSU President Gordon Gee and many of his senior leadership team. Beatty won the primary rather comfortably and was elected to Congress in November and very quickly became an important player and a close confidante of House Speaker Nancy Pelosi—and also, of course, a continuing friend of The Ohio State University. Today, Representative Beatty is the chair of the Congressional Black Caucus.

Deregulation

When Gee returned in 2007, he very quickly commissioned general counsel Chris Culley and me to prepare a plan whereby the university could gain major regulatory relief from the State of Ohio. The motivation for this directive was at least two-fold. First, Gee simply could not abide silly, costly, unnecessary regulations that impeded university operations, whether imposed by the state itself or by the university's own internal bureaucracy. Second, Gee believed that the less encumbered by state restriction, the more money the university could save and the more money it could generate. If we had been very successful in this enterprise, this topic would have required an entire chapter. But unfortunately we were not.

Culley's team did a fantastic job reviewing deregulation efforts in other states and carefully analyzing the Ohio Revised Code to see where OSU might seek relief. Culley's group examined both very detailed proposals and very broad scenarios that would actually change the legal/constitutional relationship between Ohio State University and the State of Ohio. There was one very significant reform we accomplished in freeing the university from incredibly burdensome, illogical construction restrictions (see chapter 15 on the medical center and the discussion of Project One). Most of our other proposals were shot down, some summarily. One proposal, which we did not expect to get, was the freedom to set our own pricing for tuition and fees. Even with private assurances that we would not abuse this freedom, Ohio's elected officials were worried about the political fallout should tuition increases get out of hand. And as the cost of higher education became a more salient issue in this time period, the barriers to tuition freedom became much steeper.

There were other proposals made that on their surface looked eminently reasonable. Many involved administrative and regulatory functions that were being performed by the state on the university's behalf for which we paid the state; we said we could do these things more cheaply and just as well. But this was not a winning argument since it meant that various state agencies would be losing a revenue stream, and no bureaucracy likes that outcome. Another idea put forth by the university was to give the Board of Trustees more power to run its own affairs, but that was not to be. Yet another proposal was to allow the governor to select trustees to the Ohio State Board of Trustees who were not residents (technically electors) of the State of Ohio. We argued that Ohio State is a national, even international university, and should have some representation on its board from places in addition to Ohio. We always raised the prospect of getting a Bill Gates or a Warren Buffett on the board, which would not be permissible under current restrictions. This proposal went nowhere, although the university was later allowed to select a limited number of out-of-state charter trustees to serve on the board, albeit without voting privileges. The final nail in the coffin to our deregulation efforts came when the chancellor of the Board of Regents, the coordinating body for higher education, said at a public meeting with college and university trustees that if deregulation proposals were adopted that did save colleges and universities money, the state would claw back some of that money. It was as if efficiency and rationality were being financially punished.

And thus the battle continues. If we find something in Ohio Revised Code or the Ohio Constitution that might prevent Ohio State from contributing to some universally agreed upon goal such as economic development, the university will go quietly to key legislators and the governor to see if something can be done. Or if some state agency or department has rules and regulations that are so outrageously stupid or counterproductive, we will go quietly to the appropriate authorities to see if it can be changed. Thus, the current strategy is one of chipping away at impediments and not a full-frontal assault. But if the political climate should ever change, Chris Culley has locked away a full menu of deregulation for higher education in Ohio. Unfortunately for Ohio State, Culley left Ohio State in 2019 to take a senior leadership position at Georgetown University.

OTHER INITIATIVES AND ACTIONS

The Regional Campuses

One of the variations in Gee's "One University" theme was the term "Six Campuses, One University." The six campuses referred to the main campus in Columbus, the Agricultural Technical Institute in Wooster, Ohio, and the four regional campuses in Lima, Mansfield, Marion, and Newark. The regional campuses were created decades ago when civic and business leaders and residents of these four smaller cities worked hard at the grass roots level to provide land and financial resources in order to have a direct Ohio State University presence in their communities. Over the decades, the main campus administration in Columbus has had differing perspectives about the importance and necessity of the regional campuses. In his first administration, Gee recognized that the four regional campuses were in small cities surrounded by rural areas and represented by state legislators who otherwise might not have a close relationship with Ohio State. Gee saw the regional campuses as an important political asset. Moreover, even at a time of open admissions and the beginning of the selective admissions era, Ohio State could not possibly accommodate all the Ohio students who sought admission to the main campus in Columbus. Thus, the regional campuses became a safety valve; students who were not admitted to the main campus as part of the fall quarter freshman class could start at one of the regional campuses and then later transfer to the main campus assuming satisfactory academic progress. These advantages of being a political asset and providing a safety valve were widely acknowledged, but one had the sense that in earlier decades this was more of an afterthought, that the regional campuses were not fully integrated into the academic planning of Ohio State University. But this changed dramatically in Gee's second term, in part because of his heightened awareness of the value-added provided by the regional campuses and also because of the work of the Office of Academic Affairs, especially Mike Boehm, the Vice Provost for Academic Planning, to ensure that the regional campuses were a more integral part of the university's strategic academic planning.

    The four regional campuses are responsible for their own revenues and expenditures. The major sources of revenue are driven by enrollments and consist of tuition dollars and the state subsidy (which is distributed by the Columbus campus to the four branches.) Each of the regional campuses is headed by a person with the dual titles of dean and director; the major responsibility for oversight of the four campuses rests with the provost and the Office of Academic Affairs on the Columbus campus. The regional campuses were each originally co-located with a two-year technical college, an arrangement that provides benefits, but also creates problems when the regional campus and the technical college have disagreements about resources, use of facilities, and the like. The head of the technical college has the title of president, while the head of the regional campus is "merely" a dean. There was a period many years ago when the long-serving former president of Marion Tech would not work with the dean of OSU Marion and would only want to speak with the OSU president in Columbus. Today the relationship between the two institutions is much more cooperative. The Lima campus is co-located with Rhodes State College, formerly Lima Technical College. OSU Mansfield shares its campus with North Central State College, while OSU Newark shares a campus with Central Ohio Technical College. The OSU Newark/COTC relationship has long been an outstanding collaborative partnership and has been recognized as a model for cooperation, efficiency, and success.

Degrees earned by students at the regional campuses are conferred by the appropriate college within Ohio State. That is, the degree is an Ohio State degree, not a regional campus degree. The most frequently earned degree is the Associate of Arts, but in recent years there have been expanded opportunities to earn a four-year degree entirely on the regional campus, making it a much less expensive degree for students, not only because of the lower tuition costs on regional campuses but also because many students are place bound and/or live at home, thereby saving on room and board fees.

The courses offered at OSU regional campuses are the same as those offered on the main campus. The responsibility for course content and degree requirements rests with the academic department on the Columbus campus; academic content is not at the discretion of the regional campus. Tenure-track and tenured professors on the regional campuses are full members of their appropriate departments on the main campus. And, technically, associated faculty such as lecturers and senior lecturers would only be hired at regional campuses with the concurrence of the home department on the main campus. And the process by which a regional campus faculty member earns tenure runs through the process utilized on the Columbus campus.

I mention all of the processes above to demonstrate that the regional campuses provide a high-quality education offered by highly qualified professors. As admissions to the main campus became more selective and more students needed to have an alternative, that alternative became increasingly the regional campuses. The university's commitment during the second Gee administration to the academic quality of the regional campuses made them an attractive alternative for students who could not begin their Ohio State education on the Columbus campus. In some ways, the regional campuses resemble a small liberal arts college with small class sizes and courses taught largely by regular faculty. They differ from small liberal arts colleges in that they are far less expensive and do not in most cases have a major residential component with substantial co-curricular offerings.

Columbus State Community College

During the Jennings administration in the 1980s, Columbus Technical Institute (CTI) announced that it was seeking approval from the Ohio Board of Regents to become Columbus State Community College (CSCC). The proposed new entity would continue its wide array of technical offerings and certificate programs and would now add the associate of arts and the associate of science degrees to its curricular offerings. Some high-level administrators at Ohio State expressed misgivings about CTI's proposal, fearing that it might be a threat to Ohio State's enrollments. Immediately, President Jennings disagreed and expressed strong public support for the creation of Columbus State Community College. Jennings argued that CSCC was critical for the educational needs of central Ohio. He asserted that central Ohio was likely to continue to experience rapid growth (which it did) and that Ohio State could not fully accommodate the demand for education in the region. Moreover, as Ohio State had started down the path to becoming a more selective institution, it would be vital to have an institution such as CSCC to provide the first two years of a BA or BS degree for those students who could not start at Ohio State.

From that point on, the State of Ohio and the Ohio Board of Regents promoted articulation agreements between the community colleges and the public universities to facilitate transfers across the two sectors so that students who began at a community college and earned their AA (or AS) degree could more readily move on to a four-year institution and earn their bachelor degree with the credits earned at the community college counting toward their degree requirements. These articulation agreements worked reasonably well, but there were still some bumps in the process of moving from a two-year community college to a four-year university and earning the bachelor degree.

Thus, in the second Gee administration, Columbus State and Ohio State worked collaboratively to develop a better pathway by which Columbus State students could move more smoothly and successfully to Ohio State and earn their undergraduate degrees. The Preferred Pathway Program was created; it outlined many different academic areas of study whereby students would complete both an associate degree and a bachelor degree. There were different configurations in terms of how many years a student spent at each institution. The most common pattern was a 2+2 where students spent two years at Columbus State and two years at Ohio State. There were variations such as a 1+3 program; students who wanted the associate degree could transfer credits back to Columbus State after earning them at Ohio State and thereby satisfy the requirements for the associate degree. The Preferred Pathway Program was initially approved by the Ohio State Board of Trustees in 2011 and in 2019 the board reaffirmed the program. The program provided Columbus State student academic advising for the various academic areas offered by the program, assistance in transitioning to Ohio State, and a special orientation program. As of 2018, there were 82 well-defined pathway programs. And between 2011 and 2018, the number of Columbus State students transitioning to Ohio State under the Preferred Pathway Program increased from 400 to 569. In its television advertising throughout central Ohio, Columbus State talks enthusiastically about its participation in the Preferred Pathway Program and typically features a Columbus State graduate who is now enrolled at or having already graduated from Ohio State. And that student points out how much money she saved by starting at Columbus State. Prior to the creation of the pathways program. Gee announced in 2009 at the annual meeting of the American Council of Education that Ohio State, in partnership with Columbus State Community College, would establish a pilot program called Pipeline to Medical Colleges Initiative. The aim of the program was to improve access to health-care fields for community college students by "creating a pipeline from community colleges to four-year colleges to medical schools." This pipeline program and the pathways program discussed earlier demonstrated how Ohio State University and universities more broadly could become meaningful partners with the two-year sector to advance educational opportunities.

12

Alternative Resource Strategies

Introduction

With the major exceptions of the medical center and the athletics department, which have their own unique funding streams, the key funding sources for the core educational and instructional activities of the university are State of Ohio support and student tuition and fees. As we discussed in chapter 1, there are many constraints and pressures on state funding and tuition dollars. The demands placed on the state budget by primary and secondary education, Medicaid, the prison system, and emerging crises such as the opioid epidemic make it highly unlikely that higher education will ever see dramatic increases in its state funding. And indeed, the overall pattern of support for higher education nationally and in Ohio in the last twenty-five years has been a growing reliance on tuition to pay for the cost of educating students and a lesser reliance on state support. This does not mean that state dollars have been declining (although see below); it does mean that tuition increases have far outstripped the increases in state support to pay for a college education. Thus, twenty-five years ago one would see that state support paid for two-thirds of the cost of educating a student and tuition only one-third. Today the proportions are reversed, with tuition carrying an ever-higher share of the cost of providing an education.

Moreover, state support for higher education is more vulnerable to budget cuts than other major parts of the budget when the state is facing economic woes. In the past, many state officials believed that colleges and universities could more readily address budget cuts by raising tuition and cutting pro-

Chapter 12

grams. Comparable options were not available for health care and the prison systems. Moreover, primary and secondary education had more political clout than higher education to fight state budget cuts. Gee learned a very important lesson about the fragility of state support during an economic downturn in his first term. In the 1990s recession, the state of Ohio found itself with substantial state budget deficits. The state constitution requires a balanced budget, so that meant that difficult choices had to be made about cutting spending and/or raising taxes. In a budget crisis, the state gives the governor the unilateral power to cut program budgets any way he chooses. Thus, Governor Voinovich cut higher education disproportionately more deeply in three rounds of budget cuts in the 1990s. That is, if higher education spending comprised 13 percent of the overall state budget, in all three budget reductions, higher education received cuts far in excess of its share of the budget. These cuts were real. They were not "Washington DC cuts," which often were reductions in the rate that budgets were increasing. The Ohio cuts meant that colleges and universities would have fewer dollars the next year than they currently had, and this was not even accounting for the effects of inflation.

In the 1990s, there was less resistance by public officials to universities' raising tuition to help offset some of the losses of state dollars. But twenty years later there was widespread opposition to tuition increases as issues of affordability and student debt came to the fore. Now it was likely that state governments would impose artificial caps or even freezes on tuition increases. This was particularly frustrating to Gee and to Ohio State since OSU had the lowest tuition increases in the nation among public flagship universities in a four-year period in Gee's second term. Thus, universities now faced a situation in which their most important sources of revenue—state support and tuition—would be constrained, and institutions had to start thinking more creatively about how to generate the revenue they needed.

One response by universities was to recognize that tuition freezes and caps only applied to in-state undergraduate students and not to nonresident students. Thus, one stratagem was to increase the number of out-of-state students who were already paying a nonresident surcharge and also increase the number of international students at the undergraduate and graduate levels. And one could simply increase the size of the entering freshman class and also increase the number of transfer students it accepted, which by definition would bring in more tuition revenue. But this approach could only be taken so far if one wanted to ensure that the student body had a high-quality educational experience. Some universities tried to get creative by imposing specialized course and college fees that they did not view as tuition. Sometimes legislatures allowed this; in other cases they saw it as an illegitimate end run around tuition caps. Other universities led by Ohio University and later adopted at other institutions in Ohio including Ohio State gave the entering freshman class a tuition guarantee that would result in students paying the same tuition rate for the next four years. This gave students and their families a high degree of predictability about the cost of their own higher education in the next four years, and also encouraged timely completion of their degrees since that tuition guarantee was only for four years. The next entering freshman class would also have a four-year tuition guarantee but at a measurably higher rate than the previous freshman class. When fully implemented after four years, a university would have four different tuition rates for each of those four entering classes. This became a way for universities to generate some additional tuition revenue (but not too much) and still give individual students and their families some stability and predictability in the costs of their higher education.

Gee certainly supported being as creative as possible on tuition, but he also knew that tuition could not be the salvation for universities' budget problems. And so he looked to other traditional sources of revenue for Ohio State such as private fundraising and capital campaigns as discussed in chapter 8. During his second term, Ohio State had a very successful capital campaign. But capital campaigns are episodic and typically do not generate the needed continuing revenues to support ongoing programs, unless they grow the university's endowment. And indeed, Ohio State's endowment did grow in Gee's second term and in the subsequent Drake administration. But the endowment itself was small in comparison to that of most major prestigious private institutions and did not generate that much in earnings annually to support continuing programs. And annual philanthropic giving also rose, but much of that was designated dollars rather than unencumbered funds to be used as needed.

Other Approaches to Generating Revenue

Another possible source of revenue was the redistribution of dollars generated by internal cost savings and efficiencies to be reinvested in core academic priorities. This had been a recurrent theme in Ohio State's financial management. For example, during the Holbrook administration, Provost Ed Ray and Vice President for Finance Bill Shkurti proposed major cost savings initiatives and some different revenue generation ideas. But when Gee returned and hired Geoff Chatas as senior vice president and chief financial officer, a different approach, one that was more urgent and more comprehensive, was taken to financial management of the university. It was an approach motivated by the recognition of the potential frailties of many of the university's revenue streams, especially those coming from the state and federal government. As mentioned before, the primary source of state support was a direct subsidy to support the instruction of students. There were also smaller amounts in various budget line items that partially supported certain university functions, such as the Ohio Agriculture and Research Center, Ohio State Extension (formerly Cooperative Extension), the Lake Erie Sea Grant program, and other small line items. There was also a small state program that provided financial aid for students. The other way that major state dollars came to the university was through reimbursements paid to the university for treatment of patients, mainly through the Medicaid program. The three major ways that federal dollars came to the university were through federal student financial aid programs that became payments to the university for tuition and other costs, research grants from major funding agencies such as the National Institutes of Health; the National Science Foundation and various US departments such as Agriculture, Transportation, and Defense; and payments to the medical center for patient care through Medicare, Medicaid, and other programs. Table 12.1 shows the overall sources of the university total budget for FY2011. Note that federal and state funding totaled 2.36 billion, or almost 43 percent of the total budget, while private sources totaled over $2.7 billion, or about 49 percent of the total with net investment income of 365.1 million, constituting about 6.6 percent of total income.

An examination of these totals showed that the university would be very vulnerable to cuts in government funding in bad economic times, although ironically the Great Recession of 2008 did not wreak havoc because of all the stimulus money the federal government was sending to the states to hasten recovery. But in "normal" economic crises, the university is indeed subject to the harsh decisions of federal and state government. Should the federal government ever get serious about deficit reduction, undoubtedly budget cuts will be part of the solution. Look at the three numbers in the table that relate specifically to the medical center and patient care. The $679.2 million from the federal government is primarily Medicare and Medicaid reimbursements. The $180.5 million from the state is mainly Medicaid reimbursements. And the $1,237.2 million in the private category is mainly patient and insurance company payments. Imagine if budget deficit battles and/or ideological warfare in Washington, DC, ever resulted in major cuts to Medicare and Medicaid. Ohio State and other health systems would be facing major threats. And further imagine if major federal funding agencies such as NIH and NSF were ever

TABLE 12.1. Sources of Funding for Ohio State University in FY2011 (in millions of dollars)

SOURCE	AMOUNT
PUBLIC	
Federal	
Medical Center	679.2
Research	379.9
Tuition/Student Financial Aid	479.4
Capital	5.0
Other	99.3
Subtotal	*1,642.7*
State	
Medical Center	180.5
Research	25.8
Tuition/Student Financial Aid	363.6
Capital	62.7
Other	82.6
Subtotal	*715.3*
Local	
Other	18.0
Subtotal	*18.0*
PRIVATE (non-federal, non-state)	
Tuition	732.7
Grants and Contracts	177.5
Patient Care	1,237.2
Sales and Service	432.8
Gifts	151.0
Subtotal	*2,731.1*
INVESTMENTS	
Net Investment Income	365.1
GRAND TOTAL	***5,472.3***

Source: Table constructed from a June 2012 OSU report on federal and state dependency risks.

cut substantially. It is likely that such a move would have a negative impact on Ohio State's research totals.

But there is also some potential good news in Table 12.1. The categories of grants and contracts, sales and services, and gifts are all areas in which the university can improve performance through its own actions. For example,

CHAPTER 12

the gift totals have risen dramatically since this FY2011 report was prepared, in part due to the implementation of the advancement model. Likewise, as we will see shortly, the grants and contracts and the sales and services numbers can be grown substantially by new initiatives of the university. Finally, the net investment income (the earnings from the endowment) can be grown if the university can raise more money for the endowment and invest the proceeds wisely. Again, we will see later in this chapter that the university had indeed done this.

The university's approach was also motivated by the realization that even in good economic times, the traditional sources of funding, especially from government, could not keep up with the university's growing aspirations and growing need for funds. Certainly one of the first things that Gee and Chatas examined was how to become more efficient and save dollars to reallocate to university priorities. Chatas and his team were very creative in proposing ideas. For example, they saw that many functions and services were provided by every college and unit. Could not some of these services be consolidated and be provided more centrally at a lower cost? For some services such as human resources or purchasing, most faculty did not care who provided these services as long as they were available in a timely and competent fashion. And if it saved money, all the better. But there was one service—computer/technology assistance—that faculty were very worried about should they lose their own departmental tech support to a more centralized operation.

Chatas and his team also examined the purchasing side of the university. Too many different units were purchasing their own supplies and equipment. Would it not save money if purchasing were centralized so that the university could negotiate better contracts with suppliers and vendors? Such contracts were negotiated with the claim that they indeed saved the university money, although there was always some doubt as it related to specific items. The university simultaneously reduced the number of suppliers in its vendor database by 20 percent, thereby enhancing its ability to negotiate for quality goods and services with vendors better known to the university. The university also developed a series of e-tools to improve operational efficiencies throughout the university and to enhance sustainability by moving to paperless systems for many operations and functions. Travel planning (e.g., airline tickets, hotels) was another service that was highly decentralized, worrying Chatas and his team that perhaps university travelers were not getting the best airfares or hotel rates, especially if the individual travelers were not paying their own expenses. Thus, travel became another opportunity for consolidation and cost savings. There was also some outsourcing of custodial jobs that, albeit low paying, still saved the university money. This was not very popular among some groups on campus.

The point is that the university was looking for savings everywhere. And savings tended to be ongoing as opposed to one-time. And ideally the savings would accumulate as the university continued to make its own operations more efficient and cost-sensitive, and would therefore generate even more dollars to invest in university priorities. (Note: Chatas also had the opportunity to chair a statewide task force on college affordability and efficiency.) There were many thoughtful recommendations, which ultimately could lead to making college more affordable. But Gee knew that cost savings alone could not produce the revenue needed to support university ambitions. The university itself would have to take steps to become more creative and entrepreneurial to generate additional revenues. Gee and Chata worked well together in this endeavor, Gee being the cheerleader and vision setter who could explain why additional revenues were needed, and Chatas, with his nontraditional, non-academic background, being the financial expert who could make these ideas work. Thus, the rest of this chapter will focus on actions that Ohio State University took to generate revenues. Some of these approaches were not new to higher education; others were.

Tech Commercialization

Tech commercialization, or more specifically, the revenue generated from tech commercialization has not been successful at Ohio State, although there has been some recent improvement. When Gee returned to Ohio State, the university was very near the bottom of the Big Ten in revenues from tech commercialization, earning little more than $1 million annually, mainly from the patent it held on the feline leukemia vaccine. When that patent expired, Ohio State had very little revenue coming in. There were many critics of the university, including former trustee Les Wexner, current trustee Alex Fischer, and Governor Kasich, all of whom wanted to see much higher earnings from the commercialization of university invention and discovery, i.e., its intellectual property. As mentioned earlier, Wexner believed the university needed to do a better job of identifying what among its intellectual property had the best potential for commercialization and licensing. The governor also hoped that if commercialization did happen on a larger scale, much of it would occur in Ohio and therefore be a source of jobs and wealth in the state. Commercialization was especially important to Wexner and Fischer since Wexner was a

CHAPTER 12

FIGURE 12.1. Board of Trustee member Alex Fischer meets with United State Senator Sherrod Brown. Credit: The Ohio State University.

founding member of the Columbus Partnership and its current chair, while Fischer was president and CEO of the Partnership (see Figure 12.1). One of the high priorities of the Columbus Partnership was to advance economic development in central Ohio, a goal that would be furthered if the university's commercialization activities ever gained momentum.

Ohio State's poor performance in tech commercialization was somewhat of a puzzle because the university always ranked among the top three universities in industry-sponsored research and was always among the top ten public universities in its research and development expenditures, much of that supported by grants from NIH, NSF, USDA, and many other federal departments and agencies. With all that research being conducted, surely there must be many opportunities for commercialization that could return a revenue stream to the university. If one wants to create new, ongoing revenues streams that are relatively unencumbered, industry-sponsored research does not provide that. It is basically contract research, a sort of fee for service operation, the fruits of which go to the contractor and not the university, although it may help support some staff salaries, provide opportunities for student employment on research projects, and help fund the purchase of equipment and supplies. It is the R&D expenditures where one must look to primarily for licensing opportunities as well as individual faculty and staff activities that perhaps were not funded by major grants.

Gee put a great emphasis on tech commercialization and brought in Brian Cummings to lead the effort to grow Ohio State's commercialization and revenue portfolio. But initially there was little progress despite substantial investments being made. The university did support faculty and staff in getting patents for their discoveries, but the patent process was a lengthy and costly one. And just because a discovery or invention received a patent did not mean it had commercial applications. At the time, Provost Joe Alutto described the situation very openly and honestly. Most universities that try to improve their commercialization revenues wind up spending more money in hiring staff and putting programs in place than they receive from commercialization income. In short, for most universities, including Ohio State, it had been a losing proposition. Relatively few universities earned "big money" from commercialization, but those that did sometimes hit gold. For example, Northwestern University ranked number one in the nation in FY2010 with almost $180 million in licensing revenue; Ohio State earned just under $2 million that year. Other Big Ten universities did well: Minnesota with just under $84 million, Wisconsin with about $54 million, and Michigan at just under $40 million. The University of Florida did well with Gatorade and various medications, but when its patent on a glaucoma medication expired, its licensing revenues fell from about $54 million in 2009 to $29 million in 2010.

In 2010, a report submitted to Provost Alutto titled "Technology Commercialization at The Ohio State University: A Call to Action" confirmed how the efforts at university commercialization could be a money-loser, at least in the short to middle term. The report was prepared by Christine Poon, dean of the Fisher College of Business, Michael Camp from the Fisher College, and Caroline Whitacre, senior vice president for Research. The report made a number of sound policy proposals to enhance commercialization. It also recommended some investments to build the infrastructure for commercialization on campus. It stated by year four or five after the new investments were made, licensing revenue would cover the costs of the new initiatives—about $1.2 million annually. And by year seven to ten, the university would be making a "profit," with a revenue stream estimated at $7 million annually. Note that this total is far less than the amounts some of the institutions mentioned earlier were already earning in 2010.

As Ohio State examined how and where other universities generated substantial licensing income, it observed that often it was pharmaceuticals, medical devices, and related inventions that generated much revenue. And so the

CHAPTER 12

university began to focus on the medical center even as it recognized that it could do a much better job throughout the university to help faculty and staff through the licensing process as well as help identify the potential commercialization prospects of the intellectual property of faculty and staff. The university changed its patent approach somewhat by focusing on intellectual property that seemed most conducive to commercialization and therefore was most in need of patent protection. This meant that the university and the colleges and departments had to do a better job identifying these targets of opportunity. It also meant that faculty and the research community itself had to play a more active role in identifying these promising prospects. These efforts could not be concentrated in a central university office; the responsibilities needed to be distributed throughout the layers of the university. The university also needed to identify where its own internal procedures, rules, and regulations might hinder the commercialization process. And the university had to work with the State of Ohio to make sure that the statutory and regulatory environment was more conducive to commercialization activities and investments by the university and its employees.

With these new procedures in place, it certainly increased the chances that Ohio State might hit it big on some invention or discovery and earn huge dollars. Imagine a new drug for treating cancer or a new antibiotic or a new medical device for ailing hearts or a new process to improve energy efficiency and reduce pollution. Inventions of these kinds could greatly increase university revenues. But without hitting the "big one," the growth in revenue will be more gradual and be due to a larger number of smaller (revenue-wise) successes. Indeed, the increases in revenues have come slowly. In FY2016, Ohio State earned $2.66 million, ranking it 13th out of 14 Big Ten schools. In FY2017, the total rose to $3.2 million, the highest ever for Ohio State, but still leaving Ohio State far behind the leaders. But by FY2018, the total income rose to almost $8 million, the highest ever, leaving Ohio State officials hopeful that steps taken in earlier years were beginning to pay off and the growth in tech licensing income was accelerating. But again, the tech licensing income totals are still low and do not (yet) provide Ohio State with a major new revenue stream to support the university.

Asset Monetization—The Parking Lease

In contrast to the tech-licensing situation, Ohio State's efforts to monetize some of its assets have yielded substantial dollars to support university pri-

ALTERNATIVE RESOURCE STRATEGIES

orities. The university began reviewing many of the "businesses" it was in and asked itself whether it should remain in that business or try to lease it or sell it to outside entities in exchange for a healthy influx of dollars. One such asset was Ohio State's parking system, which entailed parking garages, surface lots, on-street campus parking, and the thousands and thousands of faculty, staff, and students who paid for the privilege of parking their vehicles on campus. Gordon Gee questioned whether the university should be in the parking business. If not, could we spin off our parking assets to some private company, perhaps through a lease, and receive a substantial payment from the new lessor in exchange for its newly gotten opportunity to run the parking system and collect the revenues. This thinking led to a major initiative on campus led by Senior Vice President Geoff Chatas to see if there were external entities that wanted to run OSU parking and pay the university an appropriate price for the right to do this. After an extensive discussion on campus and a bidding process, the Board of Trustees in June 2012 approved a $483 million long-term fifty-year lease and concession agreement for OSU's parking operations with QIC Global Infrastructure and its operating partner LAZ Parking. The newly created operation would be called CampusParc.

There were a number of reactions and concerns on campus about this transaction. A few observers thought it was another sign of the corporatization of the university. Some worried about the job security of the OSU employees that had been working in parking operations. Others worried that a private entity running parking might raise parking fees by exorbitant amounts annually. Other worried that the new management might not maintain the parking infrastructure as well as the university had. Still others worried whether the price was right; had the university received sufficient money in this transaction?

Most of these concerns were fully addressed. Provisions were made for current OSU employees. Guarantees were built into the contract to limit parking rate increases to no more than 5.5 percent annually in the first ten years of the contract. After ten years, price increases were limited to either 4 percent or a five-year rolling average of inflation, whichever was more. Strong provisions were included in the contract to ensure that QIC had major responsibilities to preserve and maintain the parking assets. Most importantly, the university was transparent about how the proceeds from the transaction—the $483 million—would be invested.

All of the proceeds from this lease arrangement were invested in the university's endowment, where it was expected over fifty years to generate $3.1 billion for academic initiatives such as faculty hires, more student scholarships, and support for the arts and humanities. The proceeds would also support the university's bus services and increase the university's long-term investment pool by $4.9 billion. In the first four years of the agreement, earnings from the parking lease endowment have totaled over $105 million. In the 2016–17 year, more than 400 student scholarships were funded by the parking endowment earnings, including more than 100 comprehensive Eminence Fellows Program scholarships. Through September 2018, 141 faculty members in the Discovery Themes have been hired, and 50 additional searches are being funded through parking earnings. And $6.4 million went toward the renovation of Sullivant Hall and $5.5 million toward design work for the new Arts District mentioned earlier. And throughout this time, it appears that the new managers of parking operations are maintaining a high level of service to customers as well as maintaining parking facilities to a high standard. Thus, the parking leasing deal seems to have accomplished a key revenue goal: providing a high level of continuing dollars that can then be plowed back into academic priorities. The one sour note I heard in two interviews with CampusParc employees who previously worked for the university was that the management in the last year or two had become much more concerned about the bottom line and was putting a lot of pressure on employees to provide a lower level of service to customers.

Asset Monetization—The Energy Grid

Compared to the parking lease agreement, the initiative to monetize the university's energy grid and energy provision was a far more complicated and challenging task. After the success of the parking lease deal, the university looked for other opportunities for monetization and soon focused on energy. While the initial conversation began in the second Gee administration, most of the key decisions occurred during the one-year interim Alutto presidency and the subsequent Drake administration. Therefore I will not go into great detail on this except to provide a brief description of the process and the outcome. One will see many parallels to the parking-lease project, but also see how much more complex and ambitious the energy initiative was.

The first step in an energy privatization initiative was for the university to decide what it wanted to include in a potential deal. One element involved sustainability, a very expensive item, as the university investigated the costs associated with achieving a more sustainable, more fuel-efficient and more eco-friendly campus. The university spent months discussing the components of an energy deal with constituencies within and outside the university. When this was completed, the university was ready to send out a request for qualifications seeking businesses interested in managing Ohio State's energy system in return for a long-term lease. Forty qualified proposals were received by mid-2015, which the university had to evaluate. By February of 2016, the list was reduced to ten bidders and by April of 2016 was further reduced to six. It would be these six applicants that would respond to a request for proposals and a "winner" would be selected from these six. There was some opposition to this energy initiative. Labor unions expressed concern about the future of fifty-two OSU utility employees, some of whom were union members. The university said that every utility employee would get an interview with the winning bidder, and for those who wanted to remain OSU employees, the university pledged to find appropriate jobs at the same pay level. Some student groups such as the OSU chapter of United Students Against Sweatshops protested energy privatization on multiple grounds, many of which were actually addressed in the RFP and the proposals that were submitted. The students complained about corporatization, environmental threats, loss of jobs, and a nontransparent process. Again, most of these attacks had already been addressed or would be in the final agreement.

In 2017, a decision was made to establish Ohio State Energy partners, a private company comprised of the French energy company ENGIE and the Canadian investment firm Axium Infrastructure. The university would pay fees to Ohio State Energy starting at about $55 million per year and Ohio State Energy would fund and implement utility capital improvement projects on campus with an eye toward achieving greater efficiency and sustainability. The fifty-year deal earned Ohio State $1.1 billion up front plus $150 million to support academics. The university was planning to put a total of $775 million into the university endowment in four separate "buckets" to (1) support student scholarships, (2) support faculty and staff initiatives, (3) enhance key university strategic priorities, and (4) invest in various energy-related projects dealing with procurement, utilization, and efficiency.

Once again, by monetizing this asset, the university had secured a longer-term revenue stream to support key university priorities. And it is the earnings from the investment that are being spent; the body or corpus will continue to grow, and depending on how well the markets do and on how wisely the university invests, there could be a tidy sum at the end of this fifty-year period. It will be interesting to see how many other universities go down the path of asset monetization. Certainly because of its size, Ohio State had some valuable assets to monetize. But this would not have happened without the leadership of Gordon Gee, Joe Alutto, and Geoff Chatas and without the strong support of the Board of Trustees.

CHAPTER 12

Affinity Agreements—Huntington, Coke Renewal, and Nike Renewal

Universities are increasingly partnering with outside businesses, some local and some national, to gain additional resources and support, as those companies get the benefit of being linked to these universities. Ohio State is no exception. While probably the Cola wars between Pepsi and Coca-Cola and the athletic apparel battles between Nike, Adidas, and Under Armour may be the most familiar and publicized, there are scores of other opportunities for colleges and universities to expand their affinity agreements. In this section, I will mention only three major affinity agreements that Ohio State has negotiated: Huntington Bank, Coca-Cola, and Nike.

Huntington Bank is a major institution in Columbus and a longtime supporter of Ohio State. In 2012, an affinity agreement with Huntington benefitted the university in many ways. There was an upfront payment to Ohio State of $25 million. Faculty, staff, and students received special banking terms in their transactions with the bank. Huntington provided over 150 internships for students, funded some classroom renovations, and provided support for a student advising program. And Huntington pledged to invest $100 million in community lending and other investments in the neighborhoods surrounding the campus, thereby enhancing the university's own initiatives on neighborhood revitalization discussed in chapter 9. The portfolio of benefits from the Huntington affinity agreement meshed unbelievably well with the university's needs and priorities.

Another affinity agreement was with Coca-Cola, part of the ongoing "cola wars" between Coke and Pepsi to lock up agreements with colleges and universities. Ohio State originally contracted with Coca-Cola in 1998 and renewed a modified agreement in 2008 for another ten years. In 2018, Ohio State chose to extend its existing relationship with Coke for a fifteen-year period through 2033. Each renewal of the contract agreement resulted in more revenue for the university, with the 2018 renewal having a projected value of about $85 million.

The 2008 renewal during Gee's second term was projected to be worth at least $32 million over its ten-year life. And in the first five years of the agreement, Coca-Cola paid Ohio State about $17 million in royalties and over $4 million in commissions from the 438+ Coca-Cola vending machines located on campus. This contract gave Coca-Cola exclusive pouring rights on campus. With some minor exceptions, only Coke products could be sold on campus. In addition to the sales revenue of its products on campus, Coca-Cola also received guaranteed (paid) access to OSU athletic events, permission to use

ALTERNATIVE RESOURCE STRATEGIES

the Ohio State brand in its promotions, discounted corporate memberships at the OSU golf course, and other benefits. Students received some benefits from the Coke contract such as donations of Coke products to be served at student events, opportunities for students to have experiences in promotion activities and consumer marketing for Coke products, and annual support for student leadership programs and financial literacy initiatives. Also, $10 million of the Coke proceeds went toward construction of the Ohio Union. The 2018 renewal detailed specific benefits for students, including $2.25 million for student scholarships, $1.66 million for student projects and initiatives, and six student internships annually.

There were some controversies associated with the contract renewal in 2008. Of course, Pepsi lovers were unhappy. There were also complaints about the lack of transparency in the process used to renew the Coke contract. And there were some student organizations supported by off-campus groups upset about what they claimed to be Coca-Cola's unfair labor practices, especially as related to unionization in Colombia. But, overall, the contract renewal was greeted as an increasingly common way that Ohio State could generate additional revenues, and affinity agreements more generally were here to stay and would likely grow exponentially in numbers and dollars.

Another major competition for university partners was being waged by the shoe/apparel/equipment companies such as Nike, Adidas, and Under Armour. Ohio State initially chose to go with Nike and has since twice renewed and expanded the relationship. Ohio State and Nike signed three separate agreements that took effect in August 2007 and were extended until 2018. In this eleven-year period (2007–2018), Ohio State was expected to receive over $46 million. There was a standard licensing agreement, an equipment supply agreement, and an appearance and consultation agreement. Without going into the details of these contracts, it is fair to say that the Department of Athletics was the major beneficiary of the deals. In 2018, Nike and Ohio State concluded negotiating a fifteen-year deal worth $252 million, a blockbuster of an agreement to national observers and competitors. Ohio State will receive $103 million in cash and royalties as well as over $112 million in product such as uniforms and equipment for the athletic program. But this deal also includes about $40 million beyond the athletic department for, among other things, scholarships and internships for students who are not athletes. Gene Smith, the OSU athletics director, was also named vice president in 2014 by interim president Joe Alutto. Smith and his colleagues were very skillful in renegotiating the Nike deal. They waited to see how Nike's negotiations with the University of Texas and the University of Michigan would turn out, and then negotiated a

Chapter 12

better deal for Ohio State, in part because in this time period Ohio State was enjoying much greater success on the playing field than Texas and Michigan and would therefore be a more attractive partner to Nike. The title of vice president bestowed upon Smith meant that he now had joint responsibility with the Office of Business and Finance for the Business Advancement Division at the university, which included the Schottenstein Center, the Drake Union, the Office of Trademark and Licensing, the Fawcett Center, and others. Moreover, with his additional responsibilities, Smith would collaborate with Business and Finance to grow the university's affinity agreements.

While I only discussed three affinity agreements in detail, Ohio State has many more such deals, in part because Ohio State is such an attractive partner to so many businesses. Would-be sponsors see Ohio State's nationally prominent athletic program and its incredibly comprehensive medical center as wonderful venues to link their companies to the Ohio State brand and to promote their own products. Scoreboards, signage, print materials, ads, and much more provide businesses with great opportunities to connect with the public in the context of their support of Ohio State. Yet another advantage that Ohio State has in the affinity arena and other revenue generation initiatives is that it has the internal expertise (see especially the next section on century bonds) in areas such as business and finance, contracts and legal affairs, marketing and communication to be proactive and reach out to potential supporters as well as evaluate and negotiate proposed deals from external entities. One name that should be highlighted is Xen Riggs, associate vice president for business advancement and a key university player working with Columbus and Franklin County on the joint operating agreement between Nationwide Arena and the Schottenstein Center/Value City Arena. Riggs is a financial wizard with exceptional negotiating skills who engenders trust and confidence in those with whom he deals.

Ohio State is not at the mercy of external businesses in deciding upon affinity deals. Indeed, whenever an existing deal comes up for renewal, Ohio State has the internal capacity to decide whether the deal should be renegotiated and extended or whether it should be terminated in favor of another vendor. For example, Ohio State in 2013 ended a fifteen-year relationship with Sodexo, which ran the concessions at the university's athletic venues. There had been some criticisms about Sodexo's treatment of its workers and also some dissatisfaction with the variety of food offerings at their concession stands. The university decided to go with Levy Restaurants as the new concessionaire in a seven-year contract that will likely provide Ohio State with at least $1 million more than the Sodexo contract annually in commission income for a total of $4.5 million. The Levy contract will also provide about $3 million for improvements in the Schottenstein Center infrastructure and enhancements in food service facilities around the campus.

Century Bonds

Under the leadership of Geoff Chatas and Mike Papadakis and with the enthusiastic support of Gee and the Board of Trustees, Ohio State became the first public university to issue century bonds and only the third university in the country. Ohio State issued $500 million of century bonds in 2011 at a very favorable interest rate, the lowest ever for this type of instrument. This meant that the university now had a pool of $500 million in long-term capital, and depending upon how it was allocated and repaid by campus entities during the 100-year period, might effectively be a revolving fund that supports many additional projects and programs. The bonds require Ohio State to make interest-only payments through 2111; then there will be a bullet payment to pay the $500 million principal. This means that Ohio State will be investing funds now to raise the $500 million needed in 2111.

The century bond proceeds were allocated initially to a number of capital construction projects such as the medical center expansion as well as improved student housing. As these moneys are paid back, they could be reinvested in student and faculty initiatives. For example, it was expected that the Wexner Medical Center would be repaying $25 million annually for twenty years and then once these funds were repaid, they would be available for other university projects.

Ohio State also sold in 2010 $800 million of "Build America Bonds," part of the package of Obama administration programs to counter "the Great Recession." The federal government subsidized a portion of the interest payments on these bonds. Between the century bonds and the Build America Bonds, Ohio State almost doubled the university's debt burden. Rating services such as Moody's Investor Services and Fitch Ratings observed that there are financial risks associated with these developments, but also noted that the university's traditional conservative approach to handling debt should minimize that risk. Also lessening the risk was the relatively low rates the university would be paying on the bonds. Ohio State maintained its strong bond rating while these transactions were enacted.

CHAPTER 12

Selective Investments from the University Endowment

Ohio State had a university endowment of over $5 billion in FY2018, an all-time record amount and a total that has grown dramatically in the last five years. This money is invested in a number of financial instruments, securities, and the like with the goal of obtaining good return (earnings) on the endowment, which could then be plowed back into support for university initiatives. The process by which investment decisions are made is a complicated one, led by key university personnel such as a chief investment officer and his staff and working with colleagues at key investment firms. The university decided in 2010 that some small portion of the endowment could be invested in nontraditional ways with the hope of earning a higher than average return.

Thus, the university made separate investments in two venture capital firms. The first was Drive Capital, in which the university invested $50 million dollars in 2013, and the second the Ohio Innovation Fund, in which Ohio State University and Ohio University seeded the fund with $35 million in 2012. Both of these enterprises were motivated by providing more venture capital in Ohio and the Midwest to support startup companies and related enterprises that could bring jobs and economic prosperity to the region. Ohio State recognized that these investments could be risky and that the return on these investments might not come until ten or more years down the road. After all, these venture capital firms were investing in startup companies and that, even if successful, these companies would not be generating profits until sometime down the road. And it of course was possible that these startup companies would fail. But Ohio State wanted to allow for the possibility that these investments might result in surprising gains. These investments also had some other advantages by demonstrating that the university was willing to invest in Ohio and regional startups and thereby contribute directly to the economic development of Ohio.

There was some controversy, particularly surrounding Drive Capital, which was run by Mark Kvamme, a close friend of Governor Kasich and a close associate of Geoff Chatas. Some questioned whether the university's investment in Drive Capital was being made for political and personal reasons rather than because of the merits of the investment. Drive Capital raised its first $250 million fund by 2013, added another $300 million in 2016, and followed up with an additional $558 million in two new venture funds in 2019. Thus, it certainly seemed clear that investors were voting with their wallets in endorsing the Drive Capital initiatives. Moreover, the estimated market value of the initial $250 investment was $650 million by 2019, suggesting that Kvamme and his staff were making good choices in their support of startup companies.

ALTERNATIVE RESOURCE STRATEGIES

Pelotonia

The story of Pelotonia could have been placed in the next chapter on the medical center since it is a philanthropic initiative to raise money solely for the James Cancer Hospital at Ohio State. But I chose to put it in this chapter because it is also a very creative and inspirational way to not only generate contributions but also to link the broader Columbus and Ohio community in the fight to cure cancer. At its core, Pelotonia is a bike ride to raise money for cancer research at the Ohio State University. Michael Caligiuri, the director of the OSU Comprehensive Cancer Center and CEO of the James Cancer Hospital and Solove Research Institute, recognized that additional funding was needed to support cancer research and treatment. In 2008 Caligiuri and Tom Lennox, the first CEO of Pelotonia, bicycled across Cape Cod in the Pan Mass Challenge that raised money for the Dana-Farber Cancer Institute. And thus the idea for Pelotonia was crystallized: there would be a major bicycle ride in Columbus and the surrounding areas in which riders and individuals and groups that pledged financial support for the riders would raise money for the OSU cancer program. After the first year in 2009, the operating costs for Pelotonia have been paid for in their entirety by the three major sponsors, Huntington Bank, L-Brands, and Peggy and Richard Santulli; other corporate citizens and individuals provide additional support. This meant that every dollar raised by Pelotonia would go directly to cancer research. No moneys would be spent on overhead, administrative costs, and the like. Donors would know that their contributions were supporting cancer research and cancer research only.

As Pelotonia evolved, not only were there actual riders, but also virtual riders who pledged to raise certain amounts but did not have to actually ride a bicycle. In its first year in 2009, there were 2,265 riders and a total of $4,511 868 raised. In Gee's last year in 2013, there were 6,723 riders and $19,007,104 raised. In 2018, there were 8,470 riders and $27,400,779 raised, which meant that between 2009 and 2018 over $184 million was raised. In 2017, Pelotonia became legally independent from Ohio State, establishing its own 501(c)(3) status. The major reason for this change was to give Pelotonia more freedom and flexibility to take actions not easily done under university auspices, actions that would enhance its fundraising abilities. It still would be the case that all contributions would go to cancer research. One has to wonder how high the ceiling can be for the dollars raised by Pelotonia. In its first ten years, Pelotonia has raised an average of over $18 million annually (with that average growing each year), giving the leadership of the James the ability to respond quickly to the need for funding for new approaches or new equipment or whatever else might be on the cancer horizon.

Conclusion

This chapter certainly demonstrates the creativity and agility that Ohio State has demonstrated in seeking new revenue sources in an era when many of the existing revenue streams are constrained and limited. Indeed, the university and individuals within the university have been recognized by professional associations for their leadership on these matters. Ohio State, as discussed earlier, clearly has some advantages in the quest to develop alternative revenue sources. The size and comprehensiveness of the university opened up many possibilities that would not be available to smaller institutions. Again, as mentioned earlier, the presence of a huge medical complex and a large and successful athletic program gave Ohio State opportunities to exploit these resources, an advantage not available to most institutions.

But just as significant, if not more so, is the influence of leadership, and Ohio State had that in droves with Gee, Alutto, and Chatas and a supportive Board of Trustees. Many of the actions and decisions described in this chapter were out of the ordinary; they do not reflect how universities traditionally conduct business. Some even had identifiable risks associated with them. If the university leadership had been risk averse, many of these actions might never have been implemented. Fortunately, Gee, Alutto, and Chatas also had very able colleagues and assistants in the university bureaucracy, especially in legal affairs led by Chris Culley, which could analyze the various proposals and offer suggestions on how to improve them. The mindset was how can we make this work rather than let's not do this because there is risk. With that kind of positive attitude, Ohio State has certainly become a national leader in identifying and implementing alternative revenue streams. Of course, if things take a bad turn, for example on century bonds, no one who approved this decision will be around to face the consequences.

13

Ohio State by the Numbers

Trends in Quality and Performance

Introduction

The noteworthy story about Ohio State University is that along many dimensions the quality of the university has grown dramatically and continues to grow. Many of these changes began in the Jennings administration and the first Gee presidency, continued through the Kirwan and Holbrook years, accelerated during the second Gee presidency, and continued into the Drake administration. These trends are certainly a tribute to many university administrations, but they also reflect that once a university, especially a major, complex institution like Ohio State, chooses to move down a particular path, the momentum builds to stay on that path, assuming strong leadership and a solid financial foundation. University changes have internal constituencies committed to building upon the previous positive developments, especially if those developments can be measured by relatively simply and valid metrics. For example, if one measure of student quality is the percentage of entering freshmen who graduated in the top 10 percent of their high school senior class, and if that percentage has been increasing over time, then the university and various offices within the university such as admissions, academic affairs, and communications would not want to see a drop in that number.

Thus, in this chapter, we will highlight some of the key characteristics of Ohio State and how they have changed over time and how they continue to change. We will focus on characteristics that reflect the quality of the institution and its student body, its accessibility and affordability, and its performance.

Chapter 13

In discussing the student body, we will focus mainly on the characteristics of undergraduate students because it was these characteristics in the past that so heavily shaped (misleadingly) the public image of Ohio State University. For example, thirty-five years ago many observers would say that any university that was so easy to get admitted to could not be a strong institution academically. These observers were unaware of how challenging it was to graduate from Ohio State. Other observers equated cost and quality and asserted that any institution that was so cheap could not possibly be providing a high-quality educational experience; with that mentality, costly private institutions were by definition superior to their less expensive public counterparts. Today affordability and lower costs are good features, but that was not always the case. Other skeptics argued that a huge university with 40,000 undergraduates could not possibly serve students well; that stereotype has been shattered in the last thirty years. Finally, some elitists would assert the false dichotomy that any institution that had an outstanding football program and a comprehensive athletic program could not possibly have the appropriate focus on academic matters. The whole set of stereotypes associated with a successful football program at a large public university resulted in Ohio State often being referred to as a "football factory."

Throughout this time period when there was substantial external skepticism about the undergraduate program and the quality of undergraduate students, there was widespread (but not universal) acknowledgment of Ohio State's strengths in research, in its graduate and professional degree programs, and in its many strong academic departments and colleges. Yet, although widely recognized in academic circles, these wonderful attributes did not engender perceptions in the broader public that Ohio State was a first-rate academic institution, in part because of the stereotypes mentioned above.

Thus, Ohio State made a major, ongoing commitment to address the quality of the undergraduate student body and the strengths of its academic programs. And while one motivation for this initiative was to enhance the reputation of the university, the fundamental rationale was far more important. Faculty and administrators believed that Ohio State should have undergraduate students who could take full advantage of what a comprehensive, national land grant research university could offer them. And students who came to Ohio State needing remedial work in English or math or who experienced weak academic programs while in high school would not be prepared to benefit by what Ohio State could offer.

Thus, Ohio State modified its recruitment and admissions strategies and its academic requirements in a serious and comprehensive fashion and did not rely upon gimmicks and short-term tactics to get the job done. However, Ohio State could be entrepreneurial when necessary. For example, when Gee first arrived at Ohio State in 1990, he was told that the University of Toledo was bragging that it had more National Merit Scholars in its entering freshman class than any other public university in Ohio. And with that single indicator, Toledo tried to leave the impression that its student body was stronger than Ohio State's or Miami's or Ohio University's. Gee was annoyed and told his admissions and financial aid staff that that would not happen again, and so Ohio State got very active in recruiting National Merit Scholars. But Gee recognized that this was merely a short-term tactic and that Ohio State would have to undertake a major, coordinated effort supported by adequate staff resources as well as ample financial aid packages to attract the kind of student body that could better take advantage of Ohio State University. And Gee himself was fully involved in both his first and second presidencies in recruiting high school students to come to Ohio State. When he was on his state tours and on other travels, he would routinely visit high schools to spread the word of Ohio State. And if he heard from one of his many contacts that a particular high school senior (not an athlete covered by NCAA recruiting restrictions) was considering Ohio State, Gee would get on the phone and call the very surprised student.

Thus, the rest of the initial part of this chapter will focus on the characteristics of incoming undergraduate students over time (their input attributes) and their subsequent performance at Ohio State (their output characteristics). Then we will turn to measures of university performance in such areas as research funding, charitable fundraising, endowment growth, affordability, and other measures. But before moving to these topics, I want to offer a few comments about the use of metrics.

Some Comments about the Use of Metrics

The use of metrics to assess the quality and performance of universities has grown dramatically for a number of reasons. Certainly one key reason is the recognition by universities that they need to be more accountable to their various constituencies and one way to enhance accountability is to provide hard data and evidence about universities' performance. As institutions of higher education evaluate themselves, they often select metrics designed to measure features relevant to their core mission and goals. Different metrics may be appropriate for different institutions. But there are some external forces that

Chapter 13

push toward a standardization of metrics. As more and more external entities such as magazines have begun evaluating colleges and universities, the institutions themselves have become very sensitive to the kinds of indicators used by these external evaluators. In some instances, this means that universities are trying to legitimately alter their own performance and performance measures so as to achieve higher ratings. In other instances, a few institutions actually falsify their own internal data in order to achieve higher ratings from external evaluators. We will talk about this later when we discuss the *U.S. News & World Report* ratings, certainly the most visible and publicized ratings in higher education, and other rating systems.

Hence, as Ohio State became more committed to the use of metrics in the Gee One and Kirwan presidencies, it did this in an environment in which there was much more focus on metrics by external actors and much more competition among universities to demonstrate their value and quality vis a vis their peers. In this ratings game, Ohio State always played by the rules. The university generated accurate, valid data. It made data available for outside observers to scrutinize. It tried to measure important, substantive aspects of university life. For example, in attempting to assess the quality of the institution, Ohio State tried to generate data that indeed measured quality and not simply the reputation for quality. In many cases we do have hard data, but often our information is reputational, perhaps obtained through a survey of university leaders who are asked to rate the quality of a department, a college, or the university itself. Often one does not know what went into these qualitative assessments. A classic example of the potential pitfalls of qualitative measurement occurred many years ago when geography departments at universities throughout the nation were being evaluated. A measuring instrument was administered to professionals in the area asking them to rate geography departments. The geography department at Harvard University was rated fifth nationally, a very impressive performance. The problem, however, was that Harvard did not have a geography department. Undoubtedly, the high rating of the nonexistent Harvard geography department was simply a reflection of the overall high esteem in which Harvard was held. The point is that reputational measures can be flawed and biased, particularly against larger, less selective, and less prestigious public institutions. But even indicators based on hard data can be faulty if the data are not truly measuring what is purported to be measured.

When comparing universities, a very important caveat is that institutions may be so different along certain key dimensions that the comparisons made may not be as informative as one would hope. For example, institutions are often compared with respect to the number of international students attending the institution. Typically these comparisons are made on the basis of sheer numbers. Thus, it is not surprising that large institutions such as Ohio State often appear at the top of such rankings because of their size. A simple way to correct or modify this would be to *also* examine the percentage of the student body that is international students. By examining numbers and percentages, smaller institutions are not penalized for having a numerically small student body, but they are also not rewarded by having a high percentage when their overall numbers are actually quite small. *The Chronicle of Higher Education* has a regular section called the Chronicle List, which is simply a full-page data display on some measure in a particular year. For example, the Chronicle List presented the top producers of Peace Corps volunteers for FY2018 and presented information for three categories of colleges—those with an undergraduate enrollment over 15,000, those with an enrollment between 5,000 and 15,000, and those with a student body under 5,000. Ohio State ranked fifth (tied with two other institutions) in Peace Corps volunteers, and three of the four institutions above Ohio State were Big Ten Universities. (Year in and year out, Ohio State ranks highly in producing Peace Corps volunteers.) Notably, Ohio State's ranking came when being compared with peer institutions. Ohio State's number of 62 volunteers in FY2018 was higher than the leading college in the other two categories based upon the size of the student population. In contrast, in another example, *The Chronicle* presented information about colleges with the highest numbers of National Humanities Center Fellows from 1978–79 to 2019–2020. Ohio State ranked twenty-seventh nationally among all public and private universities. It is hard to know whether this is a good or a bad performance. It was the case that Ohio State ranked fifth among Big Ten institutions. But it is difficult to know what this ranking signifies, especially because it covers such a long time span.

Four additional examples from the Chronicle List indicate the difficulty in interpreting the significance of rankings. The first is a listing of flagship institutions with the highest percentages of older (defined as twenty-five and over) undergraduates in fall 2015. Ohio State ranked twenty-second nationally and third in the Big Ten with 8 percent of undergraduates being over twenty-five. What is this actually measuring? Is it capturing those students who had an earlier career such as the military prior to enrolling in college? Or are these students whose undergraduate careers were interrupted for whatever reason and then came back to school? The top eleven schools were all west of the Mississippi, led by the University of Alaska (Fairbanks) at 46.4 percent, the University of Utah at 38.6 percent, the University of New Mexico at 25.1 per-

Chapter 13

cent, the University of Montana (Missoula) at 24.2 percent, and the University of Wyoming at 21.7 percent.

Another Chronicle List indicator is the production of Fulbright US Scholars and Students in the 2017–2018 school year. Here the results were presented for research institutions, master's institutions, and bachelor's institutions. For Fulbright Scholars, Ohio State ranked fourth in the nation, and two of the three schools ahead of Ohio State were Big Ten public institutions. But for Fulbright students, Ohio State did not rank among the top thirty-one research institutions cited by the Chronicle List. Perhaps it was an atypical year for Ohio State, but there were seven Big Ten schools among the top thirty-one. Another Chronicle List indicator is US institutions with the greatest number (not percentage) of foreign students in academic year 2016–17. This information is divided into doctoral institutions, master's institutions, and baccalaureate institutions. Ohio State ranked seventeenth in the nation, with 7,684 students and with five Big Ten institutions having a greater number. I am not sure that this indicator is telling us a lot except that larger institutions tend to have more international students. For these numbers to be more helpful, it would be helpful to know the programs in which the international students enrolled.

The last Chronicle List indicator to be discussed is which universities granted the most research doctorates in FY2016. Here Ohio State ranks ninth in the nation with four Big Ten schools ahead of Ohio State and with nine of the top ten schools being public universities. The Chronicle List showed the top forty-nine schools and thirteen of fourteen Big Ten schools were in the top forty-nine. To me, this is a very impressive performance by Big Ten schools and Ohio State's ranking of ninth is very good, especially since Ohio State ranks very highly in doctoral production year after year. It really does demonstrate how critical Ohio State and Big Ten universities are to the creation of the next generation of scholars. But let me ask a hypothetical question: What if Ohio State had finished eleventh rather than ninth, and what if the Chronicle List had only listed the top ten schools? Certainly Ohio State's meritorious performance would not have been revealed. More important, it would show the downside in our culture to focus primarily on top ten lists. I mention this because Ohio State has historically had many academic departments ranked in the top fifteen or top twenty-five among hundreds of colleges and universities throughout the nation, yet they do not get the recognition they merit nor does the university overall benefit *reputationally* from these outstanding colleges and departments.

One type of cross-institutional comparison that is dramatically affected by the size and academic composition of the institution is the amount of research dollars raised. Clearly large institutions with thousands of faculty members would be expected to attract more research dollars than smaller institutions. If one moved from total dollars generated to dollars raised per faculty member, then smaller institutions would not be penalized as much in the rankings. In a similar vein, the kinds of academic units that make up a university have a lot to say about the availability of research dollars from the federal government and other sources. An institution with a heavy concentration in engineering and the hard sciences will likely have a better track record in attracting research dollars than one in which the arts and humanities comprise a larger share of the academic offerings. Likewise, a university that has a major medical center should clearly have a more impressive record attracting funds than an institution without a major health sciences presence. Research dollars as a measure of performance is also sensitive to factors over which the university may have no control. Federal budget crunches could result in fewer grants being awarded, diminishing a university's performance in this arena. Or if some prominent faculty members retire or move to another institution and take their major research programs with them, a university's performance and rankings may suffer setbacks. Also, the competition for external (especially federal) funding is growing fiercer as more universities strengthen their capabilities to seek external funding with the result that the rate of growth in applications seeking external support exceeds the rate of growth in the availability of research dollars. As we will see later, many of our measures of research performance are quite simple and straightforward.

The key point of this methodological discussion is to be sensitive to the strengths and weaknesses of our measures. It is a good development that universities are relying on more systematic information and data in making judgments about which programs to modify, which areas to invest in and which initiatives to trim back. Metrics can be very critical to wise decision-making and to an appreciation for where a university stands at a particular point in time. But metrics by themselves can lead to some suboptimal decisions when the metrics are not measuring the right things or when they are based on faulty data or when the actual analysis of the data is flawed.

U.S. News and Other Magazine Ratings

U.S. News & World Report calculates ratings of overall institutional quality as well as evaluations of specific programs, departments, and colleges within a university. The *U.S. News* ratings divide colleges and universities into differ-

Chapter 13

ent categories—e.g., national public universities, small private liberal arts colleges, and other classifications—in order to make comparisons and rankings within those categories more meaningful and informative. *U.S. News* is not the only player in the ratings game, but it is the most prominent. *Money* magazine rates colleges and universities with respect to the return on investment they provide students. *Money* was also among the first magazines to explicitly take into account the input characteristics of the student body when looking at output measures such as time to graduation and retention rates. For example, comparing Harvard's four-year graduation rate with that of a large, open-admission four-year public university would be silly; of course Harvard would have a higher graduation rate, in large part because of the characteristics of the incoming student body. Thus, *Money* tried to develop predictive models that took into account input characteristics. The model could then predict what the graduation rate should be for an institution with a specific kind of student profile. If the graduation rate was higher than predicted, that meant that the institution was doing better than expected, a very good sign. In essence, *Money* was trying to capture the value-added, transformative effect that students were experiencing at their university, a very important contribution to the wise use of metrics. *Washington Monthly* had a different perspective on ratings. It attempted to assess not only what institutions do for students, but more importantly what they do for the country. Thus, in examining national universities, *Washington Monthly* focused on university contributions to social mobility, research, and service.

When *U.S. News & World Report* began its ratings of colleges and universities, many observers on campuses and throughout the broader society scoffed at the magazine's efforts, criticizing its methodology, data, and interpretations, and fundamentally challenging the very premise of the work. According to the magazine, the rationale for the ratings was two-fold: to help students and their families make better-informed decisions about choice of college and to help colleges and universities make better decisions about their own enterprise through the extensive data that was being collected. There was actually a third unstated rationale—that the public would eat up this kind of story and that the visibility, circulation, and profits of *U.S. News* would soar. From the very beginning, some universities said they would not participate, but most of those threats soon fell by the wayside as the popularity of the annual ratings grew. Some universities actually cheated and misreported their data in hope of getting a higher ranking. This problem of misconduct, or at least mistaken reporting of data, has continued to the present. In July of 2019, *U.S. News* revealed that five colleges, including the University of California at Berkeley, had notified the magazine that they had initially submitted incorrect information. This mistaken data gave all five schools a higher ranking than they would have earned with the correct information. Thus, *U.S. News* put the schools in its "Unranked" category, where they would remain until the magazine's next "Best Colleges" computations were done and the schools were able to verify the accuracy of their next data submission.

On multiple occasions, Gordon Gee criticized *U.S. News* rankings as one of the worst things to have happened to higher education. He asserted that the ratings distorted university priorities, provided incentives for poor decision-making, and trivialized serious evaluations of the performance of universities. Yet higher rankings in the *U.S. News* ratings became one of the goals for Ohio State. Why *U.S. News* rather than some other publication? Because *U.S. News* ratings were the most prominent and most publicized, and were considered by many media outlets as the most credible. *U.S. News* ranks hundreds of major national universities and then ranks the public universities from within that list. One goal for Ohio State was to move to a top fifteen rating among public universities from the nineteenth ranking it then had. Ohio State also aspired to move to a top fifty ranking among all universities from the fifty-sixth ranking it then had. The Institutional Research and Planning Office of the university under the wise leadership of Julie Carpenter-Hubin did extensive analysis of the components of the *U.S. News* ratings to better understand what the ratings were actually measuring and to see where Ohio State needed to improve its performance in order to achieve a better rating.

Some of these analyses reflected core Ohio State values. For example, one indicator used by *U.S. News* was graduation and retention rates. If those indicators were improving at Ohio State (and they were), then the university's ranking was likely to go up and the university would consider additional retention and graduation strategies it might adopt. Another indicator was alumni giving measured as the percentage of alumni who gave financial contributions to their university. Ohio State and most public universities scored low on this indicator in contrast to private institutions. Ohio State should certainly strive to enhance alumni giving, and that is indeed one of the goals of the advancement model discussed in chapter 8, to be accomplished in part by better engagement with alumni after their graduation. But on this indicator, some creative personnel tried to come up with more gimmicky ways, which Ohio State did not implement. For example, if undergraduate students just prior to graduation had moneys remaining on their meal cards, then if that money could be transferred to the university, it could count as an alumni contribution and improve Ohio State' performance on this indicator.

Chapter 13

The more general point is institutions tried to game the *U.S. News* methodology. And the *U.S. News* methodology was biased from the very beginning with its reliance on many reputational measures, which clearly favored prestigious private schools and hurt large public universities. Unfortunately, the public only heard about the overall rankings and did not learn about what went into those rankings. The quality of institutions was trivialized by their ranking. Heaven forbid if a university's rank went from twenty in one year to twenty-two in the next year. Many voices might say that the institution declined in quality. But that conclusion certainly does not follow from the dip in the ratings; the only thing that went down was the rating score. Indeed, the institution might have improved in quality in that year. But if other universities were improving at a faster rate, then the institution's rating would go down.

Table 13.1 shows Ohio State University's standing among all national universities and among all national public universities as calculated by *U.S. News & World Report*.

TABLE 13.1. Ohio State's Overall *U.S. News* Rankings from 2008 to 2019

YEAR	ALL NATIONAL UNIVERSITIES	ALL NATIONAL PUBLIC UNIVERSITIES
2008	57	19
2009	56	19
2010	53	18
2011	56	18
2012	55	17
2013	56	18
2014	52	16
2015	54	18
2016	52	16
2017	54	16
2018	54	16
2019	56	17

Source: *U.S. News & World Report* College Rankings.

Note the stability of the rankings over this twelve-year period. Ohio State never quite reached its goal of being within the top fifty among all institutions and among the top fifteen among public universities. Again, these rankings are based on a collection of indicators, so it would not be clear what is actually happening from one year to another. And these numbers mask some wonderful changes occurring at Ohio State during this time period. Therefore, for the rest of this chapter, we will focus on metrics that directly measure what had been happening at Ohio State over this time period. And by having annual measures, we can observe the progress that Ohio State has made from one year to another.

Student Quality

The most dramatic and impressive trend at Ohio State has been the continuing growth in the quality of the student body as measured by the academic characteristics of successive freshman classes. The major improvement in undergraduate student quality began in the late 1980s and continued through the second Gee presidency and into the subsequent Drake administration. This improvement reflected Ohio State's transformation from being an open admissions university to a selective admissions institution. With respect to graduate and professional education, Ohio State has always had outstanding students. But at the undergraduate level, the change in the profile of the first-year (freshman) class measured by such indicators as ACT and SAT scores, rank in high school senior class, and others has truly been astounding.

As mentioned in chapter 1, this process of change began in the Jennings administration in the 1980s, accelerated dramatically in the first Gee and Kirwan administrations, and has continued through the Holbrook, Gee Two, and Drake presidencies. During the Jennings era, by state law Ohio State University was an open admissions institution, which meant that any Ohio high school graduate with a valid diploma could attend Ohio State. But Ohio State could not possibly accommodate all these Ohio high school graduates (nor would the other public universities in Ohio want to see Ohio State absorbing so many students). Thus, Ohio State in effect adopted postmark admission: applications that were received by a certain date would be accommodated. But each year that date changed and got earlier, and more importantly, was made public only about a week before the actual deadline. This process hurt students and families who did not enjoy a tradition of college participation and who were not familiar with the application process, thereby disadvantaging applicants from lower income, non-college families.

More importantly, this process helped contribute to a freshman class that was in dire need of remedial work in English or mathematics or both. For example, in 1982, 18 2 percent of incoming freshmen needed remedial work in math and 18.0 percent in English. Freshmen in the UVC100 (University Col-

Chapter 13

lege) survey course would be told to look to your left and to your right; at least one of you would no longer be at Ohio State by the end of your freshman year. One reason for this appalling statistic was the State of Ohio's open admissions policies. High school seniors knew that they would be accepted to Ohio State (and other public universities) as long as they had their high school diploma. The content of their high school coursework really did not matter. Thus, many high school students blew off their senior year, took easy, non-college prep courses, and arrived on college campuses poorly prepared academically. Under President Jennings leadership and with the approval of the attorney general of the State of Ohio, Ohio State adopted in the late 1980s a conditional/unconditional admissions policy that said that in order for students to be admitted unconditionally to the university, they had to take in high school three credits of mathematics, four credits of English, two credits each of social science, natural science, and foreign language, plus some additional credits. If applicants did not have this full complement of credits, they could still be admitted to Ohio State, but conditionally with academic deficiencies noted. Such students would have to make up these deficiencies within their first thirty credit hours at Ohio State, *and* this coursework would not count toward the credits needed for graduation. These changes got the attention of high school students, their families, and their guidance counselors. Within a few years the proportion of Ohio State freshmen requiring remedial work dropped substantially. When Gee finished his first term as university president in 1997, the remediation rate for math was 12.3 percent and for English 2.9 percent, and when he returned ten years later in 2007, the mathematics remediation rate was 2.9 percent and for English 0.7 percent. This is an excellent example of a reform that changed behaviors and did not cost any additional money. All it did was to incentivize high school students to take college prep courses that were already being offered in their high schools.

This was the start of the major improvement in the quality of the freshman class at Ohio State, and the beginning of the transformation of Ohio State from open admissions to a selective admissions institution. Other indicators of the quality of the incoming freshman class were ACT and SAT scores and the percentage of the entering class who graduated in the top 10 percent and top 25 percent of their high school senior classes. Indeed, ACT and/or SAT scores became key criteria for admission and major bragging points for the university. Table 13.2 presents some of the indicators of student quality over time. Note especially the dramatic improvement in the average ACT scores. A change of this magnitude over a relatively short period of time at a large public university is practically unparalleled in American higher education. But Ohio State did not rely solely on the quantitative measures to make admissions decisions. Instead, the full student background was considered, including noteworthy activities and skills as well as relevant background characteristics and family situations.

TABLE 13.2. Characteristics of Incoming Freshmen, 1996 to 2018

YEAR	AVERAGE ACT SCORE	% IN TOP 25%	% IN TOP 10%
1996	23.5	50	26
2008	27.3	91	54
2009	27.5	85	50
2010	27.8	89	54
2011	28.0	89	55
2012	28.1	89	54
2013	28.5	92	58
2014	28.8	95	61
2015	28.9	95	62
2016	29.1	95	63
2017	29.2	95	65
2018	29.3	95	64

Source: Ohio State University Enrollment Reports.

There were other impressive characteristics of incoming freshman classes. More and more freshmen came to Ohio State having earned substantial college credits while in high school through advanced placement tests and other programs encouraged by the State of Ohio. By the end of the second Gee presidency, about 15 percent of entering freshmen had earned a full year's worth of college credit, a percentage that continued to grow in the subsequent Drake administration. But instead of graduating from Ohio State in three years (and reducing the cost of their undergraduate degree), most chose to stay four (or more) years and earn a second major or a minor or multiple minors; students were completing their undergraduate careers with a richer, more substantial set of academic experiences. A growing proportion of students availed themselves of various academic and scholarly activities such as the Honors and Scholars program, the STEP program, study abroad experiences, internship and co-op opportunities, and many other enriching and potentially life-altering experiences. And the opportunities for students to participate in co-curricular activities, whether through student organizations and clubs or other specialized

Chapter 13

programs grew exponentially with great leadership from the Office of Student Life and Dr. Javaune Adams-Gaston. The university operated under the belief that the more involved and integrated students were in campus life, the more successful they would be academically and the more they would benefit from their university experience.

One very important output measure of student success was the retention rate of students from their freshman to their sophomore years. Whereas in the 1980s, retention rates were routinely below 65 percent, in the second Gee administration and the following Drake administration, retention rates were regularly in the range of 95 percent. Obviously, one reason for higher retention rates was the better-prepared student body. But there were also other important factors at play. The university had made a major commitment to freshman success through such programs as the First Year Experience, the Honors and Scholars program, enhanced training of residence hall advisors, improvements in the physical environment of residence life, and others. Mabel Freeman and her colleagues did a fantastic job creating the First Year Experience program and were recognized nationally for their efforts. Freeman was also instrumental in creating the Ohio State Honors & Scholars program. The effort at making the first year experience a great one for freshmen began with summer orientation for families and students and a move-in day experience that was incredibly well-organized and relatively painless for students and families. The summer orientation gave new students a portrait of college life, about what to expect, and about what would be expected of them. During orientation, students met with academic advisors and mapped out their course schedule. They also took care of a number of nuts and bolts items such as getting their BuckID cards, taking any placement tests, if necessary, and generally getting a good sense of the logistics of campus life.

The campus move-in experience was also designed to ease the transition into university life. Imagine 7,000 students moving into residence halls on the same day and the chaos and nervousness that could create. To address this, every year the university recruited over 1,000 continuing students to move into the residence halls early and serve as OWLs—Ohio State Welcome Leaders. They assisted the new students and their families with moving belongings into the residence halls. More important, they served as a face of the university to the new students to make them feel more comfortable and welcome. This was reinforced by President Gee, who was highly visible during the move-in process, traipsing from one residence hall to another and greeting students and their families. For many students (and their families), it was amazing to meet the university president on their first day on campus. It certainly made the day more memorable.

An even more significant indicator of student success was graduation rates and how these had improved over time. Certainly one of the key measures of student success is degree completion, and Table 13.3 shows the information. Typically two measures are considered—the six-year graduation rate and the four-year rate. While Ohio State has improved on both these measures, note that these measures have an implicit bias to them. If students come from wealthy families and do not have to work while in college, then graduating in four years should be more attainable than for students who are required to hold jobs while attending college. And major private universities have more prosperous student bodies than major public universities, so one should expect faster times to completion from the former set of universities. The numbers in Table 13.3 are a bit complicated. They indicate what percentage of undergraduates in their respective graduating classes finished within four and six years of their initial enrollment at Ohio State. Thus, the 79.7 means that 79.7 percent of the graduating class of 2011 were graduating within six years of their initial enrollment, while the 58.5 indicates that 58.5 percent of the graduating class of 2011 had completed their degree programs within four years of their initial enrollment.

TABLE 13.3. Four-Year and Six-Year Graduation Rates at Ohio State

YEAR	SIX-YEAR GRADUATION RATE (%)	FOUR-YEAR GRADUATION RATE (%)
2011	79.7	58.5
2012	82.4	61.4
2013	83.2	58.5
2014	83.5	58.7
2015	83.1	58.5
2016	83.6	58.9
2017	82.5	63.4
2018	83.5	64.6

Source: Ohio State Enrollment Reports.

Four points should be noted about Table 13.3. First, the graduation rates reported in Table 3.13 are higher overall than those of many comparable public

Chapter 13

universities. Second, the graduation rates are gradually improving over time. Third, the four-year graduation rate took a noteworthy jump in 2017 and 2018. Finally, the slight spike in the 2012 numbers is most likely due to students speeding up their graduation date so as not to get caught in any potential delays arising from the move to a semester system from a quarter system.

One indicator of the growing attractiveness of the Ohio State experience was the rapid increase in the number of applications for admission. Some of this increase was due to the university joining the Common Application and some due to university tactics and strategies designed to generate more applications, but the increase in applications started well before the Common Application and continued on after Ohio State joined. Moreover, applications to Ohio State from out-of-state students and international students also grew dramatically, an indicator of Ohio State's enhanced reputation on the broader national and international stage. For example, in 1997, in Gee's last year of his first presidency, the number of applications for the freshman class was 18,814. By the middle of his second term, the number was 29,247, and when he left in 2013 the number was 35,475. And in 2017, the number reached 52,427, an almost three-fold increase from the total of twenty years earlier. And since the number of enrolled students did not change much over this time period, this meant that Ohio State was looking like an increasingly selective university, although one would also have to examine how many of the much larger applicant pool were accepted by Ohio State and then chose to enroll or not enroll at Ohio State. But, again, numbers such as a freshman class of 5,861 with an applicant pool of 18,814 in 1997 versus a freshman class of 7,136 with an applicant pool of 52,427 certainly make Ohio State resemble a more selective institution. It is one of the ironies of public higher education that the more students you reject, i.e., the more selective you are, the more likely you will be viewed as a prestigious, high-quality institution. Fortunately for Ohio State and for those meritorious students who were not admitted to begin their collegiate studies on the main campus in Columbus, they had the opportunity to begin their Ohio State education on one of the four regional campuses in Lima, Mansfield, Marion, and Newark, and later transfer to the main campus.

Once the university started down the path of selective admissions, a natural momentum developed to move even more strongly down that path. But the university also adopted strategies and programs to advance the transformation to becoming a selective institution. A key step was the decision of President Gee to hire Dolan Evanovich in 2009 away from the University of Connecticut. Evanovich's official title was vice president for Strategic Enrollment Planning, which meant that he oversaw many key offices involved in the student recruitment process, including the Offices of Undergraduate Admissions and First Year Experience, Student Financial Aid, the University Registrar, the Student Service Center, and Enrollment Services Analysis and Reporting. Evanovich was a superb leader, administrator, and visionary. He was the architect of numerous initiatives to make Ohio State a national leader in the recruitment and admissions process and was very active in national organizations devoted to student recruitment. He also was instrumental in the development of the Student Academic Services building into a facility that brought many student services under one roof and made it easier for students to navigate the various offices. Unfortunately, Ohio State lost Evanovich in 2016 when he was appointed senior vice president for Enrollment and the Student Experience at Syracuse University. Ohio State was very fortunate to have had Mabel Freeman and later Dolan Evanovich to lead the university's enrollment strategies over the years.

External Research Funding

Like the growth in student quality, the trends in research funding were also very positive, although not as dramatic and consistent on a year-to-year basis. Funding from major federal sources such as the National Institutes of Health, the National Science Foundation, the Department of Education, the Department of Defense, the Department of Agriculture, the Department of Energy, NASA, the Department of Labor and other federal agencies suggest the wide scope of research being conducted at Ohio State. Whether in the health sciences or agriculture or engineering or the social sciences or the natural and physical sciences or education or the arts and humanities and many other areas, Ohio State had a research portfolio as comprehensive as any in the nation. And Ohio State had numerous faculty selected for membership in prestigious national associations. For example, in 2013, 207 Ohio State faculty were fellows of the American Association for the Advancement of Science, 14 were members of the National Academy of Engineering, 12 were members of the National Academy of Sciences, and 8 were Institute of Medicine members.

Two key points need to be made here about Ohio State's success in securing external funding. First, this funding, especially from federal sources, is typically awarded on a competitive basis. Thus, the fact that Ohio State was successful in winning large awards was a statement about the high quality of the institution and its faculty, staff, and students. Second, it was also a testament to the Office of Research led by Senior Vice President Carol Whitacre, who

CHAPTER 13

worked closely with deans and faculty to identify grant opportunities, to facilitate successful grant applications, and to lessen the bureaucratic impediments that often faced those seeking external funding. Whitacre and her team tried to streamline and expedite processes, especially when governmental and university regulations were creating unnecessary hurdles. Whitacre played an active role in national organizations advocating for increased funding for research and also for reforming research administration processes. Table 13.4 shows the research expenditures at Ohio State from 2006–07 to 2017–18.

TABLE 13.4. Ohio State Research Expenditures (in millions of dollars)

YEAR	RESEARCH EXPENDITURES			INDUSTRY-SPONSORED RESEARCH
	Total Funding	Sponsored	Rank*	Rank*
1994–95	213.5	N/A	N/A	N/A
2006–07	720.2	512.1	N/A	N/A
2007–08	792.6	481.0	N/A	N/A
2008–09	721.2	488.3	10	2
2009–10	N/A	N/A	N/A	N/A
2010–11	828.5	536.9	9	3
2011–12	N/A	N/A	N/A	N/A
2012–13	934.0	498.6	9	3
2013–14	982.5	495.2	10	3
2014–15	962.0	505.7	12	4
2015–16	847.1	515.6	12	4
2016–17	864.3	534.6	13	4
2017–18	875.0	534.7	12	3

Source: Ohio State University Statistical Profiles.

*The rank for research expenditures is based on public research universities. The rank for industry-sponsored funding is based on public and private universities.

Note that Ohio State consistently ranked among the top nine to thirteen public universities in the country with respect to research expenditures, bringing in close to one billion dollars in some years. Also note that throughout this time period, Ohio State ranked between second and fourth in the nation among all universities—public and private—in attracting support from the private sector. This is a very important achievement: it said that the private sector looked to Ohio State expertise to help its businesses be profitable and successful, thereby contributing to economic development. It also meant that Ohio State students had more opportunities for internships and field experiences with those companies supporting research and development activities at Ohio State. In 2013, the university and its faculty and staff had active partnerships with more than 340 industries across Ohio and more than 760 partnerships throughout the nation.

This support from business also helped balance a negative portrait of Ohio State when it came to revenue earned through the commercialization of university intellectual property. As discussed in chapter 12, Ohio State usually ranked near the bottom in Big Ten and other rankings with respect to commercialization revenues and royalties. This led some to say that the university was not a major player in economic development, totally ignoring all the other funds the university brings to Ohio and ignoring all of the well-trained graduates Ohio State prepares for the workforce. But this poor performance in the generation of commercialization dollars has been an ongoing sore point for the university, and the university has taken and continues to take steps to improve this situation. See chapter 12 for a detailed discussion of this topic.

Development and Advancement

Yet another way in which a university demonstrates its merit and value is its ability to raise private philanthropic dollars through annual giving campaigns and special capital campaigns. And despite starting late like many public universities in systematically raising private dollars, Ohio State has been very successful in this domain, starting with its first major capital campaign during the Jennings era designed to raise $350 million to the most recent campaign in the second Gee administration, which exceeded its stated goal of $2.76 billion dollars and finished at over $3 billion dollars. Throughout this time period, annual giving to the university grew, as did the number of friends and alumni and businesses and foundations that financially supported the university. The university's endowment also grew markedly and, though smaller than the endowments at elite private institutions, began to provide a revenue stream to support university priorities and initiatives. The advancement model is discussed in detail in chapter 8. Here we might simply note that the advancement model advocated and implemented in the second Gee administration was showing major successes, not simply with respect to fundraising, but also in engaging more friends and alumni to stay involved in the life of the university. Table 13.5 shows some of the successes of Ohio State advancement.

TABLE 13.5. **Ohio State University Fundraising**

YEAR	ANNUAL GIVING*	NUMBER OF DONORS	ENDOWMENT*
1994–95	92.9	84,212	0.639 (6/21/96)
2006–07	228	121,173	1.636 (10/31/07)
2007–08	237	115,914	2.076 (6/30/08)
2008–09	237	119,048	1.716 (6/30/09)
2009–10	215	144,016	1.869 (6/30/10)
2010–11	259.2	177,322	2.121 (6/30/11)
2011–12	335.9	211,800	2.366 (6/30/12)
2012–13	374.1	228,297	3.149 (6/30/13)
2013–14	404.1	233,180	3.548 (6/30/14)
2014–15	405.4	237,340	3.634 (6/30/15)
2015–16	454.2	245,650	3.579 (6/30/16)
2016–17	532.6	267,354	4.253 (6/30/17)
2017–18	601.9	269,420	5.211 (6/30/18)

Source: Ohio State University Statistical Profiles.

*The numbers for annual giving represent millions of dollars while endowment is in billions. Thus, the entries for 2017–18 indicate that the annual giving was $601.9 million and the endowment was $5.211 billion. The value of the endowment is for the date indicated in parentheses.

Note the steady increase in annual giving and number of donors. This is a tribute to Mike Eicher and his team and their successful implementation of the advancement model adopted in the second Gee administration. The endowment also grew substantially; the decline in the 2008–2010 period is due to the impact of the Great Recession on financial instruments. The endowment growth was due in part to wise investment decisions. But it was also due to new funds such as the proceeds of the parking lease being deposited in the endowment. The growth in the annual giving and the number of donors can certainly be viewed as an indicator of support for Ohio State University by its alumni and friends. By 2017, Ohio State's endowment was the sixth largest among public institutions; the annual giving was also the sixth highest among public universities.

Access and Affordability

Throughout Gee's first and second presidencies, he recognized that the governor and the General Assembly were concerned about the costs of higher education, especially the increasing rise in tuition costs. And even though there was a direct relationship between the state's investment in higher education and the need for tuition increases, the state typically did not adopt budgets that provided ample dollars to higher education so that tuition increases could be kept low. Instead, the state would impose arbitrary limits on how much universities could raise tuition in a particular time period. The typical tuition increase limit was two percent over the biennium. (Ohio has a two-year budget.) This tuition cap applied only to resident instate undergraduate students; there were no caps for out-of-state undergraduates or for graduate and professional students. The focus on instate undergraduates was a political and a policy statement. Ohio students and their families are the voters who select the state's leaders. Moreover, these are the students who are more likely to be experiencing financial stress; graduate students and many professional students had assistantships and stipends of various kinds. And Ohio families are paying taxes to the state to help fund higher education.

Gee recognized, particularly in his second term, that the cost of higher education had become a salient national issue. To the chagrin of some members of his own administration and to the dismay of many of the other pubic university presidents in Ohio, Gee decided not to increase instate undergraduate tuition for two consecutive biennia, or four years. This was a very powerful statement about affordability and, even though some other costs such as room and board did go up, the fact that tuition was frozen was welcomed by students and their families and by Ohio public officials. Indeed, Ohio State was the leader among the fifty flagship universities in the nation in limiting the increase in tuition. *The Chronicle of Higher Education* noted that Ohio State was the most successful flagship institution in limiting tuition increases for resident students between 2007–08 and 2017–18, in large part because of the tuition freezes imposed by Gee. This led to Ohio State moving from the tenth highest flagship tuition in 2007–08 down to the twenty-ninth highest in 2017–18. Furthermore, in this ten-year period, Ohio State had the fourth lowest increase in tuition and fees for out-of-state students. It is unfortunate that media stories about the soaring costs of higher education do not give greater acknowledgement to those universities that are doing a better job reining in costs and expanding

CHAPTER 13

financial aid for students. In both the second Gee presidency and even more so in the Drake administration, there were numerous initiatives to increase financial aid and make Ohio State more financially accessible.

Conclusion

In summary, throughout the second Gee presidency, the trajectory of Ohio State continued to soar along many key dimensions. The academic profile of the undergraduate student body became increasingly impressive as the transformation from an open admission university to a selective admission institution was completed; the input characteristics of each succeeding freshman class became ever more outstanding. And the outputs also became more impressive with respect to retention rates, graduation rates, and time to graduation. Appendix C, the 2016 Enrollment Report, provides an informative graphical presentation of many of the trends and developments we have discussed.

In this time period, the students' academic experiences while at Ohio State became richer and more stimulating in terms of multiple major and minors, more internship and co-op opportunities, more students experiencing travel and study abroad, and more students participating in co-curricular activities that complemented their academic programs. In this same period, the faculty continued to shine with respect to external research funding, publications, membership in prestigious academic societies, major participation in national and international conferences, leadership roles in their own academic associations, and so many other ways. And throughout this time period, Ohio State continued to improve in national rankings or at least to hold its own in a very competitive academic environment. And financial support from friends and alumni throughout the nation continued to grow. When Gee left Ohio State for the second time, he left behind a university on the rise.

14

Athletics

Introduction

Intercollegiate athletics and especially the football program have long been a major part of the culture of Ohio State University. The athletic program garners an amazing amount of attention in the media, from fans and critics, and from the public at large. Before the arrival of the Columbus Crew (soccer) and the Columbus Blue Jackets (hockey), Columbus had been one of the largest cities in the nation without a major league professional sports franchise. That gap was filled by Ohio State sports, especially the football program. Ohio State had had the iconic Woody Hayes as its head football coach from 1953 to 1978, a period of great success and sometimes sharp controversy. The ten-year war between Ohio State and Michigan, between Woody Hayes and Bo Schembechler, raised an already intense rivalry to new heights and visibility. Even after Woody's departure, the rivalry remained keen, and the success of future OSU football coaches would be judged by their record against "that team up north." And as college football moved to the Bowl Championship Series and then to four team playoffs for the national championship, the importance of football grew even more, particularly at institutions with traditionally strong football programs in power conferences such as the Big Ten and the Southeastern Conference.

Ohio State football also played an unusual unifying role at the state level in Ohio. Ohio is a unique northern industrial state in that it has multiple media markets and major cities dispersed around the state rather than having one overwhelmingly dominant city such as Chicago in Illinois or Detroit in Michi-

Chapter 14

gan or New York City in New York or Philadelphia and Pittsburgh in Pennsylvania. In addition to the Columbus, Cleveland, and Cincinnati metropolitan areas, Ohio has smaller cities such as Toledo, Akron, Youngstown, Dayton, and others. The state is also divided with respect to its professional sports loyalties, with southwestern Ohio supporting the Cincinnati Reds (baseball) and the Cincinnati Bengals (football), while northeastern Ohio favors the Cleveland Indians (baseball) and the Cleveland Browns (football). And sitting in the middle of the state is Franklin County and Columbus, which had no major league professional teams until the Columbus Crew SC in 1996, but did have the Ohio State Buckeyes football team and also the men's basketball team. But the reach of Ohio State football was statewide with friends and alumni of OSU living throughout the state. And nationally, there were huge pockets of Buckeye fans in South Florida, Arizona, southern California, the Chicago region, and in the Middle Atlantic States.

Thus, Ohio State football was a focal point of media coverage and popular interest throughout Ohio. When all was going well, the Ohio media coverage was extensive and overwhelmingly positive. But when there was a crisis or scandal, the media coverage expanded to the national scene, and the intensity and harshness of the coverage could be daunting. Ohio State athletics, especially football, could be a source of incredible pride and spirit or a cause for great controversy and disappointment. Gordon Gee knew this firsthand from his first stint as president of Ohio State when football coach John Cooper, who had come to Ohio State two years before Gee, lost his first four games to Michigan despite having an overall strong win-loss record. Finally in 1992, Cooper's four-year losing streak was broken when the Buckeyes tied the favored Wolverines. Gee had the misfortune to proclaim the tie as a great victory and immediately heard to the contrary from outraged fans.

Gee and OSU Athletics

When Gee was at Vanderbilt prior to returning to Ohio State, he had surprised the world of college athletics and certainly his fellow SEC institutions by bringing athletic administration more closely into central administration and linking it more closely to the chancellor's office. He did this by naming David Williams as athletics director and vice chancellor for University Affairs and Athletics. Many observers wondered whether Gee would want to do a similar restructuring when he returned to Ohio State, and the answer was a clear no. Gee inherited a high-performing athletics department under the leadership of

ATHLETICS

FIGURE 14.1. Director of Athletics Gene Smith and Board of Trustee member Alex Shumate. Credit: The Ohio State University.

athletics director Gene Smith and the talented team of assistants and coaches he had assembled (see Figure 14.1). Gee and Smith worked in close collaboration in good times and in the rare, but significant bad times.

Gee saw the athletics program, especially football, as a key resource in promoting the university. As noted in chapter 5, Gee saw football Saturday and the events surrounding it as unique venues to advance the agenda of the university. The pregame events with a strategically selected guest list always had a program that highlighted some the accomplishments of faculty and students. The guests invited to sit in the president's box during the game were able to converse with the university's senior leadership team. And at halftime, other guests not sitting in the box were invited to come to the box for refreshments so that Gee could schmooze with them. Similar events were planned for basketball games, although on a smaller scale. The Ohio State University Marching Band (TBDBITL—the best damned band in the land) would present incredible pre-game and halftime shows, many of which went viral with millions of hits on YouTube and elsewhere and highlight the musical talents of the band members. In many instances, recipients of university honors, be they faculty, staff, students, major philanthropic donors, and others, would be honored on the field at halftime. The impressive scoreboard would often showcase major achievements of the university family. In short, all of the events surrounding a football game were skillfully exploited to promote the university.

Athletics: Scope, Funding, and Facilities

One of the impressive features of the OSU athletics departments is the scope of the intercollegiate varsity sports it supports. Ohio State has one of the most comprehensive programs in the nation. In Gee's second term, it fielded 36 varsity sports teams with a full complement of women's sports. It achieved equity in opportunity for men and women under Title IX, not by dropping men's sports, as has occurred at other colleges and universities, but by expanding opportunities and growing the number of women's teams. And the facilities to support student athletes are first-rate and not just in football. There were ongoing initiatives to enhance the facilities for nonrevenue sports such as men's and women's volleyball and wrestling and others. The McCorkle Aquatics Pavilion, dedicated in 2005 and for which the initial planning began in the first Gee administration, provides a world-class natatorium and is the home of the men's and women's swimming and diving teams.

Ohio State is also unique in the funding of its athletics program. It is one of the few athletics programs in the country that is fully self-sustaining. It does not draw money from the university treasury; indeed, it returns money to central university coffers. One of the worries about many athletic programs throughout the country is that they are being heavily subsidized by student fees and other central university support. And that central university support for public universities may include taxpayers' dollars. Ohio public universities have an instructional fee (tuition) and a general fee, mandated by the state to support non-instructional student services. At Ohio State, the primary purpose of the general fee is to foster students' emotional and psychological well-being as well as their social and cultural development. Thus, at Ohio State, the general fee supports such entities as the Counseling and Consultation Services, the student unions, the Student Health Service, and others. It does *not* go to athletics. At other Ohio public universities, the general fee goes heavily to subsidize athletics; indeed, the business model for athletics at smaller institutions simply does not work without using general (student) fees. Students at these institutions do get free admission to football and other sporting events, but it is not a good trade-off given that the cost of the general fee is approaching $400 for the academic (two semesters) year. And what if you do not want to attend football games and other sporting events? At Ohio State, students can choose to buy tickets at $32 each for a total of $224 for all seven games, but this is far less than the general fee. And, again, students can choose to not purchase tickets.

The athletics program at Ohio State has many revenue streams that enable it to be self-sustaining. First and most obvious is the revenue generated by ticket sales in a 100,000-seat stadium and 19,000-seat basketball arena. But ticket sales are more complicated; there are special incentives and programs such as the Buckeye Club which generate more revenue. There is all the revenue generated by concessions, parking, and related activity. And of course, there is the revenue generated through television contracts and athletic events such as the NCAA March Madness—Road to the Final Four and the College Football Playoffs. The revenue generated by the Big Ten Network is substantial for each of the member institutions. The Big Ten Network was formally launched in August 2007, just before Gee's return to Ohio State, but Gee was actively involved in working with Big Ten Commissioner Jim Delaney in shaping the Network. The Big Ten Network is owned by Fox Sports Media Group (Fox Corporation) with 51 percent ownership and the Big Ten Conference with a 49 percent share. This arrangement is far more advantageous to the Big Ten Conference than its earlier relationships with ESPN and other entities, not just with respect to income, but also to the coverage given to Big Ten universities beyond the major sports of football and basketball. Indeed, when the Big Ten expanded to include Nebraska, and then later to bring in Maryland and Rutgers, one of the major drivers of these decisions was to expand the viewership population of Big Ten sports. Increased ratings and more generous television contracts go hand in hand. And the addition of Maryland and Rutgers brought the Washington media market and the New York City and Philadelphia media markets into Big Ten territory. These many revenue streams (plus others) enabled the athletic department to return funds to the university. For example, in FY2012–13, the department provided almost $30 million to the university, including $16 million in grant-in-aid reimbursement for student athletes. Nationally, Ohio State has typically been among the top three universities in generating money from its athletic program, typically trailing only Texas and Texas A&M. In Gee's last year as president, athletics generated over $140 million in revenue, with the major sources being ticket sales (about $54.6 million), contributions (about $22.2 million), and rights and licenses such as television and the Big Ten Network (about $45.8 million). The Nike apparel contract is also a major source of support. By 2019, athletic revenue went over $200 million, once again placing Ohio State third nationally behind Texas and Texas A&M. The fastest growing revenue source was rights and licenses, suggesting the financial wisdom of expanding the Big Ten into East Coast markets.

CHAPTER 14

The Ohio State athletic program is blessed with outstanding facilities, and not just the iconic Ohio Stadium, which seats over 100,000 fans, or the Schottenstein Center/Value City Arena, which houses basketball and hockey and hosts concerts and other special events. The athletic program also has state-of-the-art training and practice facilities. The medical and rehab services provided players are unparalleled. The academic support services provided student-athletes are also impressive. Of particular note is the Younkin Success Center, which houses the Student Athletes Support Service Office—SASSO. SASSO provides assistance on academic, athletic, personal, and professional development with particular emphasis on academic advising, tutoring, and study skills.

The Performance of the Athletic Program

The performance metrics for the athletics program are superb, both on the field and in the classroom. During the second Gee administration, the three major revenue-producing sports—football and men's and women's basketball—were consistently competitive for league championships and post-season participation. It was not just the major sports that fielded strong teams. Volleyball, tennis, wrestling, crew, gymnastics, hockey, and others all were competitive in the Big Ten conference and sometimes on the national scene. The men's volleyball team won the NCAA national championship in 2011 under longtime coach Pete Hanson (who subsequently won two more championships, in 2016 and 2017) and demonstrated that championship volleyball was no longer limited to the West Coast. Likewise, the men's tennis team achieved national prominence before, during, and after the second Gee administration. Ty Tucker, coach since 1999, made men's tennis at Ohio State into a consistently elite program that dominated the Big Ten and almost always qualified for the NCAA tournament. By 2012, the team had reached the NCAA quarterfinals seven consecutive times and in 2013 reached the NCAA semifinals. Tucker was regularly named Big Ten Coach of the Year and in 2009 was named Wilson/ITA National Coach of the Year. Individual athletes also excelled in such sports as tennis, swimming and diving, golf, wrestling, and track and field, even when their teams did not secure championships. One sport that mostly performed below the radar screen was the synchronized swimming team. Synchronized swimming received official NCAA recognition in 1977. Since that time, Ohio State has won the national championship in 32 out of 42 years, the most recent win coming in 2019.

The performance of student athletes in the classroom has also been impressive. Typically when the Big Ten announces its all-conference academic team, Ohio State student athletes are abundantly represented on the list. In 2012–13, 74 Ohio State student-athletes were named Big Ten Distinguished Scholars, more than any other school in the conference. The football and men's basketball team regularly meet the NCAA's APR—academic progress requirements. And the NCAA typically honors multiple Ohio State teams (including football) with public recognition awards for academic performance.

Another significant point to note is that there were no serious academic scandals in the Gee years, nor before and after. Such scandals can be devastating to the external reputation and the internal morale of a university. One reason for such a good record is strong integrity and compliance initiatives within the athletics department. Another reason is strong monitoring by the athletics department and by coaches of their players' attendance in classes. Yet another factor is the strong support services such as SASSO provides to student-athletes.

The Tressel Resignation

With all the monitoring and compliance mechanisms mentioned earlier, they were inadequate to head off the major athletic scandal of the second Gee administration. It is a truism that the quickest way for a university to get major bad publicity is to have something go seriously wrong in its athletic program or in its medical center. Scandals in other domains are of course serious and harmful, but an athletic or medical center scandal really captures the attention of the media and the public. Over the years Ohio State has had controversial conclusions to its football coaches' careers both before and after Jim Tressel, with the most prominent ones being the dismissal of Woody Hayes, Earl Bruce, and John Cooper and most recently the retirement of Urban Meyer. Few people care if the coach of a "minor" sport is dismissed or unexpectedly retires for whatever reason. Indeed, there were a number of less visible athletic personnel decisions that Gee and Gene Smith had to resolve, but these largely flew under the radar screen. But when it is the future of the football coach that is in question, the sports writers, media analysts, and especially the talk radio hosts and the broader public all feel that this is significant news that must be covered in excruciating detail. And so when the mistakes of football coach Jim Tressel became public, controversy erupted about what steps the university should take (see Figure 14.2).

Chapter 14

FIGURE 14.2. In happier times, Gene Smith, football coach Jim Tressel, and Gordon Gee. Credit: The Ohio State University.

Tressel was a widely admired and successful football coach and a respected member of the university community and the broader central Ohio community. His teams were highly successful, having won the national championship in 2002 and with one exception having won all the rivalry games against Michigan. They also performed well academically. The Tressel controversy stretched out over months as more information dripped out over time. In December of 2010 six OSU football players were suspended by the NCAA for selling or trading football memorabilia such as conference championship rings in exchange for various benefits, a violation of NCAA policy. The players would be suspended for the first five games of the 2011 season. At that time, Tressel expressed surprise at the news, but it later came out that he had known about these transactions since April 2010 and failed to inform university officials and the compliance office, an NCAA violation. He lied in writing to the NCAA when he signed a compliance document in September 2010 stating that he knew of no infractions in the football program. As more information came out about Tressel's actions and inactions, the university held a press conference on March 8, 2011, to announce that Tressel would be suspended for the first two games in the 2011 season and fined $250,000. Tressel himself requested that his suspension be increased to five games to match what his players had received.

ATHLETICS

Assistant coach Luke Fickell was named the interim head coach during Tressel's absence.

Tressel, Gene Smith, and Gordon Gee were all in attendance at the news conference even though Gee had been wisely advised by a prominent trustee to stay away from the event. At the event, Gene Smith said, "At the end of the day, Jim Tressel is our football coach," suggesting a strong endorsement of Tressel despite his mistakes. A reporter asked Gee whether he had been considering firing Tressel and Gee quipped, "Are you kidding? I'm just hopeful he doesn't dismiss me." To everyone in the room, Gee's comment was clearly a joke designed to ease some of the tension. But when that comment went viral online, all context was lost and readers and listeners throughout the country actually thought the OSU president was afraid of being fired by his football coach. This incident damaged Gee and the university and angered the trustees who thought that Gee had committed an unforced error. When all the details of Tressel's misdeeds became known, it was clear that he lied to the university and to the NCAA. And as more information came out, it was clear that Tressel needed to retire or else he would be dismissed. Trustees were upset with the communications strategies and tactic employed to address Tressel's mistakes and in hindsight, many trustees thought a decision to remove Tressel should have occurred months earlier.

Because Tressel retired in May of 2011, it was too late in the year to recruit a permanent coach, so assistant coach Luke Fickell was named interim coach for the upcoming season. His regular season record was 6–6, which enabled Ohio State to be invited to a bowl game, which it proceeded to lose to South Carolina and thus finish with a 6–7 record. As this mediocre season was unfolding, Gee and Smith were searching for a prominent coach with a great track record and quickly settled on Urban Meyer, who had retired from the University of Florida a year earlier, in part because of health issues. Meyer's appointment was enthusiastically welcomed, and as Meyer's teams enjoyed success on the field, the bitter and angry memories of Tressel's downfall began to fade. However, there was still some anger about how Gene Smith handled the NCAA sanctions that were later handed down. Ohio State had self-imposed some sanctions on itself in hopes of heading off severe penalties from the NCAA. But when the NCAA sanctions were handed down, the most painful one was that Ohio State would not be eligible for post-season bowl participation in 2012, Urban Meyer's first year. This really frustrated Ohio State fans, since the Buckeyes were undefeated in Meyer's first season and would have been likely challengers for the national championship. Critics of Gene Smith said that Ohio State should have voluntarily declared itself bowl ineligible in Luke Fickell's

CHAPTER 14

year as coach. Perhaps that would have headed off the NCAA's disqualification of Ohio State for the next year.

Conclusion

The Tressel situation was the major problem in OSU athletics in Gee's second term. Otherwise the program was in great shape on the field, in the classroom, financially, and in the hearts and minds of Ohioans. The Urban Meyer appointment helped many people who were disappointed about Tressel's fate or mad about Ohio State's handling of the whole matter to move on. And Meyer's initial successes told Buckeye Nation that the football program was once again on the right track—until the next crisis. The Tressel events reminded university leadership how a scandal in the football program can undermine the good things that are happening in the athletics department and in the university overall. And it also reminded the university that effective crisis communications are an absolute necessity in the contemporary social media environment where news goes viral instantly, especially on topics such as misdeeds in the athletic program. There is much less time to sit back and watch things unfold before taking actions.

15

The Ohio State University Wexner Medical Center

Introduction

In 2012, the university renamed the Ohio State University Medical Center to the Ohio State University Wexner Medical Center (see Figure 15.1), in honor of Les Wexner and his family and all that they have contributed to Ohio State. The immediate impetus for the renaming was the transformative $100 million gift the Wexners and the Limited Brands Foundation gave to the university in 2011, a gift that mainly benefitted the OSU Medical Center and the James Cancer Hospital and Solove Research Institute. But as President Gee said at the renaming ceremony:

> Les has been among Ohio State's most dedicated leaders and most passionate supporters for many decades, and someone who continues to make an indelible impact on our community. His generous contributions, both in time and resources, have been wholly transformational, but his most valuable gift has been his extraordinary leadership. He has a firm and unequivocal vision for our academic medical center, and that is to be a world-class institution, period.

Wexner's leadership contributions to the university took many distinct forms. He served for sixteen years on the Ohio State University Board of Trustees and was a founding member of the University's Foundation Board and its

CHAPTER 15

FIGURE 15.1. The Establishment of the Wexner Medical Center. In the front row center are Gordon Gee, Abigail and Leslie Wexner, Dr. Steve Gabbe, and on the far right Dr. Michael Caligiuri, head of the cancer programs at Ohio State. Credit: The Ohio State University.

first chair. Wexner also served as the first chairman of the newly constituted Wexner Medical Center Board, a major change in the governance structure of the medical center that we will discuss later.

Decades ago, the OSU Medical Center had been a source of pride for the university, but as discussed in chapter 1, that pride rested more on outstanding patient care and superb preparation of the next generation of health-care professionals, including doctors, nurses, medical technicians, therapists, and so many others. But in the past, the medical center was not as renowned for its signature medical programs or its outstanding research or its path-breaking innovations in treatment protocols. In some ways, the medical center was seen as a sleeping giant forty years ago when compared to academic medical centers at other universities. But that all began to change during the Jennings administration, and the pace of change continued to accelerate during the administrations of his successors: Gee One, Kirwan, Holbrook, Gee Two, and Drake. In the Jennings administration, the university moved forward on the first James Cancer Hospital and Solove Research Institute, a major commitment to having a nationally prominent cancer treatment and research facility. Moreover, as one moved forward to subsequent administrations, especially Gee Two, there was much new focus on "signature" program initiatives for which Ohio State made the decision to be a national leader and to invest accordingly. In addition to cancer, these programs were heart, critical care, imaging, neuroscience, and transplantation. But these signature foci should not obscure the fact that the Ohio State University Wexner Medical Center is one of the most comprehensive centers in the nation. It has grown tremendously with respect to programs, staff, research grants, and facilities, and currently its revenues constitute more than half of the university's total budget.

On the academic side, in addition to the College of Medicine, there are seven other health sciences colleges: Allied Medical Professions, Dentistry, Nursing, Optometry, Pharmacy, Public Health, and Veterinary Medicine. In addition, there is an extensive hospital system as well as walk-in, urgent care, and ambulatory facilities and other assets throughout central Ohio. On the main campus are University Hospitals (Rhodes and Doan), the new James Cancer Hospital and Solove Research Institute (we will say much more about its construction when we discuss Project One shortly), the original James Hospital that has been repurposed into the Brain and Spine Hospital, the Ross Heart Hospital, and the Dodd Rehabilitation Hospital. Located off-campus are Harding Hospital and OSU East Hospital. OSU East is located in the Near East side of Columbus, a neighborhood with major economic challenges and a substantial need for social and health services. The decision by Ohio State to convert what had been St. Anthony's Hospital into OSU East and to make major investments in the facility provided an important boost to the Near East Side neighborhood. Furthermore, just up the street from OSU East is Carepoint East, formerly a Veterans Administration facility taken over by Ohio State that also addresses neighborhood health-care needs. There is also a Carepoint Gahanna and a Carepoint Lewis Center. In addition, there are many other OSU medical facilities throughout central Ohio, such as the Havener Eye Institute, the Jameson Crane Sports Medicine Institute, the Martha Morehouse Outpatient Care facility, and the Upper Arlington Kingsdale facility.

The medical center is a wonderful asset for the university community and for the broader central Ohio region and beyond to the State of Ohio. Most OSU employees receive their health care from Ohio State professionals and at Ohio State facilities. The many citizens from throughout Ohio who come to the medical center become new friends for the university.

In recent years, medical center personnel have played a more active role in public policy discussions about important health-care issues such as the opioid crisis, restraining health-care costs, Medicaid expansion, and accessibility to health care in rural areas. Through the second Gee administration, Jerry

CHAPTER 15

FIGURE 15.2. Attending a policy conference at the Wexner Medical Center are (front row) Columbus Mayor Michael Coleman, Dr. Michael Caligiuri, and (back row right) Jerry Friedman. Credit: The Ohio State University.

Friedman, advisor for Health Policy and associate vice president for External Relations and Advocacy, represented the university skillfully as he worked with state officials on Medicaid-related issues. Friedman was instrumental in assisting the state to find creative ways to draw down more Medicaid funding to Ohio, thereby enhancing patient care and also helping the OSU medical center's bottom line. Friedman was also centrally involved with university initiatives with the city of Columbus (see Figure 15.2) and with the successful effort to receive a major federal grant, topics discussed shortly. Another member of the medical center advocacy staff, especially with respect to the James Cancer Hospital, was Jennifer Carlson, who was routinely called upon by political leaders for her policy advice and who was always seeking ways to advance the interests of the James in governmental and private settings.

Culture and Governance at the Medical Center

The issues of culture and governance of the medical center have been challenges to many OSU presidents, including Gee in his second term. As mentioned in chapter 4, some of Gee's colleagues would tease him when he talked about "One University" by asserting that before you could have one university, you needed first to have "one medical center." The medical center was beset by many divisions, some of them due to internal competition for resources, others due to the clashing of the strong personalities in charge of different units of the medical center, and yet others due to the natural tension between the values and priorities of the academic medical departments versus the emphasis of much of the medical center's leadership on the financial bottom line of the enterprise. Probably the greatest, or at least most obvious schism was between the cancer program and other units of the medical center. Some of this friction was based on the perception that the cancer program was the favored child of the university, while the other medical center programs were stepchildren, especially in the competition for resources and recognition. These tensions were exacerbated by the sharp elbows of many in leadership positions, especially within the cancer program.

Facing this dysfunction within the medical center, Gee decided to bring back Dr. Steve Gabbe to Ohio State in 2008 as the chief executive officer of the Ohio State Medical Center and senior vice president of Health Sciences at Ohio State. Gee thought that Gabbe would be the right leader to address the culture conflict within the medical center for a number of reasons. First, Gabbe had been at Ohio State once before in his career and thus knew the university well. Second, Gee knew Gabbe very well from his first term as Ohio State president; Gabbe worked well with Gee until he left for the University of Washington in 1996. Gee later convinced Gabbe to leave Washington and join him at Vanderbilt, where Gee was chancellor. Thus, when Gee convinced Gabbe to return to Ohio State in 2008, he knew he was getting a person of great integrity and fairness who would be his trusted partner in fixing problems at the medical center. Gee would have brought Gabbe back to Ohio State even sooner, but Gee had an agreement with Vanderbilt that he was to do no recruiting from Vanderbilt for a year after his decision to leave. Gabbe was brought back to Ohio State not only to address the culture of the medical center but also to lead Project One, the university's most complex and ambitious plan for the medical center (to be discussed shortly). Upon his return to Ohio State, Gabbe worked tirelessly to bring unity and collegiality to the medical center with mixed success and also did a superb job on the Project One implementation. In my interview with him, Gabbe said that Gee had tasked him with rethinking and restructuring Medicare, mentoring College of Medicine Dean Chip Souba, giving Gee at least four years as leader of the medical center and then helping find his successor, and working to heal the breach with Michael Caligiuri and the cancer center.

Chapter 15

Michael Caliguiri was an extremely talented and effective leader of the cancer program at Ohio State. During the Gee years, Caligiuri was the CEO of the James Cancer Hospital and Solove Research Institute and director of the OSU Comprehensive Cancer Center, as well as a professor with a very active and well-funded research program. He was a very prominent national leader in the fight against cancer and left Ohio State to become president of the City of Hope National Medical Center and soon thereafter in 2016–17 became president-elect of the American Association for Cancer Research. I mention all these accomplishments of Caligiuri to indicate that he was a very prominent and powerful leader of the cancer program at Ohio State with many resources to try to chart his own independent course.

Moreover, the governing structure for the James Hospital at Ohio State also fostered a separation from the overall medical center and its leadership. The James was one of eleven members of the Alliance of Dedicated Cancer Hospitals. In 1983, Congress adopted special rules governing Medicare payments to Dedicated Cancer Care Centers. The rationale was the prospective payment system (PPS), which Medicare typically used to reimburse hospitals for their services, did not work well for Dedicated Cancer Centers; thus, cancer centers needed a PPS exemption. The overly simplified explanation is the PPS system "underfunded" cancer centers since their mix of cases was so different and more costly than the average case in non-cancer hospitals. One of the rules that Congress built into qualifying for the PPS exemption was a degree of separation from the main medical center. Caligiuri and his team used this provision extensively to try to gain as much independence as possible from the OSU Medical Center. This meant that Caligiuri, instead of reporting to Gabbe, would report to the central university leadership—the president and the provost. This mindset led members of Caligiuri's team to behave as though they could act independently of central university preferences across a number of areas. One example of this came when Jennifer Carlson (mentioned earlier), the vice president for External Relations and Advocacy for Caligiuri, attempted to secure an increase in the state tax on cigarettes to generate additional funding for cancer research and cancer education. When the university government relations team (of which Carlson was a member) learned about this, it shut down this effort to the consternation of Carlson and some of her supporters. The reasons for shutting it down were many, but a key one was that university employees should not single-handedly be seeking tax increase, especially without the knowledge of the university president. The potential blowback by legislators who would not favor tax increases, no matter how noble the cause, could be very harmful to the university. A second reason was the lack of sensitivity to university priorities. Many university leaders would have placed funding for state-provided financial aid for students as a higher priority for the university should additional or new tax revenues become available.

Thus, this quasi-independent status for the James and reporting arrangements caused much stress, leading Gee to raise two questions. Was this reporting arrangement absolutely required by federal regulations? And even if it were, was the value of the enhanced reimbursements worth the harm it caused to teamwork, cooperation, and "One Medical Center"? When these questions were raised, it began the process of bringing the James back into the medical center family and setting the stage for a change of leadership in The Ohio State University cancer program.

Another contributing factor to increased divisiveness within the medical center was the unusual governing arrangements for the hospital system overall and not just for the James. Each hospital had its own advisory board composed of university employees and external members. As university president, Gee was an ex officio member of every advisory board. Because he could not possibly attend every meeting of every advisory group, Gee appointed designees to represent him on these advisory boards. I was appointed as Gee's designee to the University Hospitals Board, and to this day it was never very clear what our responsibilities and actual powers were. The typical meeting was a dog and pony show or show-and-tell affair in which hospital administrators gave reports on a variety of interesting and important topics, but in which many important matters were left to the end of the meeting with little time for discussion. For example, at my first meeting, a budget resolution for about $850 million was brought up for voting approval. It was the last item on the agenda and came up at 11:50 a.m. at a meeting that was scheduled to end at noon. There was little time for questions, but Betty Montgomery, a public member of the board and former Ohio attorney general asked what I thought were the key questions. What assumptions is the budget resolution based on? How cautious are the revenue and expenditure numbers? What numbers are you most worried about? After some less than complete responses, noon was approaching, and it was time to vote. I voted yes for the resolution with little confidence that mine was a sufficiently informed vote. I then went back to Bricker Hall (the administration building) and told Geoff Chatas, senior vice president and chief financial officer that I had just voted for an $850 million resolution in which I had little confidence and then said that I was fully confident that he could remedy any sins of omission or commission that I had committed.

The decisions of these advisory boards were by no means the final word; they went to the central administration and ultimately to the Board of Trust-

Chapter 15

ees. When Gee returned in 2007, the board committee that dealt with medical center issues was the Medical Affairs Committee. At the time, the board met five times a year for a two-day (actually a day and a half) period, and the typical committee meeting was around ninety minutes. Obviously, schedules could be adjusted and reprioritized, but the key point was that the Medical Affairs Committee was like every other committee of the board. By the time Gee left in 2013, the governance of the medical center had been changed for the better. The hospital advisory boards were gone, and more important, the Board of Trustees structure had been dramatically altered as it related to the medical center. The Board Medical Affairs Committee was replaced by the Wexner Medical Center Board, which met for longer sessions the day before the full Board of Trustees meeting. Moreover, the Wexner Medical Center Board established a Quality and Professional Affairs Committee. The Wexner Medical Center Board reported to the full Board of Trustees, but with Leslie Wexner chairing the Medical Center Board, this board now became the site for serious discussions and decisions about the priorities and finances of the medical center.

As I mentioned before, the meetings of the old hospital board advisory committees were largely show-and-tell affairs. Let me tell one story in which the show-and-tell aspect had a wonderful benefit for the university and for the neuroscience program headed by Dr. Ali Rezai. At one meeting, Dr. Rezai gave a presentation on deep brain stimulation and the treatment of Parkinson's. I had not been aware of this research and was stunned by some of its successes. Parkinson's patients received brain implants and were now leading normal lives with no tremors or shakes. I was so impressed by this that I went to Gee and said we need to give Governor Kasich a firsthand presentation of the research. And so Gee, Dr. Rezai, a patient named Roger who had received one of these implants, and I went downtown to meet with Governor Kasich about this research. The governor was appropriately impressed and asked insightful questions. Roger explained that he used to enjoy carpentry, but with the onset of Parkinson's and the associated tremors, he could no longer do it. Now, because of Dr. Rezai's research and surgery, he could engage in his favorite pastime again. Roger then presented the governor with a laminated cutting board that he had created the previous week. Everyone was moved by the demonstration of the efficacy of Rezai's brain implant. The governor said that he wanted Rezai to do a presentation of his research at one of the governor's cabinet meetings. A few weeks later, I escorted Rezai to the cabinet meeting. He made his presentation and almost instantly about half the cabinet directors had questions about the application of Rezai's research to their own areas of responsibility such as health, veterans affairs (PTSD), mental health, rehabilitation and corrections, education, and more. The end result of this was a state investment in Rezai's research program. Unfortunately, this story does not have a happy ending for Ohio State. When Gee became president of West Virginia University (for the second time), he was able to recruit Dr. Rezai to join him in Morgantown and to become the director of the newly created Rockefeller Neuroscience Institute.

Project One

Gabbe and his team accomplished much during Gee's second administration. Gabbe invested in management and culture training for the medical center. There was a major emphasis on quality and safety when Gabbe put together a working group led by Pete Geier and Jay Kasey. Gabbe's emphasis on patient safety and quality was recognized nationally when the Wexner Medical Center was ranked third among 104 academic medical centers by the University Health System Consortium (UHC) in delivering top quality health care to patients. Another of his major accomplishments was integrating the physician's practice plan into OSUP. Outside consultants came in to help, and internally Chris Culley and Almeta Cooper were very critical to the process.

Gabbe also led a major change with the installation of electronic medical records through the EPIC system. EPIC said at the time that it was the biggest and best conversion that they had ever seen. This was an incredibly complex process that had to go right lest there be chaos at the medical center. Pete Geier and Jon Stone played key roles, and the end result was to put Ohio State in a national leadership role as other medical centers switched over to electronic records. There were genuine time costs for physicians learning the new system. There was some resistance in going in this direction, but Gabbe kindly explained to people that if you did not want to make this change you did not need to work here. About 14,000 people had to be trained. Patient records and the billing system were converted to the new system. There was a dramatic moment when the old system went down at 11:58 and the new one was successfully launched at 12:03. Gabbe gave credit to many people for the successful transition and specifically cited Phyllis Teater and Beth Niecamp.

The most ambitious, complex, and significant accomplishment in the medical center under Gee's and Gabbe's leadership was the successful completion of Project One. Project One was a $1.1 billion investment in the construction of new facilities and the renovation of others at the medical center. The largest single project was the new James Cancer Hospital and Solove Research Insti-

CHAPTER 15

FIGURE 15.3. The new James Cancer Hospital and Solove Research Institute. Credit: The Ohio State University.

tute, estimated originally to cost about $700 million (see Figure 15.3). Incorporated within the new James were critical care beds. Project One also filled out three floors in the Biomedical Research Tower and three floors in the Ross Heart Hospital, completely remodeled McCampbell Hall, doubled the size of the emergency department located in the new James Hospital, and enhanced the external environment of the medical center with the Spirit of Women Park, new benches, sitting areas, and landscaping.

The new James Hospital was certainly the most complicated and challenging part of Project One. It went through a lengthy planning process that changed direction multiple times. Bill Shkurti led the planning process originally, and in October 2008 Steve Gabbe succeeded Shkurti as head of the Executive Sponsors Group, which had the responsibility for shepherding the OSU planning and design process. The plan was presented to the Board of Trustees in 2009, and ground was broken in June 2010. Throughout this process, Les Wexner was very involved, weighing in on many aspects of the design. Two other board members made substantial contributions to the planning and success of Project One—Ron Ratner and Alan Brass. Ratner (see Framework discussion in chapter 11) brought important planning and construction expertise to the project. Brass was the OSU trustee with the most extensive experience and success in the health-care industry. Brass was the chief executive of

FIGURE 15.4. In the right in the photo is Dr. David Schuller, who over the years was one of the most passionate advocates for the cancer program at Ohio State. Credit: The Ohio State University.

the ProMedica Health System in northwest Ohio when appointed to the OSU Board of Trustees. Under his leadership, ProMedica thrived financially and programmatically. Brass also had extensive experience in health-care systems and hospitals in Saint Louis, Ann Arbor, and Columbus. In addition to his extensive professional experience, many years earlier—in 1973—Brass earned a master of science degree in hospital and health services administration from Ohio State University. Thus, Brass was a key player in the deliberations surrounding Project One.

Ultimately, the chosen design for the new James cancer hospital reflected a superb recognition that hospitals, especially cancer hospitals, should not be gloomy, institutional-looking places. The final design incorporated openness, light, and optimism and had a zigzag (indented) pattern that divided each floor of the hospital into "neighborhoods," thereby creating a sense of intimacy among patients, visitors, and staff. Whenever Dave Schuller (see Figure 15.4) would lead individual and group hard-hat tours of the new hospital during construction, he would point out so many major and minor design features intended to lift the spirits of cancer patients, their friends and families, and the medical staff that was caring for them.

Chapter 15

This massive project was finished on time and under budget. In fact, the final cost was about $30 million less than estimated, so more floors were built out as well as four more operating rooms than originally planned. One reason for the timely completion of the new hospital was the university's successful effort to change the state-mandated process governing construction of public facilities. Ohio had been one of very few states to require the use of multiple contractors and prohibit the use of single prime contractors. The multiple prime process was a disaster that fostered delays, litigation, and finger pointing in trying to resolve disputes that arose in the construction process. With multiple primes, no single entity had responsibility for problems. The concrete contractor might blame the steel contractor for a problem; the electrical contractor might blame the plumbing contractor on a different problem. Often these disputes resulted in lengthy delays and even litigation. In contrast, with a single prime contractor, there was one entity in overall charge that had the responsibility to resolve disputes and to bring the project in on time and on budget.

One would have thought that the notion of a single prime contractor would be a slam-dunk, especially for Republican officeholders, since it promised cost savings and efficiencies. But for political reasons, neither political party had supported it in the past. Republicans worried that many small contractors (small businesses) in their districts would lose business if the prime contractor sought out larger subcontractors. Democratic legislators worried on behalf of their labor union supporters that a single prime contractor would find it easier to seek out nonunion labor.

This issue was one that universities, especially Ohio State, had battled for years. It was one major item in the deregulation agenda mentioned in chapter 11 where the university was not successful. Gee had also tackled the issue in his first term with little success. But in his second term, he led a full-scale offensive supported by Jack Hershey, myself, Board of Trustee members, newspaper editors, many business groups, and others to make the case that the multiple prime contractor requirement was bad for economic development. Given the size of the hospital contract and the number of jobs it would create, Gee could throw out cost-savings percentages that added up to real dollars. For example, if single prime could save 10 percent on a $700 million project, that was real money that could be reinvested for other purposes. And the lengthy delays associated with multiple primes would not only add to costs, it would also harm the patients whose treatment in the new facility would be delayed. Likewise, the economic benefits of the project would also be delayed. Gee took his case directly to Governor Strickland and the legislative leaders. Strickland convened a panel to identify how to increase the speed and efficiency of public sector construction projects. The panel concluded that construction reform that would allow new ways to manage projects might conceivably save the state over $320 million annually. The panel proposed reforms that allowed the state to continue to use the current method of multiple primes, or one of three other methods that gave more control to a lead contractor with enhanced power and authority. Project One then was designated as one of three selected Construction Reform Demonstration Projects that could utilize an alternative construction management process, and Ohio State chose to go with the single prime contractor approach with great success. Note that the state did not abandon multiple primes nor did it allow Ohio State to choose its preferred method for all of its projects. But since Ohio State got what it wanted for its massive cancer hospital project, it was very happy with the result. But even with this new flexibility, the university and its selected prime contractor Turner Construction had to be sensitive to certain external interests and provide ongoing reports and summaries about the dollar volume of contracts that went to instate versus out-of-state companies, majority and minority vendors, and union and nonunion contractors. Ongoing totals were kept about the number of women and minorities working on the project. Years later, in 2019, Don Brown, former Franklin County administrator and now executive director of the Franklin County Convention Facilities Authority, thanked me and Ohio State University for gaining flexibility in the construction management for Project One and demonstrating that it worked. Because of this achievement, the state of Ohio granted construction flexibility more broadly, which benefitted Brown and his colleagues in the building of convention facilities.

As the new hospital was under construction, a major development occurred in Washington, DC, that eventually provided a $100 million grant for radiation oncology in the new James. Jerry Friedman identified a $100 million appropriation that Senator Christopher Dodd (D.-Conn.) had successfully gotten into legislation. Many observers who read the accompanying legislative language thought the $100 million was wired for the University of Connecticut, Senator Dodd's home state flagship university. But as he read the legislative language, Friedman thought that Ohio State could qualify to compete for the money. Dodd himself had said that the money was not an earmark, that it would be awarded competitively. Friedman mentioned this opportunity to David Schuller, who having recently left the James leadership, was now tasked with finding additional funding for the new hospital. Before going all in on trying to win this grant, Schuller wanted to be sure that Ohio State was indeed eligible for this funding. The initial response from the Health Resource and

Chapter 15

Services Administration (HRSA), an agency of the US Department of Health and Human Services (HHS), was that Ohio State was not eligible since the legislative language seemed to require that applicants have a combined medicine and dentistry program, which Ohio State did not and the University of Connecticut did. Friedman did not stop there. He went up the chain of command at HHS and successfully argued that Ohio State had the equivalent capability, only in two separate colleges—the College of Medicine and the College of Dentistry, and both colleges were integral parts of the university's medical center. HHS decided that Ohio State was indeed eligible for the competition, and Schuller put together an outstanding team to develop an incredibly strong proposal. As this process was underway, I raised the possibility of splitting the funds with the University of Connecticut, to which Dave replied (as I knew he would), "I want all the money." (It turns out that it would have been legislatively impossible to split the funds.) After a proposal was drafted, it was given to a team at Battelle, whose job was to tear it apart. The Battelle involvement resulted in an even stronger proposal, one that resulted in Ohio State receiving the $100 million.

Throughout this process, US Senator Sherrod Brown and his staff were very involved and worked to bring the entire Ohio congressional delegation on board, although Ohio State won the award on merit and not on any political pressure exerted. But Brown did get all members of the delegation to endorse the need for greater access for Ohioans to cancer care at the medical center. Ironically, one advantage that Ohio State had over other applicants is that having already started construction of the new James, it had more detailed information about specifications and facility details that other applicants did not. But when Ohio State won the grant, it had to stop construction and redesign and strengthen the foundation of the building to accommodate an extremely heavy fifth floor radiation facility.

After the new James was completed, the medical center went through a fascinating and drawn out discussion about the appropriate signage for the building and other medical center facilities. This discussion got difficult at times and reflected some of the still remaining tensions at the medical center. After all, it was the James Cancer Hospital and Solove Research Institute at the Wexner Medical Center of The Ohio State University. The new James Hospital was in a prime location. To the north was Ohio Stadium, to the west was SR 315 with its high traffic volume, to the east was the heart of the campus and campus neighborhoods, and to the south was more campus neighborhoods, the Short North, and ultimately downtown Columbus.

There was one final exciting aspect of Project One and that was how many new jobs it was bringing to Columbus. This prompted Gabbe and Friedman to ask whether there was some way that a portion of the city income taxes generated by the new jobs could be recaptured for university and medical center purposes. There was a recent precedent for a recapturing—the major expansion of Nationwide Children's Hospital in the southeast section of downtown. In that project, Pete Cass, a very creative and effective staffer at Columbus City Council, helped the Council and Mayor Coleman find a way to rebate some of the additional income taxes generated by the Children's Hospital job expansion back to the hospital for reinvestment. With Cass's help, and with excellent cooperation between the city and university leadership teams, a similar deal was arranged for Project One. The university pledged to spend some of these recovered dollars in the PACT neighborhood mentioned in chapter 9 with an emphasis on housing, health, employment, and education. In general, throughout the second Gee administration, the working relationship between the university and the Coleman administration was outstanding. Gee and Coleman and their staffs would meet regularly to address issues of common concern such as economic development and job growth, infrastructure, policing and public safety, and many others.

Conclusion

At the end of Gee's second term, the Wexner Medical Center was in very good shape (see Figure 15.5). Project One had been successfully completed. Some of the culture issues that Gee had encountered on his return in 2007 had been ameliorated. All of the major indicators were strong—reserves, cash on hand, hospital bed occupancy, safety and quality control, patient satisfaction, and many others. Moreover, the influx of research dollars into the medical center continued to grow, as did the dollars generated by Pelotonia for cancer treatment and research at the James. There was a constant churn in staffing with the arrival of new personnel and the departure of others, with the medical center enjoying success in attracting new talent to Ohio State. The focus on specific priorities and signature programs became sharper, thereby guiding the investment of resources into these programs.

There were still problems in the culture and leadership of the medical center that continued after Gee's departure, including the unhappy decision to have Sheldon Retchin succeed Steve Gabbe. The situation seemed to improve by the

CHAPTER 15

FIGURE 15.5. The photo shows four individuals who were instrumental to the success of the medical center. From left, Dr. Hagop Mekhjian, chief medical officer of the medical center who held numerous academic and administrative positions and was a passionate and caring physician; President Gordon Gee; George Skestos, a former member of the Board of Trustees who with his spouse, Tina, donated to many worthy causes at Ohio State; Dr. Steve Gabbe. Credit: The Ohio State University.

third year of the Drake presidency. The selection of a chancellor (a new title for Ohio State) of the medical center in 2018 initially seems to have had a calming effect on the medical center. There were some concerns expressed to me about the loss of talented faculty and staff to other universities and medical centers because of the leadership problems at the medical center. And there were a few financial caveats expressed about potential volatility in medical center finances due to the dysfunction of the Congress and the whims of the president as well as the magnitude of the annual federal budget deficit and the overall national debt. Should Congress and the president ever severely shrink Medicaid and Medicare reimbursements or even cut their rate of growth sharply, this could create great stress for the medical center. Likewise, if the federal government should ever tighten eligibility requirements for Medicare and Medicaid so that patient volume went down, this too would be a worrisome development. And should there ever be major reductions in funding for NIH, NSF, and other federal agencies, many research programs at universities could be devastated.

While major reductions in federal support for health care may seem unlikely, it is wise to keep such a scenario in mind, given the dysfunction and instability in Washington, DC. Most planning assumptions at the university assume a more steady state to modest growth in federal support. The final financial concern expressed to me independently by two high-ranking, knowledgeable university employees were legally binding financial obligations of the medical center that do not appear on the books or show up in public documents. Examples of obligations are startup packages offered to doctors and scientists to entice them to come to the university. Each of these packages could total millions of dollars for equipment or laboratory space or bringing an entire research team to Ohio State. One prominent startup package at the medical center purportedly totaled $30 million, yet nowhere did it show on the budget documents even though it was a legally binding commitment.

One final area in which policies of the federal government could have a harmful effect on Ohio State is receptivity to international students studying at American universities as well as receptivity to international talent joining the American workforce. At the undergraduate level at many universities, international students are a revenue source to help balance college and university budgets. At the graduate level at Ohio State, many PhD programs rely on international students, particularly in the health sciences, the physical sciences, and engineering, to support course offerings and serve as RAs and TAs. And with respect to medical centers specifically, international talent is a crucial component of the workforce throughout the entire enterprise.

But the cautionary observations made above should not hide the fact that along many fronts the Wexner Medical Center is prospering and thriving. The facilities for doctors, researchers, and patients are first-rate. The financial situation is very strong (with the caveats noted above). Morale seems to be improving, and the recruitment of new talent is going well. Research and invention are proceeding apace. The medical center is likely to be the source of future major growth in Ohio State's commercialization efforts. Overall, the news from the Wexner Medical Center in upcoming years is very likely to enhance the reputation and relevance of The Ohio State University to citizens throughout Ohio and the nation.

16

The Changing Dimensions of Diversity at Ohio State

Introduction

Over the past four decades, Ohio State has consistently made diversity a core value in its various mission statements. A diverse and inclusive academic environment with respect to faculty, staff, and students was seen as essential to enhance the academic environment, yield better academic outcomes, and fulfill the university's obligation to the broader Ohio society. But in this time period, the notions of diversity and the populations to which it referred became more expansive and inclusive and resulted, for example, in the Office of Minority Affairs becoming the Office of Diversity and Inclusion in the second Gee administration.

In the first Gee administration and even earlier, when diversity was discussed, it was most often in terms of gender and race. With respect to the student body, the primary focus was on the composition of the undergraduate student body. There were certainly programs designed to increase the number of Black PhDs graduating from Ohio State, such as the Graduate and Professional Visitation Days program, led by Dr. Frank Hale, focused on historically Black colleges and universities. There were also programs designed to increase female participation in areas such as the sciences and engineering, where women had not enrolled in high numbers. At the undergraduate level, the overall proportion of women in the student body was consistently high—about 49 to 50 percent (although low in certain disciplines), and so the major focus was on how to increase the proportion of Black undergraduate students. The typical metric used at Ohio State and in many states and most public flagship universities was to compare the percentage of Black residents in Ohio's population with the percentage of Black students in the undergraduate student body. And with that metric, Black students were underrepresented and remain so. For example, if Black citizens were 12 percent of Ohio's population, their percentage in the student body was typically about half that number. This was the situation in most states. And in those states (unlike Ohio) that had large Hispanic, and/or Native American populations, the situation was the same: Hispanics and Native American representation on campuses was much lower than in the overall state population. Often, the one minority group to be represented in the student body in excess of its overall population proportion was Asians. Table 16.1 shows the minority group composition of the total Columbus campus enrollment (undergraduate, graduate, and professional).

TABLE 16.1. Minority Percent of the Columbus Campus Enrollment, 1996–2013

RACE	1996	2007	2008	2009	2010	2011	2012	2013
Total Minority	14.2	14.6	14.4	14.4	14.4	14.4	16.4	17.2
African American	6.8	6.5	6.3	6.1	5.9	5.8	5.8	5.5
Asian American	4.2	5.2	5.2	5.3	5.3	5.3	5.4	5.5
Hispanic	1.7	2.5	2.6	2.6	2.8	3.1	3.1	3.4
Other	.3	.4	.4	.3	.3	.2	.3	.2
Two or more races	N/A	N/A	N/A	N/A	N/A	N/A	1.9	2.6

Source: Constructed from Ohio State University Statistical Summaries.

Note that the percentages in Table 16.1 remain fairly stable over time with an increase of about 3 percent in the total minority population between 1996 and 2013. But this growth is not due to an increase in African American students, but instead modest growth in the Asian and Hispanic student numbers. Indeed, the percentage of African American students remained fairly stable, with a decline between 1996 and 2013. If one were to examine only undergraduate African American students and further divide them by gender (male undergraduate and female undergraduate students), one would learn that the percentage of Black male undergraduates is particularly low, a situation all too common in universities around the country. This underrepresentation of Black male undergraduates is one of the major reasons why the Todd Bell Center is so vital to the university.

Chapter 16

Table 16.2 shows the place of residency—Ohio, out of state, international—for the total Columbus campus between 1996 and 2013. Note that there is a notable decline in the percentage of students who claim Ohio as their home, while there is a comparable increase in the percentage of students from the other 49 states and from other countries. Public state universities have to be careful to not let their out-of-state numbers creep up too much, lest they be accused of rejecting qualified home state applicants in favor of out-of-state applicants. Yet out-of-state students do provide a significant benefit to the university; the fees they pay the university far exceed those paid by instate students and help keep the university's budget healthy.

TABLE 16.2. The Geographical Home of Columbus Campus Students, 1996–2013

HOME	1996	2007	2008	2009	2010	2011	2012	2013
Ohio	79.2	82.4	81.7	75.3	73.2	71.4	69.5	69.0
Out of State	12.9	10.7	11.0	17.6	18.7	19.7	20.8	21.5
International	7.9	6.9	7.3	7.1	8.1	8.9	9.7	9.5

Source: Constructed from Ohio State Statistical Summaries.

Out of state and international students certainly contribute to a more diverse and inclusive campus, but they are not typically thought of as minority groups. But as the university traditionally tracked distinct student subpopulations, it was Blacks, Hispanics, and Asians as well as nonresident and international students that received the major focus. As the university moved further into the 21st century, many other student subpopulations became visible and central to the notion of diversity and inclusiveness. We will discuss these groups later in the chapter.

Universities have historically tried to do a better job of recruiting underrepresented student populations, focusing especially on the undergraduate student body. But President Jennings in the 1980s observed that it was not sufficient to simply recruit the existing pool of students harder. If one truly wanted to increase minority representation, one had to increase the pool of eligible minority students. And thus, the Young Scholars program was created at Ohio State, a program supported by every university administration since then. The Young Scholars Program focused primarily though not exclusively on academically talented first-generation students with major financial need from nine of the largest urban school districts in the state; these students were primarily African American. The program celebrated its 25th anniversary in 2012. In that period, almost 3,000 participants who most likely would not have attended higher education let alone graduate enjoyed success at Ohio State. The program was a resource intensive initiative; students were formally inducted as Young Scholars in the tenth grade. In the early years they would come to the Ohio State campus for a few weeks in the summer to enhance study skills and become more comfortable with a university environment. The Young Scholars had to take college preparatory courses in high school and maintain a 3.0 grade point average. Students who successfully completed the program requirements were guaranteed admission to Ohio State along with a financial aid package that would enable them to attend. The Young Scholars Program was widely recognized as a path-breaking initiative, and in 2013, the Association of Public Land-grant Universities awarded it the C. Peter Magrath University Community Engagement Award.

With respect to female participation in disciplines not traditionally welcoming of or attractive to women, universities, including Ohio State, knew they had to take positive steps to attract female students to these disciplines, including mentoring programs and the recruitment of more women faculty in these areas to serve as role models and inspirations for the next generation of female students. As the years went by, greater focus was given to attracting women to the STEM disciplines.

When diversity was discussed with respect to the composition of the faculty and staff, two primary questions were asked: How do we increase the percentage of women and minorities in the university workforce, and how do we ensure women and minorities are appropriately represented at the top levels of the faculty and staff? On the faculty side, many incentives were adopted to increase the hiring of women and minorities, such as the creation of additional positions and the adoption of spousal hiring programs. In the last thirty years, some of the pool questions were addressed as the number of women who went into law and medicine and the sciences grew dramatically and therefore the pools from which universities could recruit from also grew dramatically.

Just as universities were making some progress in enhancing traditional diversity goals in the student body and in faculty and staff, the contemporary discussion of diversity became more complex, especially at the student level, as other underrepresented groups came to the fore with legitimate needs for inclusion and as universities themselves recognized that their missions required a broader, more inclusive approach to diversity. Thus, at Ohio State, the Office of Minority Affairs became the Office of Diversity and Inclusion, and today there is much more attention to underrepresented populations in general that go beyond race and gender and ethnicity. For example, there is much more concern about students who would be the first in their families to ever attend college and about students whose family financial situation makes college unaffordable. There is also greater attention to "late-starting students" and to students who have had their education interrupted for whatever reason. In particular, there is much more attention to students who are leaving the military and transitioning to civilian life and higher education. There is also much greater attention given to the disabled community and the kinds of accommodations needed to enhance their success. There is much greater attention given to student athletes and what their post-college careers would look like, especially for those athletes who are not going pro in some sport and have to make a living elsewhere. There is also concern about ensuring a welcoming campus climate for the LGBTQ community, although Ohio State and the city of Columbus have been widely recognized as being very supportive of LGBTQ students, faculty, and staff. In general, there is a heightened awareness of the needs of students with challenging economic and social backgrounds and with difficult life circumstances, and this awareness goes beyond the traditional categories of gender, race, and ethnicity.

Achieving Student Diversity

In this section, we will discuss some of the programs and initiatives designed to enhance student diversity in its many forms. First and foremost, diversity is now much more embedded in the academic curriculum. The general education program requires one course in social diversity in the United States and two courses in global studies and options for coursework in such areas as culture and identity, service learning, education abroad, and foreign languages. Ohio State also has significant academic programs and majors with a diversity focus, such as African American and African Studies, Women's Gender and Sexuality Studies, International Studies (undergraduate only), and many foreign language and country culture areas of study. The university now has a certificate program in Diversity, Equity, and Inclusion. The co-curricular opportunities for students to enjoy diverse experiences are limitless, with hundreds of student organizations, many of them focused on race, gender, gender identity, domestic and international cultures, military experiences, religion, and so many others.

There are many offices and programs that provide support for underrepresented groups. Chief among these is the Office of Diversity and Inclusion (ODI), which supports the recruitment, retention, and success of students, faculty, and staff. As of 2019, the office is headed by Dr. James Moore III, the vice president for Diversity and Inclusion and chief diversity officer for the university. ODI oversees many significant initiatives, including the Frank W. Hale, Jr. Black Cultural Center, the Todd Anthony Bell National Resource Center on the African American Male, the aforementioned Young Scholars program, and others as well as being home to a full array of retention, mentoring, scheduling, and access programs. Moore is also the executive director of the Bell Center, the initial focus of which was to improve the retention and graduation rates and the overall academic experience of African American undergraduates. Ultimately, the Bell Center broadened its domain to conduct research on the unique problems experienced by African American males throughout their life span.

The Hale Black Cultural Center is named in honor of the late Dr. Frank W. Hale, former associate dean of the Graduate School, vice president for the Office of Minority Affairs, and special assistant to the president (see Figure 16.1). Hale was the architect of the Graduate and Professional Schools Visitation Days that contributed mightily to Ohio State being one of the leading producers of Black PhDs in the United States. The Hale Center sponsors programs and activities for the development and advancement of students, especially African American students. It is a home for showcasing Black art and culture and highlights the contributions of African Americans to the broader society. When Hale died in 2011 after an extended illness, President Gee commented:

> We have lost one of the true giants of the Ohio State community. Dr. Frank Hale was a scholar, teacher, researcher, administrator, a civil rights pioneer. More than that, he was a force to be reckoned with who opened the doors of opportunity to underserved students through the sheer force of his intellect and determination. Frank Hale richly deserved the honor of having Hale Hall named for him. Indeed a small piece of the campus carries his name, but every inch bears his imprint.

There are also many programs under the auspices of the Office of Student Life that enhance diversity and inclusion in many ways. I will mention just a few of them such as the Office of Disability Services, the Multicultural Center, and the Younkin Success Center. Like many campuses forty years ago, Ohio State was not known for making it easy for students with disabilities to navigate the physical and academic world of the university. But that changed over time with changes in federal and state laws and with the office itself expanding its portfolio from physical disabilities to include learning disabilities and other

CHAPTER 16

FIGURE 16.1. Dr. Frank Hale, a long-time leader in making Ohio State a more diverse and welcoming university. Credit: The Ohio State University.

impediments to student success. Today Disability Services serves over 3,000 students with a wide range of disabilities, and as the office states, "the majority being those (students) with hidden or invisible disabilities."

The Student Life Multicultural Center today emphasizes programming that focuses on the intra-cultural needs of specific constituency groups *and* also the intercultural development across constituency groups. But in the 1969–2001 era, separate offices were created to address the needs of each separate group. Thus, the African American Student Services office was established in 1969, the Women Student Services in 1973, the Hispanic Student Services office in 1975, the Asian American Student Services office in 1988, the Gay, Lesbian, Bisexual, Transgender Student Services office in 1989, and the American Indian Student Services office in 1996. But in the 2001–2007 era, after an extensive program review and widespread internal discussions, it was determined that separate offices did not satisfy the objective of developing a truly multicultural campus, and the Center began focusing on both individual group activities *and* cross-group programming. Ohio State has been recognized by a number of organizations as having one of the best campus environments in the country for LGBTQ students.

The Younkin Success Center focuses not only on the recruitment of students to Ohio State but also their success at Ohio State as measured by graduation rates and successful entry into careers. One specific division of the Younkin Center is SASSO—the Student-Athlete Support Services Office. The primary focus of SASSO is the 1,000+ student athletes on thirty-six NCAA teams. SASSO in effect was a recognition that the university had an obligation to student-athletes, many not on athletic scholarships, but all devoting great time and effort to their respective sports, to further their academic careers. Thus, to enhance personal and professional development, there are programs in academic advising, tutoring, career planning, and many other areas. With respect to tutoring, free tutoring services are offered to all Ohio State student veterans and to all students enrolled in ROTC.

Ohio State's support for student veterans has grown dramatically, easing the transition back to civilian life from military service and also accommodating those students whose academic careers are interrupted by the call to duty. There are many services provided to assist veterans to become integrated into campus life. Of particular importance are services helping student veterans work with the Veterans Administration to ensure that their records and information are correct and up to date so that they receive the education benefits to which they are entitled. The number of student veterans continues to grow to about 1,300. When President Obama gave the spring commencement address on May 5, 2013, he stated:

> Consider that today, 50 ROTC cadets in your graduating class will become commissioned officers in the Army, Navy, Air Force, and Marines. 130 of your fellow graduates have already served—some in combat, some in multiple deployments. Of the 98 veterans earning their bachelor's degree today, 20 are graduating with honors. And at least one kept serving his fellow Veterans when he came home by helping to start up a campus organization called Vets4Vets. As your Commander-in-Chief, I could not be prouder of all of you.

The Kirwan Institute for the Study of Race and Ethnicity is a valuable campus resource for the systematic analysis of issues of race and ethnicity on campus and in the broader society. One can think of the Kirwan Institute as a think tank devoted to studying the causes and solutions for ethnic and racial disparities. Its emphasis is to be very involved in solving problems in the broader society and putting its research into action by sharing it with public officials, community leaders, and citizen activists. On campus, it serves as a hub for scholars who investigate issues of race and ethnicity to come together to share ideas and research results.

CHAPTER 16

Faculty and Staff Diversity

As mentioned earlier, in discussing the diversity of the faculty and staff at Ohio State University, the two most salient groups have been and continue to be women and African Americans. And the two key questions have been and continue to be what proportion of university positions are held by women and Black individuals, and at what level are these positions? There are many groups and offices on campus whose focus is on the professional development and advancement for women and for women of color. Two very significant entities are the Women's Place and the President and Provost's Council on Women. The idea for the Women's Place began in Gee's first term when he appointed a task force to investigate women's issues that ultimately led to the establishment of the Women's Place. Initially, the Women's Place provided a clearinghouse for information for women on campus, served to enhance networking opportunities for women, and tried to improve the overall campus climate for women. As the Women's Place developed in its early years, it became much more ambitious and intentional in fostering changes in university policies to advance women's careers and in identifying the barriers and impediments that restricted opportunities for women at Ohio State.

Most importantly, the Women's Place implemented systematic, longitudinal data collection about the status and progress of women at Ohio State and, in conjunction with the President and Provost's Council on Women, prepared an annual report on the status of women at Ohio State. This report is an important resource to learn what has been accomplished and what remains to be done as it related to women's status at Ohio State. The 2013 status report, the last year of Gee's second term, provided some key summary evaluations, starting with the observation that the proportion of women in all faculty ranks has steadily increased since 1999, but that women of color are still markedly underrepresented at Ohio State. The report also cited that 22 percent of named professorships and full professor positions are held by women, and should be higher. The report noted that within the category of non-faculty executive staff and other professionals, over 50 percent are female. But all other categories of *senior* administration positions have lower than proportional levels of women and that the numbers of women and men of color are very low. Finally, in analyzing the representation of women in senior level administrative positions and in senior academic leadership positions, the report concluded that the proportion of women was low in these high-ranking positions when compared with the proportion of women in the faculty and the professional staff and that there had been no consistent upward trend over the past fourteen years. The report also added "the proportion of leadership positions held by women of color continues to be extremely disappointing to those concerned with diversity at Ohio State."

The Women's Place and the university are addressing some of these concerns through various programs. One program in particular is to make the university community in general and the leadership levels in particular more conscious of the implicit bias that may influence personnel hiring and promotion decisions. The report attributes good will and commitment to those university officials in leadership positions to enhance diversity at Ohio State, but then wonders why given all this good will more progress has not been made. The report attributes this situation in part to the subtle influence of implicit bias, defined as unconscious attitudes that affect behaviors in ways we do not recognize. Thus, the report calls for programs and training to address the problem of implicit bias. Another initiative to address the inadequate representation of women in senior leadership positions was Ohio State University joining the Widening the Circle initiative, a program fostered by the Columbus Partnership to improve the representation of women at the highest leadership ranks of organizations throughout central Ohio. Board of Trustees member Alex Fischer is president and CEO of the Columbus Partnership and fostered Ohio State's joining the Widening the Circle Initiative. It should be noted that the Women's Place works with many university offices, including the Office of Human Resources, the president and the provost's office, the President and the Provost's Council on Women, and many others to address how to improve the status of women on campus. The Women's Place also administers Critical Differences for Women, a scholarship/grant program for women seeking advanced education and improved professional lives; funding is available to faculty, staff, and students.

The Women's Place has also worked diligently to foster a welcoming environment for LGBTQ faculty and staff and to advocate for human resource policies and benefits that fully include the LGBTQ community. The Multicultural Center discussed earlier sponsors safe zone training that offers a broad overview of issues faced by the LGBTQ community with the aim of increasing awareness and understanding of sexual orientation and gender identity and expression. Issues that might have been controversial in other settings and localities have been handled routinely at Ohio State. For example, gender inclusive bathrooms are now commonplace throughout the campus. The Ohio State University Alumni Association now has a LGBTQ club named the Scarlet and Gay Society. The Wexner Medical Center hosts the LGBTQ Employees Resource Group (ERG), open to all LGBTQ faculty and staff and allies to

Chapter 16

provide a place for people to come together to socialize and address issues of common concern. I could go on and on detailing the ways that Ohio State has endeavored to make the campus a safe and supportive environment for its LGBTQ faculty, staff, and students. One validation of this is the external recognition that the university has received for its efforts. Many entities have rated Ohio State as among the most LGBTQ-friendly campuses in the country: College Consensus ranks Ohio tenth; College Choice ranks Ohio State second. Other ratings have Ohio State anywhere between third and twenty-fifth. This is a very impressive recognition to be rated so highly among the hundreds of colleges and universities in the nation.

Ohio State is a more diverse campus than it has ever been both with respect to students and to faculty and staff. The proportion of Black undergraduate students should still be higher, just as women and women of color need to be better represented in the higher levels academic support administration. But that should not hide the fact that two highly significant developments occurred in the second Gee presidency, developments that were already taking root prior to Gee Two and have continued to grow and expand in the subsequent Drake administration. The first is a much more expansive and inclusive definition of diversity and the second is the recognition that achieving diversity is the responsibility of the entire campus community and not just a few offices that have words like *diversity, inclusion, women,* or *minority* in their job descriptions. Let me talk about each.

The More Inclusive Notions of Diversity

Today, the focus on student diversity and inclusiveness goes well beyond the traditional emphasis on gender and race. There is much broader recognition that there are many student subpopulations that have not been adequately represented in the university community. As discussed earlier, the reasons for this are many, including family situations such as financial distress and the absence of college-going participation. Or they could be life history, such as delay or interruption in higher education because of external factors such as military service or family responsibilities. Or they could be impediments created by discrimination due to sexual orientation and gender identity or physical or other disabilities. There could even be external perceptual reasons such as wondering whether Ohio State would be a welcoming environment for students for whatever reasons.

Many of these factors overlap and interact. The important point is that Ohio State is addressing these factors. For example, in the second Gee presidency, extraordinary steps were taken to slow the rise of tuition and to make college more affordable. More funds were put into student financial aid, and this effort was accelerated and targeted in the subsequent Drake administration. On campus, there are numerous offices to help students with the transition to college and to help them succeed at Ohio State. There are expanded efforts to assist students with their post-college careers, be they in the workplace or further education, or whatever paths their interests take them.

There is also growing cultural sensitivity by the university that there are many parts of Ohio where higher education is not on the radar screen, and certainly not Ohio State. Throughout my career at Ohio State, I would routinely ask students from rural areas, particularly economically poor rural areas, how they decided to come to Ohio State. I was shocked to hear some of their answers. Students would tell me occasionally that their high school guidance counselors would encourage them to not go to Ohio State and stay closer to home, perhaps to attend a tech center or a local community college. They were told that Ohio State was too large and complex for students from small rural high schools, who would be made to feel unwelcome by students from urban and suburban areas. They were also told that they were less likely to succeed academically since the rural high schools they attended were supposedly not as good as the suburban, urban, parochial, and charter schools that many other applicants had attended. This perceptual bias was reinforced by Ohio State's move to selective admissions and the recognition that applicants who attended wealthy suburban high schools had many more academic opportunities than students who attended economically poor high schools. For example, a suburban high school might offer fourteen advanced placement courses; a rural district might only offer one or two. The suburban district might teach seven foreign languages; the rural district only one. A similar narrative could be told about science labs and co-curricular activities.

It was fortunate that when Ohio State learned about these "cultural barriers," it responded in many ways. Recruitment activities were strengthened, including bringing high school guidance counselors to campus to try to correct any misperceptions they might have had. When Gee was on his state tours in his first and second administrations, he would routinely visit rural high schools to spread the word about Ohio State. Ohio State University Alumni Association clubs in rural counties (and throughout the state) played an active role in identifying outstanding students, pointing them to Ohio State, and reassuring

CHAPTER 16

them about their prospects for success. The university also channeled more money to financial aid, recognizing that poverty and income shortfalls were a rural problem just as they were an inner-city problem. The university also enlisted its local friends and alumni, its Extension Service, and others to provide information, answer questions, and assist in the successful completion of the application forms.

It is indeed the case that Ohio State today has a more diverse student body, and this is intentional, not accidental. Veterans, returning students, students with disabilities, out-of-state students, and students of racial and ethnic identities are targets of recruitment, and that recruitment was aided by the offices and support services mentioned earlier to make these students feel welcome and help them succeed at Ohio State. Let me finish this section by relating the story of Patrick Klein. It is a fascinating story because it is a case where a university program helped create a sense of cultural identity that in turn led to the creation of a program to address the situation of would-be students from Appalachia. Although Klein is from Washington County, a relatively poor area in Appalachia, Klein did not develop a sense of Appalachian identity until *after* he enrolled at Ohio State. This occurred when as an undergraduate student in 2002, he received a letter from the (then) Office of Minority Affairs awarding him a scholarship of $4,000 because he was from Appalachia. Klein, who is white, was surprised and went to the office and said, "Hey, I think this is a mistake," to which he was told, "No, you're from Washington County, you're Appalachian." Klein said that it was the first time he had been labeled with that term. "Growing up there, you don't call yourself that. It was one of those things where I said, 'You're right. I am. Four thousand dollars. I'll take it.'" This event led Klein to learn about the income and educational disparities in Appalachia. These were conditions that Klein said he was not aware of growing up because he and his brother hit the "parent lottery." His parents were professionally successful and were able to provide their children with all that they needed.

From this experience, Klein was inspired to start the iBelieve program, designed to help students from Appalachia evaluate their owns strengths and weaknesses and aspirations with the ultimate goal of helping them between their freshman and senior year of high school be ready to move on to higher education. The program is also helping to generate leadership in the Appalachian region and develop a sense of an Appalachian community that is not defined by pathologies such as the opioid epidemic or crushing poverty or dysfunctional families, but instead is defined by commitment to education, success, and pride. Gee himself was helpful to Klein's work on iBelieve, in part because of his understanding of the tremendous challenges confronting Appalachia and its residents, having been the president of West Virginia University earlier in his career (and a place and job he returned a year after his departure from Ohio State in 2013). I tell this story because the accident of giving a scholarship to a student who did not see himself as Appalachian changed him into an advocate for the region. This in turn has spun off many benefits, including the recruitment of more students from Appalachia to Ohio State and other colleges and universities. This was a case where identity followed upon an initial intervention (the grant) and led to a much broader recognition of Appalachia.

The Responsibility for Achieving Diversity and Inclusion

The other significant development about diversity is that it is now the responsibility of the *entire* campus community. While there are certain key offices and groups such as the Office of Diversity and Inclusion, the President and Provost's Diversity Council, the University Senate Diversity Committee, and many others, today there is the expectation that diversity is the responsibility of leaders at all levels and in all parts of the university. This is reflected in diversity being incorporated into the university's mission and vision statements. When colleges and departments write strategic plans, they include a diversity component. When deans and department chairs are themselves reviewed, their record in promoting diversity is very much a part of their evaluation. The Office of Academic Affairs has a Special Opportunity Hiring Fund that provides financial support to colleges and departments to enhance faculty diversity. In the 2014–15 academic year, the provost required implicit bias training for faculty search committees seeking to fill positions within the Discovery Theme areas. Indeed, all search committees are expected to have a diversity advocate and to conduct their work actively seeking to advance diversity. Along with this is careful monitoring of the diversity of the pool of candidates being considered and the efforts made to generate that pool.

Diversity is not only embedded in the academic curriculum. It is also integral to the cocurricular activities overseen by the Office of Student Life and administered through the Office of Student Activities. There are more than 1,200 student organizations on campus representing every diverse group affiliation imaginable. Every university-approved student organization must have a constitution on file with the Office of Student Activities that includes a statement "prohibiting discrimination on the basis of age, ancestry, color, disability, gender identity or expression, genetic information, HIV/AIDS status, military status, national origin, race, religion, sex, sexual orientation, protected veteran

Chapter 16

status . . ." Recognizing that this multitude of student organizations is the core of the students' campus co-curricular experiences, the Office of Student Life has established guiding principles that emphasize the growth and development that students experience with involvement in student organizations and the hope that this growth impacts students beyond their own organizations. The Office of Student Life envisions a multicultural campus arising from "student interactions across diverse backgrounds, across colleges and departments, and between student organizations . . ." The Office of Student Life of course recognizes that students will naturally gravitate to organizations that reflect their own characteristics and interests. But the office also aspires that these distinct organizations interact, their members get to know one another, and they all become members of the common Ohio State community.

Thus, diversity and inclusion are alive and well at Ohio State. Yet we have seen in recent years on campuses throughout the nation how easily and quickly a campus can be torn apart by some incident that undermines diversity and community, whether that incident be racist, homophobic, sexist, or whatever. It might be an event as simple as offensive emails or postings or outright intimidation and physical threats or even violence perpetrated against the victims. Universities may have systems in place to handle these kinds of events, but even with the best of systems, it still requires leadership to speak up quickly and forcefully to address the situation, communicate openly with the campus community, and take meaningful steps to reassure the victims and defuse the situation. When Gee immediately condemned racist graffiti sprayed on the Hale Black Cultural Center in 2012, it helped defuse the situation. But the student rally in response to this incident is a reminder of how quickly incidents of bigotry and intolerance can create turmoil and pain in a seemingly calm and diverse community. This is exacerbated in our social media age where the most disgusting or threatening or false statements can circulate widely and almost instantaneously create a crisis that requires quick and effective responses on the part of university leadership.

17

Gee and the Governors

The Voinovich Years

Gee's first term as Ohio State president largely overlapped with George Voinovich's two terms as governor of Ohio. Gee served from 1990 to 1997, while Voinovich was elected in 1990 and re-elected in 1994 and served from 1991 to early 1999. Although Gee and Voinovich ultimately became very close personal friends, their relationship started on a rocky note from which Gee learned some valuable lessons. Voinovich was a fiscally conservative person who very much enjoyed the mechanics of government and wanted to make it more efficient and more productive. He often referred to "getting into the bowels of government" to see what made it tick and how to improve its performance. Voinovich saw higher education as being fat and wasteful. He believed that faculty did not work very hard and he believed that much of what was taught at universities had little relevance to what he viewed to be the highest priorities—jobs and economic development. And the governor routinely cited anecdotes about highly paid faculty not working very hard, about recent graduates who were not prepared to hold the position of bank teller, and about wasteful personnel and purchasing practices in higher education. Some of these anecdotes were directly aimed at Ohio State. One story had Ohio State stealing a healthcare professional from Case Western Reserve University to come to Ohio State with a high salary in hand. Moreover, this faculty member taught only one formal course despite this high salary, which really irked the governor. When Ohio State tracked down the details of this case, it was true that the faculty member taught only one formal classroom course. But the faculty member

Chapter 17

also oversaw student dental clinics in the College of Dentistry; indeed, she was spending more time with students than professors in most departments and colleges. The governor also told the story of an OSU faculty member who was seen mowing his lawn midweek. The governor was angry that the faculty member was not on campus teaching students. When this story was tracked down, it turned out that the faculty member—a surgeon—had just completed a number of major surgeries and was supposed to be off-site to rejuvenate himself.

But no matter how many times the governor was told some of his stories were inaccurate and misleading, he would continue to repeat them. It was clear to Gee that Voinovich had an antipathy toward higher education and especially toward the liberal arts. Voinovich saw higher education as elitist and out of touch and not committed to the citizens of Ohio. Gee had never encountered a governor, especially a Republican governor, who had such disdain for higher education. Then in the mid 1990s, Ohio experienced serious economic problems, and the state budget had slipped into a deficit, an impermissible situation in Ohio. In such a situation, the governor has unilateral power to cut appropriations to agencies and departments to try to bring the budget back into balance. The governor does not have the power to unilaterally raise taxes to address the situation. The governor ordered three rounds of budget cuts, and in all three cuts, higher education's share of the reductions was greater than its share of the budget. For example, higher education's share of the state budget was about 13 percent, yet its share of the first round of cuts was closer to 29 percent. This disproportionately harsh treatment of higher education infuriated Gee, and one evening, while meeting with students at a campus-area bar, a student reporter from *The Lantern* asked Gee what he thought about the budget cuts and the governor, Gee instantly called the governor a "damn dummy" for slashing higher education. Needless to say, this remark went public, created a major stir, and harmed what had been a strained but improving relationship that Gee had with Voinovich. Gee instantly apologized, both publicly and personally, but damage had been done. Gee then worked hard to try to be of help to the governor and his policy objectives when he could. An opportunity arose very quickly. It became very clear that Ohio could not cut its way out of its financial predicament; more revenue—higher taxes—would be needed to avoid further cuts to state programs. And Gee volunteered to help lobby the governor's tax proposals through the state legislature. Indeed, one day Gee and Voinovich ran into each other in the halls of the legislature. Voinovich thanked Gee for being willing to step up, but then added that he still thought higher education was fat and could survive further cuts. Gee just smiled.

FIGURE 17.1. George and Janet Voinovich in the president's box at a football game. Credit: The Ohio State University.

This episode illustrated a number of key points about Governor Voinovich. He was committed to governing in a fiscally responsible way. He was willing to use his political capital to call for tax increases *after* he first tried to ensure that existing dollars were being spent wisely and frugally. Finally, the governor was willing to make tough, unpopular decisions. That's what real leaders did; they did not kick the can down the road. Voinovich knew that budget cuts would be unpopular to some Ohioans; he knew that tax increases would be unpopular with others. Yet he went forward to do what he believed to be right. And Gee learned that his governor was a principled man of strong beliefs, whom Gee had grown to respect and admire. Indeed, the two of them became fast friends, a friendship that lasted until Voinovich's death in 2017 (see Figure 17.1).

Gee also learned another lesson in his first term as president; do not upstage the governor. Recognize that the governor is the most prominent politician in Columbus and in the state. And even though you are the president of the one of the largest universities in the country, a university that has a reach throughout the entire state, and a football program that probably brings Ohioans together more so than most other activities, you are still merely a university president who needs to, where possible, be a partner with the governor. That

CHAPTER 17

Gee had learned this lesson became evident when he returned as president of Ohio State in 2007.

The Strickland Years

Gee returned to Ohio State in 2007 and served until 2013. Ted Strickland was elected Governor in 2006, took office in 2007, and served until early 2011, after being narrowly defeated for re-election by John Kasich in 2010. Gee had known Strickland for a while, since Ted's earlier service in the US House of Representatives. They had had a good working relationship, which Gee vowed to continue and improve (see Figure 17.2).

Number one on the governor's higher education agenda was the establishment of the University System of Ohio, which he accomplished through an executive order in August 2007. The executive order began with standard language touting Ohio's great higher education tradition and asserting that collaborative efforts among Ohio's colleges and universities will improve higher education in Ohio. It then initially established the University System of Ohio by directing the chancellor of the Board of Regents to refer to Ohio's colleges and universities as the University of System of Ohio. The executive order directed the chancellor "to manage the state's investment in higher education to build The University System of Ohio so that it ensures affordable, high quality education opportunities for all Ohioans." Finally, the executive order directed "the Chancellor to prepare a ten-year plan for The University System of Ohio that sets clear goals for the System and provides a timeline for accomplishing those goals."

When the USO was announced, there was not yet much content to the proposal; that would be generated in the strategic planning process led by Chancellor Eric Fingerhut. Gee had known Fingerhut in his earlier roles as a state senator and a member of the US House of Representatives. More importantly, Gee knew that Fingerhut was a person of keen intellect, insight, determination, and ambition, someone to be taken very seriously. And Fingerhut was the first chancellor to be appointed directly by the governor; previous chancellors had been selected by the Board of Regents itself. Clearly Fingerhut had the governor's ear and support. And Governor Strickland himself had demonstrated his support for higher education in his first biennial budget by not only proposing a tuition freeze, but also paying for it through additional state dollars so that it was not a financial hit to the colleges and universities.

FIGURE 17.2. Governor Strickland flanked by Provost Alutto and President Gee. Credit: The Ohio State University.

Thus, Gee and the higher education community believed it needed to work constructively and cooperatively with Fingerhut and his team. And Gee proposed that his and Fingerhut's leadership teams meet regularly, which they did at breakfasts at the university residence. These meetings were open discussions, full of substantive content about how to have the Strategic Plan meet the objectives the governor had set out for the USO. Throughout these meetings, Gee and his Ohio State colleagues always stressed their desire to be good partners, but also reminded Fingerhut and his team of Ohio State's unique mission and role as the state's flagship, comprehensive, national research institution. When I received a draft of the ten-year plan the week before it was to be released, it referred to Ohio State simply as Ohio's land grant institution with scant acknowledgement of its unique research and teaching missions, especially at the graduate and professional levels. When Gee saw this, he was irate, called up Fingerhut, and said we needed to talk. We then went downtown to Fingerhut's office and got the text changed to better reflect Ohio State's mission and contributions to the state. This incident passed over quickly, but it did raise concerns about the USO that many internal constituencies at Ohio State and many Ohio colleges and universities had already expressed quietly:

Chapter 17

What did a system mean? What decisions that had been campus-based would now be handled centrally in Columbus by the Ohio Board of Regents? What would happen to the role of the boards of trustees as the governing authorities (appointed by the governor) of their respective campuses? How intrusive would the Board of Regents and the chancellor become in the routine activities of colleges and universities? What would the commitment of future governors and legislatures be to the University System of Ohio? Gee had to perform a skillful balancing act on campus and off. His own legal affairs team worried about the USO usurping some of the university's powers. The Office of Academic Affairs leadership worried that the Board of Regents would be insensitive to traditional academic rights and responsibilities. And the business and facilities staff of the university fretted that a less expert Board of Regents might try to interfere with their normal business operations. At the same time, Gee need to reassure the governor and Fingerhut that he was indeed a reliable partner and advocate for the ten-year plan.

Ohio State did speak out about specific concerns it had with the strategic plan. Since one of the goals was dramatically increasing enrollments in higher education, would Ohio State wind up being penalized because it was viewed as being at full capacity with slight future growth being at the margins in particular programmatic areas? Another goal was to keep more of our graduates here in Ohio. Would Ohio State be penalized because many of its students graduating from highly ranked departments and programs were very competitive nationally and would receive job offers from all over the country? Would the success of our students in being attractive on the national stage hurt Ohio State in the metrics of the University System of Ohio? On this specific concern, Ohio State suggested that the greater the opportunities for Ohio-based internship and co-op experiences while a student, the more likely graduates would receive and accept an Ohio job offer and remain in the state. Yet another concern raised by Ohio State was the negative impact of many state regulations and processes that added to the costs in time and money, especially in the renovation and construction of facilities. (See the discussion of Project One in chapter 15.) The core argument here was that if the state wanted a well-functioning higher education system, there would be times when the state had to step out of the way and unleash its colleges and universities rather than keeping them bound by cumbersome, costly bureaucratic processes coming from state government. Gee would also acknowledge that Ohio State has to review its own internal procedures to remove impediments to university progress.

The University System of Ohio did get off to a good start, and that is a tribute to Strickland and Fingerhut and the leaders of the campuses. The goals outlined for the system brought focus to many of the campus-based activities and programs. The emphasis on cooperation across institutions made the colleges and universities more effective in responding to state needs. The focus on the role of higher education fostering economic development encouraged colleges and universities to be more flexible and responsive in addressing business needs in the domains of workforce, technology, and research. Overall, the USO gave greater meaning and clarity to the old saw that colleges and universities were always citing: Higher education is the economic engine of the state.

Even as Gee and Ohio State worked closely with the Strickland administration on the development of the University System of Ohio, Gee was also building his relationship with Strickland along other dimensions. One particular example is worth noting. Gee, former Senator John Glenn, and I visited with Governor Strickland and two of his senior staff to present an opportunity for the governor to take the lead on issues of political reform, particular legislative redistricting, and gerrymandering. Gee indicated that he and Senator Glenn would be willing to publicly support a gubernatorial-led initiative on political reform. Moreover, Gee told Strickland that former Governor and US Senator George Voinovich and some other Republicans were on board, making this a truly bipartisan proposal. The Ohio State team at the meeting saw this as a wonderful opportunity for the governor to exercise leadership on an issue that many civic and community and media leaders thought needed to be addressed. But nothing developed from that meeting, and it was later learned that the governor's two senior advisors at the meeting encouraged him to stay away from the issue, cautioning him that it might antagonize some interests (including some in the Democratic Party) and might not be successful. Moreover, it was not an issue he had run on and there were still other parts of his 2006 campaign platform that needed attention. Strickland had the misfortune to serve during the Great Recession, a time of great budget strains and job losses in Ohio. Although many observers believe that Strickland did a good job protecting core state functions and responsibilities, when he ran for re-election in 2010, John Kasich narrowly defeated him.

The Kasich Years

From his first term as OSU president starting in 1990, Gee and John Kasich, who was a member of the US House of Representatives at the time, had a wonderful personal and professional friendship. And when Gee returned as president in 2007 and Kasich was elected governor in 2010, that friendship became

Chapter 17

an even stronger working relationship where the two would engage in often intense conversations about issues facing higher education in Ohio and the nation and what needed to be done. This relationship enabled Kasich to turn to Gee twice to chair task forces addressing the two major funding streams that the state provided higher education—the capital budget for the renovation and construction of physical facilities, and the operating budget, particularly the instructional subsidy, which along with tuition, fees, and other income sources, paid for the core instructional activities of the university. As Gee undertook these assignments, he was supported by the superb work of Jack Hershey, a senior member of Ohio State's government affairs team and who today is executive director of the association of community and technical colleges. It is my personal belief that the accomplishments of Kasich, Gee, and Hershey in reforming the capital and operating budget processes through a collaborative approach generated outcomes that improved college and university physical plants and enhanced student educational success. These outcomes have never received the attention and acclaim that they deserve. Let me elaborate.

Unlike some other states, Ohio directly supports the capital needs of its higher education institutions. This might take the form of new buildings and facilities or the renovation and updating of existing facilities. The capital budget is considered biennially in even-numbered years and, in addition to projects for higher education, includes projects for some state agencies and departments. The capital budget also typically includes funds for community projects, which can take many forms, including money for sports arenas, arts facilities, social service sites, and the like. Community projects constitute the smallest proportion of the capital bill and are also the most politically sensitive, with communities and regions competing for scarce dollars. The non-higher education portion of the state capital bill is driven largely by the legitimate needs of state agencies as arbitrated by the Office of Budget and Management and the Office of the Governor. But the higher education portion of the capital bill had often resembled the Wild West with colleges and universities fighting for dollars for projects that in some instances seemed puzzling to external observers. How were these requested projects actually contributing to the university's mission and how were they contributing to the state overall? Each college and university would put together its prioritized list of projects and send that list to the Board of Regents. The board would then construct a budget from these many requests and send its recommendations to OBM and the governor. At this stage the governor's proposed capital budget would be forwarded to the legislature, where it would be passed by the House and Senate very quickly. No one wanted a bill that involved capital projects (some of which resembled pork barrel) to be sitting out in the public eye too long, lest others make efforts to modify the bill and add to the bill. Capital bills were mainly funded by the sale of bonds. To pay off the interest and principal on the bonds, a portion of the state's operating budget was committed to pay this obligation; typically, this portion was kept to no more than 5 percent of the general revenue fund.

Governor Kasich was unhappy with this process. He was not convinced that the individual list of projects the colleges and university prepared reflected their true needs and preferences, especially since once a project made it on a university's wish list, it tended to stay on the list until it was funded, perhaps four or five biennia, or eight to ten years down the road. And the governor was convinced that the individual wish lists of universities did not necessarily reflect the overall needs of the State of Ohio, that individual wish lists did not add up to good public policy. So Kasich called upon Gee to create a collaborative process among the two-year and four-year institutions that would better serve the needs of the state and the institutions themselves. He wanted consensus to be reached and reminded the college and university presidents that if they could not come to an agreement, higher education might not be in the capital bill at all. This warning (a few years earlier the state had skipped an entire capital budget) was credible and got the attention of the higher education leadership. Thus, Gee and especially Hershey worked closely with each campus to review its capital budget requests to see if there were any low priority items on the list for which funding was being requested for the upcoming capital bill. They indeed found such projects including a university (not Ohio State) request for millions of dollars to renovate an old building for which the university had no use. Gordon and Jack convinced the university leadership to remove the project from the list, which created some tension on that campus with advocates for that particular "bridge to nowhere." In another example, Stark State College had just established an Energy Training Center directly benefiting the Canton region's growing oil and gas industry. Gee's capital funding commission viewed this as a priority project that warranted full funding right away given the workforce needs of the industry. This center would enhance Stark's workforce training and certification offerings. But the way the capital bill process had worked in the past, Stark by formula could not get the full funding for the facility in one biennium; instead, it would have to be stretched out over multiple biennia, which would delay the start of the newly adopted program. The capital commission argued that money needed to flow to top priorities, both state and institution specific, even if that meant that other projects would not receive funding. And, indeed, in this example, Stark State did receive full funding in one biennium, a radical departure from

Chapter 17

past practices. Ohio State's own capital request got modified in this process. Originally Ohio State wanted two separate buildings for chemistry and biomedical engineering teaching and research. The Gee commission helped the university better recognize the opportunities for interdisciplinary activity and therefore OSU then requested funds for a single building that would support many chemistry and engineering faculty partnerships with business.

Gee and Hershey were successful in getting the higher education leadership to unite behind a core set of principles to guide future capital budget decision-making. Among the key factors was the acknowledgment that capital expenditures should not increase the net square footage of facilities. Dollars should be focused on renovation and not on new construction. And where new buildings are being constructed, efforts should be made to reduce existing square footage. Moreover, whether renovations or new buildings, priority should be given to projects that house programs and activities that contribute to economic development. Priority should also be given to projects that involve partnerships internal and external to the university and projects that can attract multiple funding streams. Finally, priority should be given to projects that contribute to the core research and teaching missions of the colleges and universities. The higher education portion of the capital budget should not be burdened with "glitz and glamour" projects that have little to do with the core activities of the institution.

Governor Kasich was very pleased with the unanimous support of the commission and expressed thanks to everyone who participated in the process. He invited Gee to the capital bill signing and jokingly asked Gee to dot the "i" in Kasich. But Gee's real "reward" for a successful capital budget process was to be asked by the governor to lead another commission of college and university presidents, this one to review and reform the funding formula for the operations of the state's colleges and universities. In Ohio's operating budget, the major portion (about 80 percent) of higher education funding was allocated to institutions through an instructional subsidy formula that the governor and others thought was profoundly flawed.

In every two-year budget cycle to this point, the Board of Regents would convene a consultation group to review the funding formula and make recommendations for improvement. Most proposed changes were at the margins; they did not change the fact that the formula distribution rewarded institutions for having "butts in seats" on the fourteenth day of the quarter. I am oversimplifying the formula, but it basically counted how many students were enrolled on the fourteenth day, and that head count drove the distribution of dollars. There were factors that entered into the formula, including the level of instruction, the type of course, and many more, but the essential philosophy was to count enrollments. If a student disappeared on the fifteenth day or failed to complete the course, that would not affect how much money the institution would receive for that student. Thus, Gee and his colleagues were charged with developing a more rational, policy-driven, outcomes-oriented formula to determine the distribution of funds.

The process Gee employed was very similar to the capital budget deliberations, but more complicated and challenging. There were of course numerous meetings and consultations with college and university presidents with Gee and Hershey demonstrating once again great skill and patience in getting a disparate group of leaders of disparate institutions to see the bigger picture and appreciate how a revised funding formula would better serve the interests of the state. This process was made more difficult when the Board of Regents would run proposed modifications through the funding formula so that every institution could see how much it would gain or lose under different formula changes. Needless to say, this created tension and anxiety among participants that was only partially alleviated when the governor hinted he might commit additional dollars for the instructional subsidy if the group came up with a better methodology. These additional dollars could help ensure that no institution lost (much) funding from the current biennium to the next. But these additional dollars were not to be considered as guarantees that would protect institutions from change; guarantees would undermine the entire effort to move to a more responsive funding formula.

The ultimate goal was to get institutions to move beyond a "butts in seats" mentality to a system that encouraged institutions to adopt policies and programs to help students complete their academic programs and graduate and move on to the world of work. In the fall of 2012, the commission was successful in having a new funding formula ready for the FY 2014-15 (HB 59) state operating budget bill. Essentially the new funding formula linked state support for higher education to successful student outcomes. The community college presidents agreed that all of their state funding should be based on successful course completion, degree attainment and certification completion rather than course enrollments. For the four-year universities, the share of their funding that was tied directly to student graduation rose from 20 percent to 50 percent.

This was an amazing outcome with credit going to the college and university presidents who saw (or were helped to see) the benefit of a performance-based system and to the leadership of Kasich and Gee. Kasich made it absolutely clear that the old system and formula could not and would not survive, while Gee, again with the aid of Jack Hershey, led his presidential colleagues through

Chapter 17

an arduous and principled process. By the end of the experience, Ohio had become a national leader in incentivizing its colleges and universities to adopt performance-based funding designed to stimulate student success. There were other reforms that the state and the USO accomplished in this era to foster student success, including improving credit transfer and articulation agreements, facilitating the earning of college credits while in high school, improving distance learning opportunities for adult learners and place-bound students, and many more. But the success in linking the allocation of dollars to performance measures was an achievement than many thought could never be accomplished.

After Gee stepped down as president in June of 2013, Governor Kasich called on him a third time to lead a statewide initiative called the Quality and Value Initiative for Higher Education. It raised the question of how could the cost of higher education be lowered for students while at the same time the quality of instruction is enhanced. This study was funded by the Ohio Board of Regents and was conducted by the Center for Higher Education Enterprise at Ohio State, a higher education policy think tank created for and by Gee before he left to become the president of West Virginia University for the second time. Like the previous two Gee-led initiatives, there was extensive consultation with interested parties, including Ohio's higher education leaders, faculty and students, the business community, research institutions, state government, and others. There were regional listening tours conducted around the state attended by Gee, OBOR Chancellor John Carey, and others. The team adopted a set of guiding principles to shape their work that emphasized inclusiveness, collaboration, responsiveness, diversity, and accessibility and transparency with an overarching goal of advancing economic growth throughout Ohio. There were many recommendations that related to students, including reinventing the student academic advising structure, improving innovative teaching practices, and investing in learning technologies, and rewarding faculty who are contributing to these goals. It also recommended the adoption of official standards for school counselors in Ohio's high schools. And it emphasized the linkages between higher education, the business community, and economic development by calling for students to have expanded opportunities for meaningful internships guided by the needs of industry and the economy. It also called for core competency-based degrees and certificate programs targeted to working adults who needed some additional education and training. Finally, it highlighted the role of the institutions' boards of trustees to ensure that their own institutional policies were in harmony with the overarching quality and value principles.

FIGURE 17.3. President Gee looks on at a bill signing in Governor Kasich's office. Also at the ceremony are Annie and John Glenn and Representative Tom Sawyer. Credit: The Ohio State University.

After Gee left for West Virginia and Kasich completed his second term as governor in early 2019, there were no more opportunities for the governor to ask the president to formally take on another higher education mission. But the friendship and respect that the two leaders had for each other remained strong (see Figure 17.3). When Gee came to Columbus in late 2018 for a book signing event for his latest book (co-authored with Steve Gavazzi) on land grant universities—held at the Land Grant bar in Franklinton, a redeveloping neighbor west of downtown Columbus, Governor Kasich hurried back from Washington, DC, so that he could make an appearance and say hello to his friend. Both Kasich and Gee marveled about how much change was achieved in Ohio higher education policy in a relatively short period of time. After all, higher education has not traditionally been thought of as a domain where change comes quickly.

18

The Ohio State University and the Gee Legacy

Introduction

In this final chapter, I will summarize some of the major developments that occurred during Gordon Gee's second administration at Ohio State University. I will divide these developments into two distinct groups—those that would likely have happened no matter who was the university president and those that can be more closely linked to Gee's presence and leadership at Ohio State. As noted earlier in the book, Ohio State had been on an upward trajectory prior to Gee's return, a trajectory attributable in part to the decisions and actions of his predecessors (including Gee One) and to a tendency for universities on a particular path to remain on that path assuming competent leadership, adequate resources and constructive bureaucratic behavior. Universities resemble large naval vessels in their movement; in most cases, they do not dramatically change course over a short period of time. But when a university does want to change course or least sharply accelerate its positive momentum, it requires leadership, commitment, and resources. And Gee, the leadership team he put in place, and the strategic decisions they made moved Ohio State forward in significant ways that would not have occurred had Gee not served a second term as president.

Ohio State Successes Not Dependent on Gee's Return

Gordon Gee inherited a university in 2007 that was already moving forward on many fronts because of the decisions and actions of his predecessors (including Gee One). For example, as discussed in chapter 13 and elsewhere, the continuing improvement in the credentials and preparedness of the student body reflected a trend fostered by the Jennings, Gee, and Kirwan administrations and enhanced by the actions of subsequent presidents. Every year, OSU presidents, including Gee's successor Michael Drake, could boast that the new entering class was the best ever at Ohio State, whether measured by ACT or SAT scores or by the percentage of students graduating in the top 10 percent of their high school senior class. Likewise, every year, the four-year and the six-year graduation rate continued to improve, and the number of applications for admission to the freshman class grew dramatically, although the university's decision to participate in the Common Application contributed to this increase. In short, the move from an open admissions university to a selective admissions institution was on an unstoppable path.

The university's record of attracting external public and private funds in the second Gee presidency also flourished, although the pattern of funding from federal government sources such as the NIH and the NSF showed a jagged path because of the vagaries of congressional budget appropriations and the aggressiveness and success of faculty seeking federal funds. In the area of contract research, which is typically funded by business and industry and the military, Ohio State maintained its high ranking as among the top two to four universities in the nation to earn such support. It was clear that faculty and staff working with businesses on a contract basis to help them solve problems and aid their productivity and profitability was ingrained in the culture of the institution, particularly in colleges such as business, the health sciences, agriculture, engineering and others.

The enhancement of the Ohio State medical center with respect to mission, quality and impact was another area to which the university had committed itself prior to Gee's return. Here, however, Gee played a critical role in the recruitment of talent and in reforming building construction policies, which made the construction of the new James hospital more feasible (see chapter 15). Likewise, the growth of athletic facilities and the expansion and enhancement of the Ohio State intercollegiate athletics program was in full growth mode

CHAPTER 18

prior to Gee's return. In both the medical center and athletics examples, Gee was certainly very supportive of both enterprises and pushed them to expand their horizons and build their programs and facilities. But it was clear that the medical center and the athletic department had moved up on the university's priority list even before Gee's return. Likewise, the university's capital budget priorities were largely in place for a ten-year period when Gee returned. This was largely a function of the process the state utilized to fund capital projects. Gee did, however, play a highly significant role in reforming the state level capital budget process in order to yield better outcomes for state policy priorities as discussed in chapter 17.

Gee's Unique Contributions to Ohio State and to the State of Ohio

Gee had an aggressive and ambitious agenda for Ohio State when he returned. He clearly wanted to secure Ohio State's place among the nation's best public universities. He advanced a number of strategies and approaches to expand the university's resource base so that the university could invest in high priority items. He wanted to expand Ohio State's footprint in a wide variety of areas ranging from health care to the arts to public policy. He was determined that Ohio State be more engaged in the international arena. He was committed to improving the physical attributes of the campus and the areas surrounding the university. Because of his close relationship with Governor Kasich, he became a major architect of higher education policy reform. He did an incredible job promoting Ohio State within Ohio and throughout the nation. I will now elaborate on some of these achievements and argue that but for Gordon Gee, many of these outcomes would not have happened.

Gee played a key role in a number of distinct ways in growing the university's resource base. He encouraged outside-the-box thinking and risk taking in coming up with new and creative ways to generate funds to support key university priorities. His hiring of Geoff Chatas and his support for the efforts of Chatas' team enabled such financial innovations as the monetizing of campus parking, the issuance of a 100-year bond, a major energy deal, and a more aggressive approach to affiliation agreements. These initiatives, strongly endorsed by the OSU Board of Trustees, placed Ohio State in a national leadership position for creative financing methods. In the years since Gee's departure in 2013, it seems that the entrepreneurial spirit has pervaded all areas of the university, especially the athletics department (see chapter 14), although not without some grumbling and concerns about the university focusing too much on revenue-generating opportunities (see chapter 12 for a fuller discussion of the alternative ways in which dollars were generated).

Likewise, private, philanthropic fundraising regained momentum in the second Gee presidency. As discussed in chapter 8, when Gee returned to Ohio State in 2007, he inherited a development/fundraising operation that was in a holding pattern. Gee believed that the university was missing out on millions of dollars of philanthropic contributions. And here Gee deserves much credit for moving the university from a traditional fundraising approach to an advancement model in which development, university communications, and the Ohio State Alumni Association were joined together to better advance Ohio State University (see the advancement discussion in chapter 8). The advancement model, as I said earlier in the book, reflected Gee's firm belief that universities should focus first on friendraising and build long-term relationships with its alumni, friends, and supporters. When that is accomplished, the fundraising success will naturally follow as long as there is skillful leadership in the advancement domain, which Gee provided with such appointments as Andy Sorenson and Mike Eicher. Annual fundraising totals reached record levels in the latter years of Gee's second term, and these records continued to be broken in the early years of the Drake administration. I would argue that part of the reason for this success was the university doing a much better job of staying engaged with its alumni and friends through more effective communication strategies and engagement opportunities including the creative use of social media and more innovative programming by the OSU Alumni Association—yet another part was Gee's leadership and commitment to the fundraising enterprise.

Gee also was instrumental in the most successful capital campaign in Ohio State's history, a campaign that raised over $3 billion when the tabulation finally stopped. Indeed, one of the reasons the trustees wanted Gee to come back to Ohio was to lead the next major capital campaign. Prior to this campaign, the last major effort occurred in Gee's first term at Ohio State. Gee brought his passion for Ohio State and his joy in sharing the story of Ohio State to donors of all stripes and made them feel that they were an important part of the university. He was also superb in performing his stewardship role in saying thank you to the many friends and alumni of Ohio State.

Gee also played a major role in reshaping State of Ohio public policy related to the funding of higher education. As discussed in chapter 17, working in partnership with Governor Kasich and with the able assistance of Jack Hershey, Gee helped lead the state toward a more rational process for allocating capital construction dollars that better reflected the genuine needs of the colleges and

Chapter 18

universities as well as the core priorities of the state. With respect to the higher education operating budget, Gee moved the state dramatically in the direction of performance-based funding, with much of the allocation based on successful student outcomes. This encouraged the colleges and universities to adopt internal institutional policies that promoted student success. Gee also played a key role in preparing a Quality and Value report that helped the state better recognize the importance of not sacrificing quality in order to have lower cost of higher education. A bargain, high-value education is one that is both affordable and high quality.

Gee also pushed very hard to achieve regulatory relief for higher education from many of the state's costly and unnecessary mandates and regulations. Working with Chris Culley, Herb Asher, Jack Hershey, and others, Gee prepared an agenda of reforms for the state to consider. Unfortunately, success in this area was limited. But there was one absolutely critical reform—changes in the processes that could be used in the construction of facilities. Until this point, Ohio was one of the very few states that prohibited the use of single prime contractors. Instead, the State of Ohio required the use of multiple primes, which resulted in more delays, internal disputes, and ultimately higher costs than if a single prime contractor could be in charge of the overall project. Ohio State was successful in getting the new, James Hospital to be treated as a demonstration project utilizing a single prime contractor. The university believed that this massive project was completed in a more timely fashion and at a lower cost than would have been the case under the old system. Because of this success, the State of Ohio has expanded the opportunities for builders to utilize more flexible construction management processes.

Internally, Gee aggressively led a number of initiatives, including the move to a semester system and the consolidation of the Arts and Sciences. The benefits of the semester conversion became clear right away with restructuring of courses, revisions of academic programs, and the enhanced flexibility in course offerings due to the Maymester and to other features of the adopted semester system. The Arts and Sciences consolidation experienced a bumpier path in achieving its stated goals, but ultimately some services were combined in a central office rather than having five separate college offices perform them. Ultimately, the new ASC configuration got more creative in offering career counseling for its students. But the overall goal of enhanced prominence of the Arts and Sciences at Ohio State through the consolidation may not have been achieved, even as the consolidation did foster more interdisciplinary collaborations across the Arts and Sciences. But a university budget model that essentially rewarded enrollments has not been a friend to the Arts and Sciences.

Gee also played a major role in advancing the quality of residential life on campus. He pushed hard to renovate the residence halls on the South Campus, including the installation of air-conditioning in those dormitories that had not had it. With the adoption of the semester system, the academic year was now beginning in mid-August rather than in late September under the quarter system. And Columbus in August could be brutally hot and humid. More importantly, Gee led the charge for a total remake of the North Campus residential area. Many of the old facilities were merely adequate at best, ugly in appearance, and not designed to foster community. Gee and Student Affairs Senior Vice President Jauvanne Adams-Gastin worked successfully on both the physical and programmatic aspects of the project, resulting in a beautiful new North Campus Residential District along with creative programs such as the STEP Program (see chapter 10). And with the requirement that undergraduate students spend their first two years in university housing, it was vital that those facilities be enhanced to provide a good home for students.

There were so many other areas in which Gee pushed the university, often working hand-in-hand with Provost Joe Alutto. The Discovery Themes (see chapter 11) were designed to enhance cross-disciplinary activity at Ohio State and to place Ohio State in a position of national and international leadership on issues facing the globe. Gee promoted the internationalization of the university's activities in many areas by the appointment of William Brustein as vice provost for Global Strategies and International Affairs and the establishment of four gateway cities, an effort to expand Ohio State's footprint beyond Ohio and the nation. These four gateway cities would facilitate international research opportunities for faculty and graduate students and provide more study abroad experiences for students.

Gee and the provost and members of the Board of Trustees also revved up the university's planning initiative, be it broader strategic planning, campus planning and the physical environment, directives to the colleges to prepare and regularly update their strategic plans, and much more. With respect to the physical environment of campus, major initiatives were planned for areas East of High Street and an Arts District on the eastern side of campus abutting High Street. Indeed, on all the edges of campus, planning was afoot to create better neighborhoods and environments.

Gee also strongly advocated improving the health and wellness of the campus community as well as the environmental health of the area. He appointed Bernadette Melnyk, dean of the College of Nursing, as the university's chief wellness officer, and Melnyk was fierce in her determination to improve the quality of life for members of the campus community. Gee was also commit-

Chapter 18

ted to making the university more environmentally friendly and becoming a better steward of energy resources. He asked Kate Wolford to lead a number of sustainability initiatives and created an internal, cross-disciplinary group to generate proposals for action.

I could go on and on in listing areas that Gee influenced. And even when he was the driving force, there were so many university colleagues who played key roles in implementation, starting with the Office of Academics Affairs and Provost Joe Alutto, and including talented personnel throughout the academic and administrative leadership of the university. But now I want to conclude this book by focusing on what I believe to be Gee's most unique assets—his powers of persuasion, his interpersonal and communication skills, and the passion that he brought to his performance as president of The Ohio State University. This cluster of skills was brought to bear in a number of distinct areas, including the recruitment and retention of faculty and staff, his amazing connection with the student body of Ohio State, and his wonderful ability to get external audiences, be they rank and file Ohioans or public officials or civic and business leaders, to feel that Ohio State was their university. And one reason they felt that way was because they "knew" Gordon Gee and knew that he liked and respected them. And this feeling was reciprocated: they liked and respected Gordon Gee.

In chapter 3, we discussed Gee's successful efforts to recruit outstanding individuals to staff his administration. But this recruitment went far beyond attracting people for senior vice presidential positions. It reached down to deans, other administrative positions, and sometimes faculty. Gee took great pride in many of the dean appointments he made. The story of Joe Steinmetz was told in chapter 3, but Gee's efforts brought many other outstanding deans to Ohio State, many of whom are still serving Ohio State well years after Gee's departure. Bruce McPheron was brought in as dean of the College of Food, Agricultural, and Environment Sciences, and later became the university provost. In addition to the recruitment of specific deans discussed in chapter 3, there were other deans that Gee helped recruit from other universities. Patrick Lloyd was recruited from the University of Minnesota and immediately took a leadership role in planning and fundraising for new facilities for the College of Dentistry and making dental care a higher priority for Ohio. Bern Melnyk came to Ohio State as Dean of the College of Nursing and quickly became Gee's partner in many health and wellness initiatives. There were also significant internal promotions to dean during Gee's second administration, including Alan Michaels as dean of the College of Law and Tom Gregoire as dean of the College of Social Work. There would typically be search committees when

THE OHIO STATE UNIVERSITY AND THE GEE LEGACY

FIGURE 18.1. The Ohio State University Marching Band salutes President Gee by marching into a bow tie formation. Credit: The Ohio State University.

recruiting deans. But Gee would also get involved, checking with his extensive network of contacts throughout the nation to identify strong candidates for deanship positions and injecting these names, both internal and external, into the search process. And if strong candidates were identified but were not yet motivated to come to Ohio State, Gee would work hard to convince them otherwise.

Gee's connection to the Ohio State student body was amazing (see Figure 18.1). Throughout my entire career at Ohio State and with my knowledge of many other campuses, large and small, I have never witnessed a situation where the vast majority of the student body, especially the undergraduates, not only knew who the university president was but genuinely liked and admired him. We discussed in chapter 6 how hard Gee, with the able assistance of Tracy Stuck, worked to connect with students. When he walked across the Oval, Gee was regularly stopped by students who wanted to talk to him or have their picture taken with him (see Figure 18.2).

The idea that a university president could relate so personally to students on a campus with more than 40,000 undergraduates is simply unheard of and a great credit to Gee. The continuing attachment and regard for Gee was aptly demonstrated on November 16, 2018, more than five years after Gee's depar-

CHAPTER 18

FIGURE 18.2. An impromptu O-H-I-O occurs as Presdient Gee walks on the Oval. Credit: The Ohio State University.

ture from Ohio State, at the Land Grant Bar in the Franklinton neighborhood of Columbus. Gee and Steve Gavazzi had coauthored a book on land grant colleges and universities published by Johns Hopkins University Press. Book promoters and friends of Gee thought it would be fun to have a book on land grant institutions celebrated at the Land Grant Bar. The event was held in a side room at Land Grant just off of the main bar space. Many of Gee's friends and former colleagues were in attendance. At one point, the door between the book event and main bar opened and customers in the bar saw that Gordon Gee was present. They shouted for Gee, he went out to say hello to them, and soon a happy throng of Land Grant patrons surrounded Gee. Gee worked the entire bar area, saying hello to everyone. It was as if a long-lost friend had returned. And it reminded many of us in attendance at the book event how strong the connection was between Gee and the citizenry.

Finally, Gee's ability to personalize Ohio State, to make citizens from all over Ohio feel that Ohio State was their university was incredible. In a state with thirteen four-year public universities and many wonderful private universities and community colleges, the fact that Gee was able to engender support for Ohio State among Ohioans for whom the university was not their alma mater was impressive. This indeed was part of Gee's game plan and his travels. His messaging and his genuine love for all things Ohio and Ohio State were designed to make Ohioans feel good about themselves and about Ohio State University. Ohioans of all persuasions loved having a university president who reached out to them, who loved his job, and exhibited so much pride in and affection for the people of Ohio. Ohio was a state undergoing a wrenching economic transformation and facing challenges on many fronts. To have a university president express optimism about Ohio's future and pride in her people was a significant morale booster to his audiences. Even today I have people from all walks of life asking me how Gordon is doing and wondering if he will come back to Ohio and to Ohio State. This personal regard for Gordon Gee was also demonstrated from tough audiences such as journalists and public officials. When Gee announced his departure from Ohio State, the General Assembly and the governor quickly put together a reception at the Statehouse Atrium to honor their friend and wish him the very best. The event was heartfelt, and the tears were genuine. Everyone in the Statehouse felt a collective sense of loss even as Gordon was still firing off quips and demonstrating his sense of humor at a very emotional event. And when Gee returned to Columbus in the summer of 2019 to speak at the midweek forum of the Columbus Metropolitan Club, a packed house demonstrated its warmth and affection for the former president. It was clear that Gordon Gee had left his mark on Ohio State and the State of Ohio. And the university community and the state had reciprocated with their affection and respect for President Gordon Gee.

Appendix A

Gee's Rules of Engagement

Office of the President

205 Bricker Hall
190 North Oval Mall
Columbus, OH 43210-1357

Phone (614) 292-2424
Fax (614) 292-1231

TO: Executive Leadership Team
FROM: E. Gordon Gee
DATE: October 29, 2007

Rules of Engagement

I have shared some of my views regarding how I believe we should work together as a team and my own general philosophy regarding the administration of the University. Now that I have had more time to reflect on my return to Ohio State, I want to share with you the things that I believe are most important in order for us to have a successful tenure *together*. These are not new ideas—rather, as you talk to my colleagues at other institutions and those who worked with me previously at Ohio State, you will find them consistent with how I have previously managed my leadership responsibility.

APPENDIX A

I. WE MUST HIRE AND KEEP EXTRAORDINARY PEOPLE
The single most important thing that we do as a University is to hire and retain extraordinary people. That goes without saying. But what should be some of the characteristics of these extraordinary people—which, of course, *includes* the people in this room?

   A. First of all, this person must be smart. That should be self-evident to everyone here today. But, for those who are to engage in administrative leadership (perhaps as opposed to regular faculty members), I do not mean that this person must act smart; I do not mean that this person must have a stilted, polysyllabic vocabulary; I do not mean that this person should be laden with obtuse jargon. I do mean that this person should be smart. Smart enough to listen carefully. Smart enough to exercise common sense. Smart enough to exercise good judgment and discernment. This person should have the ability to tell the important from the unimportant. And the ability to take complexity and distill it into simplicity. The surest sign to me personally that someone is smart is how clearly, directly, and plainly they express ideas.
   B. The second thing I look for in a person is someone who gets things done—and gets them done at the pace the new world requires. If you are bright, but you do not get things done, I do not have any use for you. To get things done quickly, you must be decisive, you must understand that all decisions involve risk, and you must be courageous enough to take these risks intelligently. You must be dependable. You must be relentless and willing to defy and overcome any obstacle, whether internal or external. You must be self-sufficient— able to gather to yourself the resources required to get something done and not waiting for me or for permission—to move forward. My view is that people who get things done do not have the time, or interest, to spend time feeling sorry for themselves or for obsessing over circumstances or mistakes, theirs or others, that cannot be changed.
   C. The third thing that I believe characterizes extraordinary people is that they are nice. Now, there are clearly many extraordinary people in this world who are not nice. But this is our University and will be our administration, and we get to exercise our prerogative on this one. I think life is already tough enough without having to be around a lot of egotistical, abrasive, duplicitous people. I believe

extraordinary people are respectful. I believe they are courteous. I believe they have the proper perspective. I believe they have the proper touch of humility. I believe they genuinely celebrate the success of their peers. I believe they are not irritable nor are they arrogant. They do not engage in academic politics. They are not rude. They take their job seriously. They take their colleagues seriously, but they do not take themselves too seriously. And, perhaps as important as any of this is that they are not status-conscious—they are not the kind of people who will not spend time nor do business with people who have a lesser title than do they.

Now, I insist that you insist on this attribute. It cannot just be words, and it cannot be just the preference of one or two of the leaders of this institution. The organization itself—*you leaders*—must insist that people be this way.

D. The fourth expectation that I have is that you develop the habit, courage, and ability to be straightforward. We should have the ability to speak plainly and naturally with each other because, as I have emphasized, we are colleagues—we are a team.

II. THE ACID TEST OF LEADERSHIP IS THE ABILITY TO HIRE AND KEEP EXTRAORDINARY PEOPLE.

This brings me to my second main point. If it is indeed important for this University to hire and retain extraordinary people, then it should be readily apparent that the acid test of your own leadership will be the ability to hire and retain extraordinary people. What do you have to do, therefore, to meet that goal?

A. First, you have to be smart, results-oriented, nice, and straightforward. By and large, the type of people we want to attract to this University are not going to work with you if you do not have these characteristics.

B. Second, you have to deal with non-performers, because great people are not going to want to be around if you cannot deal with the people issues in your areas of responsibility. I can assure you that a great person will not stay with us if people who are known to not work, and who do not achieve results, are carried by the University. And not only will great people leave, something equally intolerable will happen: by keeping non-performers around, we will lower the standards of the organization. It will be acceptable to be mediocre. That, unfortunately, is the tragedy of many universities in this country.

C. The ultimate litmus test for you and your success is whether you have been hiring and retaining extraordinary people, people stronger than yourselves. Notice I did not say that you have the *potential* to hire and keep great people—but whether, in fact, you have actually been doing it. The people with whom you work and surround yourself will be the tangible evidence of all the intangible qualities we require and covet in our academic and administrative leadership. The evidence of whether or not, ultimately, you will be successful at Ohio State *tomorrow* will be the existence *today* of a high percentage of extraordinary people in your areas of responsibility.

Now there is a corollary of which I must remind you. We have all come across a senior leader where it is well known that no person wants to work for that individual—whether it is because that person is incompetent or indecisive or arrogant or obtuse or thoughtless. Can this happen at Ohio State? Of course it can. But it should not, because this is a University that truly aspires to the highest standards of greatness. And that is why we must develop tools to appropriately monitor the success of our leaders and to allow us to make change when necessary.

III. FULLY BE YOURSELF

My third major point is that each of you has an obligation to yourself, to this University, to your colleagues, to your family, and to your friends to fully be yourself. To bring, directly or indirectly, your beliefs, your passions, your interests—all that you are—fully with you to your job. All too often I have found that those in academic leadership spend years or even decades adding artificial elements to their personalities, and in so doing, begin to leave at home certain things that are a fundamental part of themselves. As a result, they often become a little bit more dull and predictable and passionless and joyless.

I want us to have fun. And I am not just talking about superficial fun—though that is certainly part of it. I am talking about intellectual, substantive fun. And while I understand no assignment is without its less-than-fun aspects, I am urging each of you to develop a thoughtfully conceived plan and process of aligning your real interest, passions, abilities, and values—indirectly or directly—with your assignment. You cannot accomplish this mission of bringing your whole self to work by simply thinking about it. You must put together a concrete plan. Develop a list, honestly and thoughtfully, of the things that give you the most intellectual pleasure in your work. Then recruit and develop people with whom you work with talents and interests that balance yours, thus giving yourself the opportunity to spend more time at the things that give you the most satisfaction by delegating those things that are not as well aligned with your interests and strengths. And if you have chosen your colleagues well, you will be accomplishing the same thing for them.

You asked the question, and I have given the answer in terms of my own values for people with whom I work. My sense about the majority of you in this room is that you represent a pervasive, overwhelmingly obsessive, almost pathological will to do well. You would not be in these positions if, but for all practical purposes, you were like addicts when it comes to making decisions and getting meaningful, substantive, real things done. My only urging to you is that an obsessive will to win must be coupled with other powerful notions of the human experience—of humor, of deep caring, of traveling the extra mile for the other person, of humility, and of having the courage to fully be yourselves. The results, in my view, will be explosively powerful.

IV. NOW, LET ME TURN TO SOME GENERAL OPERATING PRINCIPLES THAT I BELIEVE ARE NECESSARY FOR OUR SUCCESS
   A. The key to our effectiveness as leaders rests on the simple decision of how we decide to work together. I have made the decision that we will not continue as a collection of people with different goals and agendas who happen to share a common table. We must decide to set aside our individual aspirations and motivations and to truly function as one. By the way, that will be a very hard decision. I submit that the decision to work together for common goals is not natural. In fact, it flies directly in the face of your desires for individuality, control, and territory. It requires each of us to unlearn years of organizational bad habits—bad habits that have never served this institution well. We must work as one team and drive ourselves toward operating as one University. That compact of the common, I believe, will be one of the major reasons for future success and progress at this University.
   B. *Trust* is the oxygen of teams. Without trust, the team, like most organisms, will die. Trust does not automatically exist in a team environment. Trust must be built and nurtured and given time.

Appendix A

I believe, in candor, that we do not yet have a high level of trust among ourselves. We must now work very hard to build that trust. We must start by returning to the expectation that we will be forthright and truthful with each other. We must return to an expectation of *transparency* with each other. We must do away with gossip and petty sniping. As senior officers, you need to learn to speak directly with each other about specific problems. You cannot always expect me to act as a referee. But if I am, I will expect my decisions to be final. Of course, I expect you to speak directly with me about specific issues that cannot be managed among yourselves or in which there are issues with me directly.

C. As part of our commitment to the team, we must learn to *value conflict*. Conflict means that we trust each other enough to disagree. Conflict also means that ideas are valued and discussed. Conflict means ideas are aggressively debated. And, conflict means that decisions, once made, are adhered to with a passion. Once a decision is made by the team or by me, I expect total support of that decision as a team. And, I also will expect that decision to be supported actively, and not passively.

D. We must learn to *collaborate* even better. Each of you is highly talented and opinionated. Each of you is accustomed to independence and running your own units. Therefore, your first inclination is not to collaborate. I submit that the lack of collaboration is one of the reasons why so many teams are marginalized and do not achieve greatness. Let me be clear: there is no such thing as friendly competition in the executive suite. At any level, competition is toxic, and it undermines trust. When you become competitors rather than collaborators, you then will start to withhold information and resources from one another. Rather than cooperation, you will start to seek advantage. That possibility, at this University, at this time, is unacceptable.

E. As part of our rededication to team, we must learn to make good decisions in a timely fashion. In this regard, I pledge to each of you that I will not delay the decisions that I should make, but I will also not usurp the decision that you should make. At the same time, I do expect to be consulted or informed about the major strategic decisions that are yours to make. I will hold you accountable to make tough decisions, as I expect you hold me accountable to support those decisions and to make timely decisions on behalf of the University. We must all remember that we will not be judged on how many ideas we have—only on how many we make happen.

F. We must hold each other accountable. In order to be effective, we can tolerate no one who underperforms. While not everyone within our own teams may have the same ability, they should have the same level of commitment that we expect of ourselves as a team. As I will speak to each of you about your own performance, I expect you to speak to each other about performance concerns, rather than always bringing them to me for resolution. That is how we learn to work and play with each other.

G. We must *manage to the middle*. Right now I believe this is one of our most important failings and challenges. We must insist that our middle managers work cooperatively with each other and support each other. This requires us to make certain that middle managers in your own areas work cooperatively, share resources, and support middle mangers in other departments and divisions throughout the University. This will require each of you to diligently oversee and intervene to undo years of silo-based behavior. By insisting on cooperation and collaboration among our middle managers, we also must identify those who might some day be members of the senior team or be able to take on significant additional responsibilities. Each of you must be willing to help advance the careers of those with whom you work. You must be both a leader and a teacher. Talent abounds at Ohio State, and we must take the time to grow it.

H. I also want to remind each of us to manage our gatekeepers. Those who manage our time and resources must understand how important it is to cooperate with their peers across the institution. Although I believe that we have little of this, occasionally gatekeepers can assume the cloak of those for whom they work and act imperially. These individuals have the responsibility to execute our vision, not to derail or delay projects that have already been decided. We cannot tolerate such behavior.

I. We must learn to *keep score*. By that I mean that we must measure our progress. This will make certain that we are accountable. It shows a true commitment on our behalf to stewardship. It also allows us to show clear results to a sometimes doubting campus community, alumni, legislators, and of course, our Board of Trustees. And, learning to keep score will also require us to constantly

Appendix A

check our course of action and to make course corrections when necessary.

My final thought is that I need you to rekindle your shared enthusiasm, energy, and passions for the institution. I will expect your loyalty to our goals, to each other, and to me. *Loyalty* does not mean that we do not tolerate dissent, but it does mean that I will not tolerate *disloyalty*. Loyalty, passion, energy, enthusiasm, a sense of urgency, and a clear-minded commitment to excellence will allow us to be the architects for the future of this University.

Appendix B

Gee and Alutto Memos to the Board of Trustees

To: Sharkey, Maureen
CC: Alutto, Joe; Asher, Herb
Subject: Gee Confidential BOT biweekly report
Sensitivity: Confidential

TO: Board of Trustees
FROM: E. Gordon Gee
DATE: January 22, 2008
RE: Biweekly Report

CONFIDENTIAL

I have not had an opportunity to correspond with you since our bowl game in New Orleans. Despite the game, it was a wonderful time for our fans and our students. Our students participated in a project, along with Louisiana State University students, rehabilitating a community center. A large number of students, faculty, staff, and alumni supported that project. Our team played well, but ultimately beat itself through unfortunate penalties. It was a great disappointment to our coach, with whom I spoke at length after the football game. Of course, as I pointed out to numerous people, there are 124 university presidents who would love to have my problems in terms of athletics.

Appendix B

And, speaking of athletic achievement, I did want to note that all but one of our eligible juniors decided to return to our football program. Their statements in the press were magnificent in support of the values of this University. We should take some pride in their decision. The net result is that we are already being ranked by a number of sources as a pre-season favorite to play for the national championship next year.

Now to the business of the University. The beginning of a quarter is always quite busy. And, our quarter is off to a very strong start. We are meeting or exceeding our projections in almost all categories, academic and financial, that we measure. Our bottom lines remain strong. Our student numbers remain consistently strong. We have an outstanding pool of applicants. And our Medical Center is performing with considerable strength. I say all of that realizing that we are in tumultuous financial times. Therefore, we are planning very conservatively in terms of our financial obligations and expectations. We are also working very hard to make a strong case to the state that, as it faces its own financial dilemmas, the continuing support of our University should be a very high priority. I believe they hear our message. I am also asking our senior officers to devise plans as to how we can be of immediate help or support to the state in terms of economic activity. For example, we have tremendous infrastructure needs and deferred maintenance problems. In conjunction with the state and our own resources, we could substantially increase, almost immediately, our infrastructure support activities. This would be very useful to the University and, of course, of significant economic activity for the state. We will be looking at all of our options.

As you have been reading, the proton/particle therapy issue is again front page news. I can assure you that we are working very hard to make certain that we are not outmaneuvered or outsmarted on this issue. There is significant concern as to whether or not this therapy actually works. Yet, M. D. Anderson and the Cleveland Clinic now appear to be convinced that such therapy is workable and available. While we review the science, we also need to look at the potential of partnerships that may serve us well. We also want to make certain that we would participate in any potential state support for such a project, if it made sense. This whole process is fast moving and non-transparent. I do not want to be in a reactive mode, but I also want to make certain that we are not being log rolled.

Our search for talent continues. I am very focused on developing the strongest pool of candidates possible for the senior vice president for health affairs. I am encouraged by the work that I have been doing with our consultants. We have identified a very rich talent pool and have narrowed it to a small number of candidates. I am quietly pursuing several of those candidates in order to determine their interests. As with the Peter Weiler search, I am determined to be very focused on a limited number of individuals in order to be as flexible and agile as possible. We are also in the process of searching for a chief investment officer, and I am encouraged at the beginning of this process. Finding such an individual for this assignment will require a national sweep. Allen Proctor, who has worked with us on other financial matters, will lead this search, but we will keep it also very focused.

On February 1, I will spend some time with the board in executive session talking about our executive compensation and master planning process. I have spent a good deal of my own time focusing on this issue. I have had the help of Jerry McCue, who has served as a consultant to the University over the past 15 years. I have also returned to Sasaki Associates out of Cambridge, Massachusetts, who did a master planning process for us in the mid-90s. I have asked for Ricardo Dumon, Sasaki's lead planner, to work with us to again look at both our campus planning and our community planning. Although I do not want to evidence an edifice complex, I am very concerned about our deferred maintenance, the need for renovation and new facilities in order to sustain the momentum of the University, and clearly the status of our off-campus neighborhoods and how they relate to the overall planning of the city. And, of course, all of this is tied very closely to the quality of student life, including our residence halls and the availability of good housing off our campus.

At our board meeting, I will also ask Joe Alutto to give an overview of the strategic planning and alignment process. We have been working very hard over the past three or four months to make certain that we do have a clear, precise, and creative strategic planning process in place and one that will integrate our academic, capital, financial, and master planning processes together. Joe, as the provost and leader of our integrated financial planning group, has done an excellent job in leading this effort, and we are now much better positioned to manage the University's academic plan and my strategic goals.

I had the opportunity this past week to visit our campus at Wooster and then to speak at the Akron Roundtable. I am now starting to move throughout the state and will spend this coming Friday and Saturday in Cincinnati. Our agricultural research center at Wooster is one of the best research centers of its kind in the world. I am struck, again, at the leadership role that Ohio State plays in this state and in enhancing the quality of life in this state, nationally, and beyond. I was also struck in visiting Akron how important it is for us to assert, time and again, that we are *The* Ohio State University and that we serve the people of this state in all corners of Ohio. I am also encouraged by how much people are yearning for leadership from the University, which I intend for us to provide. In these turbulent times, I believe the role of this University is even more significant and important.

I look forward to our Board meeting.

aw

c: Dr. Joseph A. Alutto
   Dr. Herbert B. Asher

GEE AND ALUTTO MEMOS

CONFIDENTIAL

July 27, 2009
TO: Board of Trustees
FROM: Joe Alutto
SUBJECT: Bi-Weekly Report

It is truly a delight to be back in sequence with reports to the board. To begin with, thanks to all of you for your expressions of concern. As you may know, I've been battling two degenerative disks in my lower back for the past year or so. It reached a point where it was decided that it would be best to fuse four lower vertebrae and insert a titanium cage to stabilize things, thereby allowing the full fusion to complete as desired. Dr. McGregor completed the surgery and I returned home after three days in the hospital. I've been in a "brace" since then and will be for another six weeks. It is uncomfortable but does have one redeeming virtue. My grandsons love to tap on it and laughingly say "abs of steel!"—which makes me wonder what videos they are watching! I managed to stay in fairly constant touch working via e-mail and telephone. Starting two weeks ago I have been coming into the office for 4–5 hours and then working from home after that. That pattern will continue for another week or so and then I should be able to spend more time in the office, particularly while Gordon is out of the country.

As Gordon has noted in his bi-weekly message, this has been a very busy and productive time for all of us. A focus on resolving budget issues made sense and generated very positive results. But we also managed to use this time to make sure we had the "right people in the right seats on the bus."

To begin with, we informed you that the dean of the College of Social Work had resigned and was being replaced with Interim Dean Tom Gregoire. That was a very difficult discussion on multiple dimensions, some having to do with the dean's performance, some being generated by internal college problems that seemed intractable and some a function of rethinking the future of the college. We will have more conversation about this as time goes on but it was necessary to facilitate a change and there is general relief that we were able to make that happen.

With your approvals, we will be making three very important new appointments effective September 1, 2009. To begin with, we greatly strengthened our focus on undergraduate programs building on the foundation developed by Martha Garland. Dr. Wayne E. Carlson will be appointed Dean for Undergraduate Education and Vice Provost for Undergraduate Studies. Wayne, a member of the Ohio State faculty since 1988, is completing his second term as chair of the Department of Industrial, Interior, and Visual Communications Design. From 1991 to 2000, he served as director of Ohio State's Advanced Computing Center for the Arts and Design (ACCAD). Previously, he was the executive vice president of operations for Cranston/Csuri Productions, a Columbus company producing special effects for the international television and advertising industries. Widely published in computer graphics literature, Wayne is a professor of design technology, with joint appointments in the Departments of Art, Art Education, and Computer and Information Science. His research interests are in the areas of computer animation, geometric modeling, interactive museum installation design, the use of computer graphics and multimedia in education, and visualization.

Wayne earned his B. S. degree from Idaho State University, M. S. degrees from Idaho State and Ohio State, and a Ph.D., also from Ohio State. We expect Wayne to become actively involved in new undergraduate program development, undergraduate program assessment, general education redesign, program support (e.g., advising), honors programs, etc. In effect, Wayne is being asked to redefine this position to parallel that of Pat Osmer, Dean of the Graduate School and Vice Provost.

The second appointment of note is that of M. Dolan Evanovich, Vice President for Strategic Enrollment Planning. Currently the Vice President for Enrollment Planning, Management and Institutional Research at the University of Connecticut, Dolan has vast experience in all aspects of undergraduate student enrollment. At U-Conn's main campus and five regional campuses, he has directly supervised the offices of Undergraduate Admissions, Student Financial Aid Services, Scholarship Programs, Student Employment, Veteran's Programs, New Student Orientation, Institutional Research, Student Services Center, and the University Registrar. His portfolio has also included oversight of $11 million in annual budgets, $111 million in private and institutionally funded financial assistance, $22 million in state and federal aid, and $118 million in student loans. Prior to his work at the University of Connecticut, Dolan served as the Director of Undergraduate Student Admissions at Arizona State University and as Director of Admissions at Eastern Michigan University. He earned his bachelor's degree in urban planning and a master's degree in geography and regional planning at California University of Pennsylvania. We expect him to fully integrate our enrollment planning and implementation activities with overall strategic plans of academic units and the university as a whole.

At the college level, I am delighted to report that Dr. Lonnie King has agreed to serve as Dean, College of Veterinary Medicine, with tenure as a Full

Professor of Veterinary Preventive Medicine. Lonnie has served as the Senior Veterinarian and Director, National Center for Zoonotic, Vector-Borne, and Enteric Diseases, Centers for Disease Control and Prevention, since 2005, and was the CDC's first director of the Office of Strategy and Innovation. He served as dean of the College of Veterinary Medicine at Michigan State University for ten years and, during his 19 years with the US Department of Agriculture's Animal Plant Health Inspection Service, also served as the country's chief veterinary officer and worked extensively in global trade agreements and protecting the nation's plant and animal resources. He earned his B. S. and DVM at Ohio State; an M. S. in epidemiology at the University of Minnesota; a master's degree in public administration at American University; and completed the Senior Executive Fellowship Program at Harvard University. He also worked in private practice for seven years.

As Gordon has noted, this was an extensive search in which the search committee found itself unable to recommend for the deanship candidates who had been reviewed on campus. However, the search committee identified Lonnie as one of two candidates they really wanted to consider but who neither they nor the search firm involved could interest in becoming candidates. After receiving the committee report and reviewing the backgrounds of the two reluctant candidates, Gordon and I agreed that we would take the initiative in recruiting Lonnie to Ohio State. Gordon visited Lonnie in Atlanta and I continuously expanded the discussions as Lonnie warmed up to the possibilities inherent in our deanship. At the end we had a very enthusiastic candidate for the deanship. Given his prior experience as a dean, his federal experience, his private practice time and his outstanding scholarship, Gordon and I were delighted to secure his commitment to serve as dean. We are now coordinating public announcements with the CDC and you will hear more about Lonnie as that unfolds.

In summary, it has truly been an "interesting time" for me and the university. The fact that we can move forward on so many fronts and attract such outstanding talent says a great deal about the excellence you have helped develop and Gordon has been able to lead.

c- President Gee
    Vice Provosts

Appendix C

Ohio State University Enrollment Report

Graphs excerpted from 2016 Enrollment Report. For this and other enrollment data, see http://oesar.osu.edu/.

2016 Enrollment Report

Undergraduate applications and enrollment, Columbus

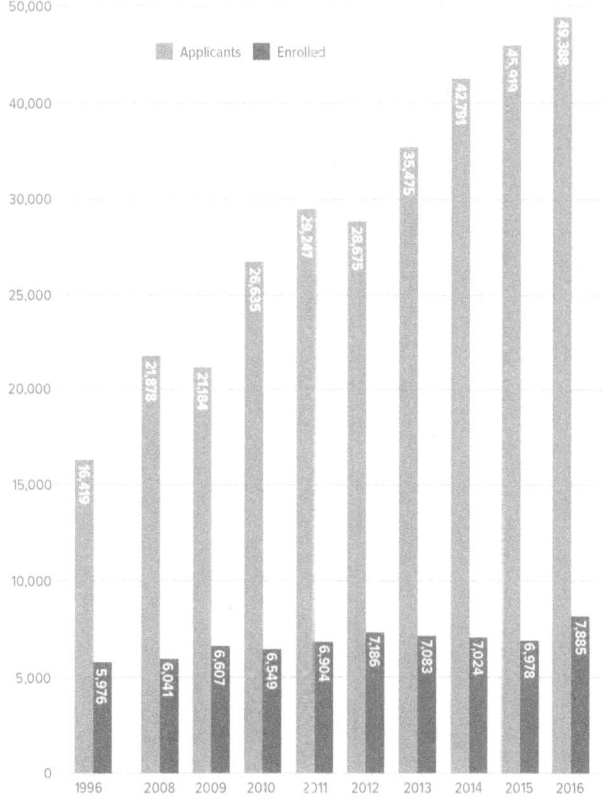

Percent in top 10% of high school class

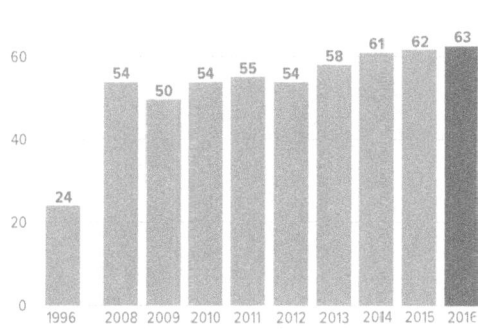

Undergraduate trends, 2008–2016, Columbus

Average ACT composite

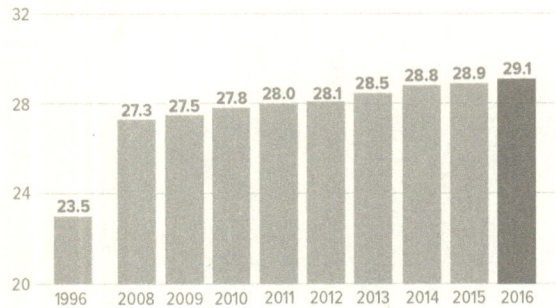

Average SAT combined critical reading and math

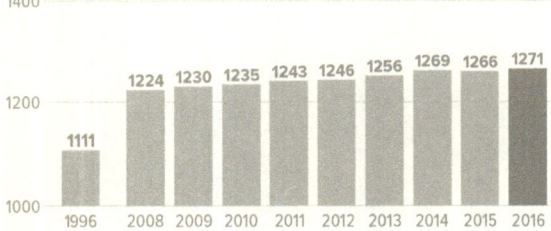

Percent in top 25% of high school class

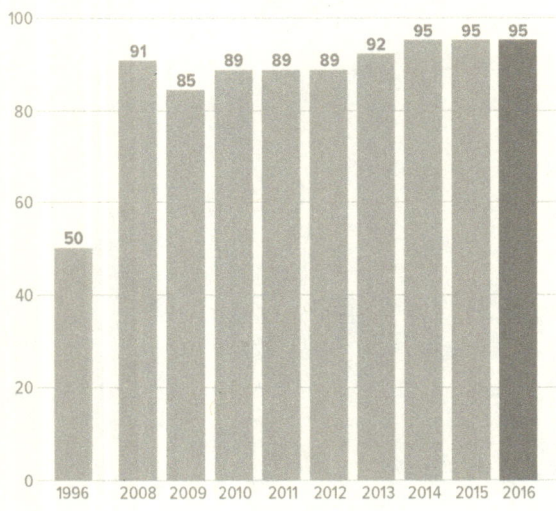

Enrollment counts

Total university enrollment, all levels, all campuses (2015)

Total	66,046
Undergraduate	52,349
Graduate	10,529
Professional	3,168

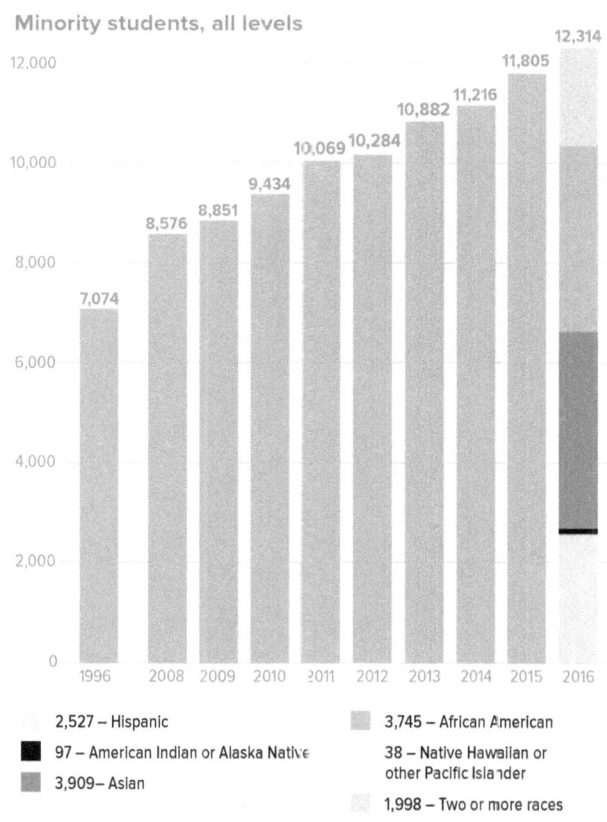

Minority students, all levels

- 2,527 – Hispanic
- 97 – American Indian or Alaska Native
- 3,909 – Asian
- 3,745 – African American
- 38 – Native Hawaiian or other Pacific Islander
- 1,998 – Two or more races

Enrollment counts

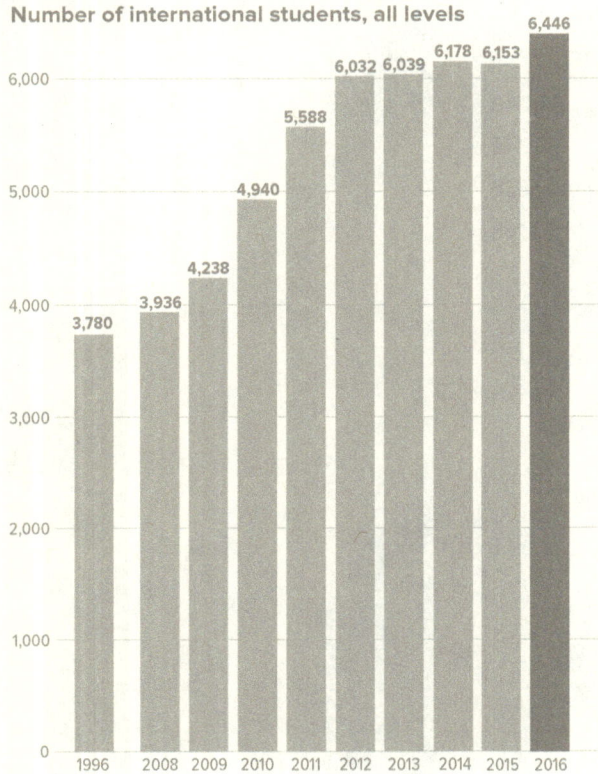

Degree attainment and graduation

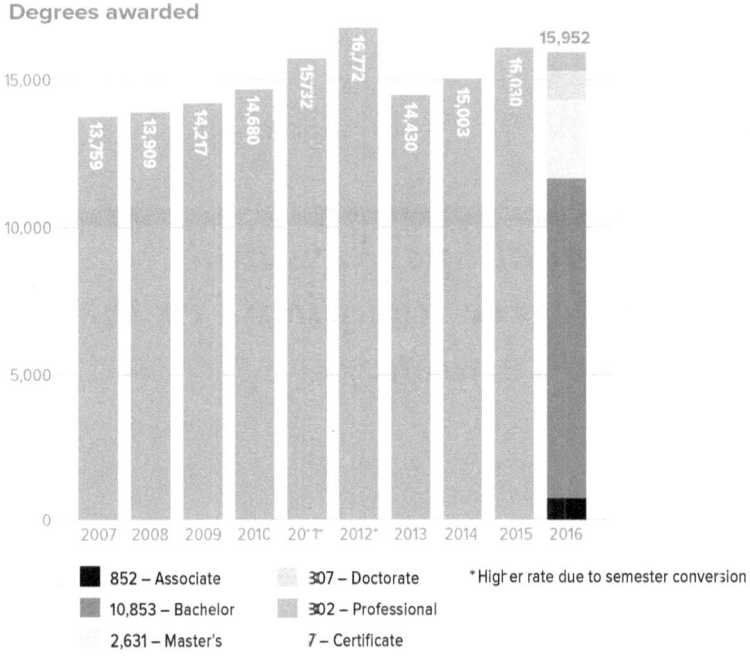

Degrees awarded

- 852 – Associate
- 10,853 – Bachelor
- 2,631 – Master's
- 307 – Doctorate
- 302 – Professional
- 7 – Certificate

*Higher rate due to semester conversion

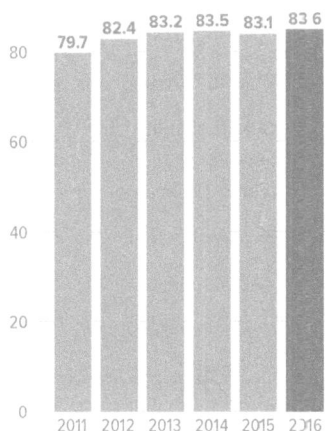

Percent of undergraduates graduating within six years of enrolling

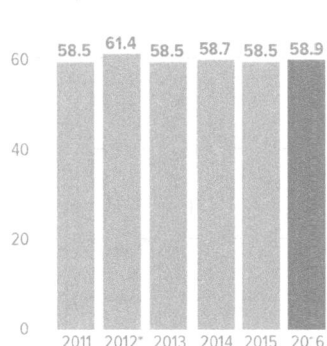

Percent of undergraduates graduating within four years of enrolling

*Higher rate due to semester conversion

Appendix D

Commencement Speakers and Honorary Degree Recipients in the Second Gee Presidency

COMMENCEMENT DATE	SPEAKER	HONORARY DEGREE RECIPIENT(S)
December 2007	Brian Joseph	Wolfgang Ketterle
		John M. Opitz
March 2008	Steven A. Davis	Roy J. Glauber
June 2008	Brian Williams	Brien A. Holden
		Brian Williams
August 2008	David L. Denlinger	John L. Hall
		Frank Wilczek
December 2008	Richard Hollingsworth	William E. Evans
March 2009	Yvette McGee-Brown	Charles K. Brain
		Jules Pretty
		John G. Thompson
April 2009		Ruth Bader Ginsburg
June 2009	John H. Glenn	Anna C. Glenn
August 2009	Thomas J. Moyer	George A. Olah
December 2009	Kevin Boyle	Olafur Ragnar Grimsson
March 2010	John P. Monton	

COMMENCEMENT SPEAKERS AND HONORARY DEGREE RECIPIENTS

COMMENCEMENT DATE	SPEAKER	HONORARY DEGREE RECIPIENT(S)
June 2010	David R. Gergen	Francisco J. Ayala David R. Gergen
August 2010	Alfred Dodge Cole	Michael B. Coleman Charles Henry Plumb
December 2010	David Tomasko	J. Tinsley Oden Carl J. Schramm
March 2011	Donna James	Solomon H. Snyder
June 2011	John A. Boehner	John A. Boehner J. Lyle Bootman Carter G. Phillips
August 2011	David Frantz	David Frantz Lino Tagliapietra
December 2011	Cheryl Krueger	Zdenek P. Bazant
March 2012	Richard K. Herrmann	Keith L. Moore
June 2012	Susan E. Rice	Donald Harris Douglas S. Massey
August 2012	Terry Stewart	Terry Stewart
December 2012	Jack Hanna	Jack Hanna Vikki Haywood Ray Jackendoff Tobin J. Marks
May 2013	Barack H. Obama	Annie Liebowitz Barack H. Obama Thomas D. Pollard Reinhard Rummel

Appendix E
Members of the Board of Trustees in the Second Gee Presidency

Until the early 2000s, there were nine trustees on the Ohio State Board of Trustees, all of whom were Ohio residents appointed by the governor for nine-year terms. A law passed in the 1990s expanded the board by two student trustees, an undergraduate student, and either a graduate or professional student, also appointed by the governor and each serving a two-year term.

In the 2000s, the university requested that the legislature and the governor expand the Ohio State Board to fifteen members, all of whom were still appointed by the governor and served nine-year terms. The argument for this was that a university as large and complex as Ohio State needed more trustees and the more diverse skills that they brought to their assignment. This expansion of the board from nine to fifteen led to a change in how the board chair was selected. When there were nine trustees serving nine-year terms, the member of the board in his or her ninth year automatically became the board chair.

Finally, the university sought and received permission from the State of Ohio to allow the board to select up to three charter trustees to serve on the board. Charter trustees are non-voting, non-Ohio residents selected by the board to bring additional skill-sets to address the challenges of governing a massive institution like Ohio State. The Governor of Ohio is prohibited by the state Constitution from appointing non-Ohio residents to the Board. Yet many observers felt that a national university like Ohio State should have non-Ohio representation on the Board and charter trustees helped accomplish this.

MEMBERS OF THE BOARD OF TRUSTEES

2007–08

Trustees: Gil Cloyd, Chair. Douglas Borror, Alan Brass, Jo Ann Davidson, John Fisher, Karen Hendricks, Brian Hicks, Algenon Marbley, Dimon McPherson, Walden O'Dell, John Ong, Robert Schottenstein, Alex Shumate, Leslie Wexner
Student Trustees: Christopher Alvarez-Breckenridge, Debra Van Kamp

2008–09

Trustees: Gil Cloyd, Chair. Douglas Borror, Alan Brass, Jo Ann Davidson, John Fisher, Brian Hicks, William Jurgensen, Linda Kass, Algenon Marbley, Dimon McPherson, Walden O'Dell, John Ong, Ronald Ratner, Robert Schottenstein, Alex Shumate, Leslie Wexner
Student Trustees: Debra Van Kamp, Jason Marion

2009–10

Trustees: Leslie Wexner, Chair. Douglas Borror, Alan Brass, Jo Ann Davidson, John Fisher, Brian Hicks, William Jurgensen, Linda Kass, Algenon Marbley, Dimon McPherson, Walden O'Dell, John Ong, Ronald Ratner, Janet Reid, Robert Schottenstein, Alex Shumate
Student Trustees: Jason Marion, Alexis Swain

2010–11

Trustees: Leslie Wexner, Chair. Douglas Borror, Alan Brass, John Fisher, Brian Hicks, William Jurgensen, Linda Kass, Clark Kellogg, Algenon Marbley, Walden O'Dell, Ronald Ratner, Janet Reid, Robert Schottenstein, Alex Shumate, Jeff Wadsworth
Student Trustees: Alexis Swain, Brandon Mitchell
Charter Trustee: Gil Cloyd

Appendix E

2011–12

Trustees: Leslie Wexner, Chair. Alan Brass, John Fisher, Brian Hicks, William Jurgensen, Linda Kass, Clark Kellogg, Algenon Marbley, Walden O'Dell, Ronald Ratner, Janet Reid, Robert Schottenstein, Alex Shumate, Tim Smucker, Jeff Wadsworth
Student Trustees: Brandon Mitchell, Evann Heidersbach
Charter Trustees: Gil Cloyd, Corbett Price

2012–13

Trustees: Robert Schottenstein, Chair. Alan Brass, John Fisher, Brian Hicks, William Jurgensen, Linda Kass, Clark Kellogg, Cheryl Krueger, Algenon Marbley, Ronald Ratner, Janet Reid, Alex Shumate, Tim Smucker, Jeff Wadsworth
Student Trustees: Evann Heidersbach, Benjamin Reinke
Charter Trustees: Gil Cloyd, Corbett Price

Index

ACT, 187, 188, 255; average, 282 fig.
Adams-Gaston, Javaune, 17, 21 fig. 3.8, 23, 70, 126, 128, 259; leadership of, 190; protests and, 64–65
Adidas, 170, 171
admissions, 4, 193; decisions on, 189; open, 188; scams, 141–42, 205; selective, 187, 192, 198, 237; strategies for, 178
Advanced Computing Center for the Arts and Design (ACCAD), 278
advancement model, 36, 87, 88–92, 97, 98, 150, 195–96, 257; development of, 93–94; impact of, 92–93; implementation of, 96, 162, 196
affinity agreements, 170–73
African American Student Services, 232
African American students/faculty/staff, 104, 227, 228, 231, 234, 236
Agricultural Technical Institute, 48, 153
Alliance of Dedicated Cancer Hospitals, 214
Alutto, Joseph A., 13, 17, 17 fig. 3.1, 28, 38, 54, 57, 138, 168, 171, 245 fig. 17.2, 259, 260, 276; arts and sciences consolidation and, 83; commercialization and, 165; Discovery Themes and, 137; leadership of, 169,

176; memo from, 277–79; organizational changes and, 82; planning and, 135, 136; Senior Management Council and, 53; strategic plan and, 133, 275; trustees and, 70–71
Alvarez-Breckinridge, Christopher, 10 fig. 2.1
American Association for the Advancement of Science, 193
American Association for Cancer Research, 214
American Council of Education, 156
American Indian Student Services, 232
American Planning Association, 107
Anderson, Carole, 79 fig. 7.1
Animal Plant Health Inspection Service (USDA), 279
Anstine, Julie, 134
Anthony, Ben, 119 fig. 10.1
applications, 183, 187, 192; grant, 194; undergraduate, 281 fig.
Archie Griffin Ballroom, 38, 118
Arts District, 111–15, 115–16, 268, 259
Aschenbach, Doug, 102, 107
Asher, Herbert B., 13, 17, 20 fig. 3.7, 29, 32, 54, 71, 258, 276; alumni association and, 91, 92

Asian American Student Services, 232
Association of Public Land-grant Universities, 229
athletics, 2–3, 171, 176, 178, 199, 200–202, 208, 233, 256, 273–74; Coca-Cola and, 170; facilities for, 202–4, 255; funding for, 202–4; performance of, 204–5; revenue from, 203; scope of, 202–4
Axium Infrastructure, 169

Bartley, Trudy, 54, 108, 109, 110
Bartter, Kate, 147
Basinger, Mary, 44 fig. 5.3
Beatty, Joyce, 22, 27 fig. 3.12, 28, 29, 150, 151; recruitment of, 26–27
Bell, Karen, 54, 113, 113 fig. 9.3
Bickel, Kathy, 48
Big Ten Conference, 2, 71, 72, 163, 165, 166, 181, 182, 195, 199, 203, 204, 205
Big Ten Network, 203
Billy Ireland Cartoon Library and Museum, 113, 114, 114 fig. 9.4
Biomedical Research Tower, 218
Black Studies Community Extension Center, 109
Board of Medical Affairs Committee, 216
Boehm, Mike, 135, 136, 153
Boehner, John A., 47 fig. 5.7
Borror, Douglas, 10 fig. 2.1

291

Index

Box-Steffensmeier, Janet, 66 fig. 6.2, 84
Brass, Alan, 10 fig. 2.1, 218–19
Bricker Hall, 215
Brook, Peter, 112
Brown, Don, 221
Brown, Sherrod, 164 fig. 12.1, 222
Brown, Trevor, 143
Bruce, Earl, 205
Brustein, William, 138, 139, 259
Buckeye Club, 203
Buffett, Warren, 152
Bugala, Shea, 57
Build America Bonds, 173
Business Advancement Division, 172
"But for Ohio State Campaign," 93–96, 94 fig. 8.3

Cage, John, 112
Caligiuri, Michael, 175, 210 fig. 15.1, 212 fig. 15.2, 213, 214
Camp, Michael, 165
Campus Collaborative, 104–5
campus life, 127, 129–30, 190–91
Campus Partners, 105, 106–7; creation of, 99, 100, 103; impact of, 101–3; initiatives by, 107–8
CampusParc, 167, 168
cancer program, 175, 213, 214, 215, 219, 221, 222
Caniff, Milt, 113
capital budget, 169, 247–49, 250, 251; campaigns for, 3, 4, 159, 195, 257
Carey, John, 252
Carlson, Jennifer, 212, 214
Carlson, Wayne E., 277–78
Carpenter-Hubin, Julie, 185
Cass, Pete, 223
Castaneda, Jorge, 39
Caswell, Lucy, 113
Cecilia, Sister, 50, 51 fig. 5.11, 52

Celeste, Richard, 27
Center for Aviation Studies, 147–49
Center for Higher Education Enterprise, 73, 252
Centers for Disease Control and Prevention (CDC), 22, 279
Chaitt, Richard, 68, 133
Chatas, Geoff, 19 fig. 3.5, 22, 23, 38, 54, 70, 159, 162, 163, 167, 173, 174, 215, 256; leadership of, 169, 176; recruitment of, 25–26
Chatas, Kate, 19 fig. 3.5
Cheng, Bill, 38
Chronicle of Higher Education, The, 181, 297
Chronicle List, 181, 182
Church, Melinda, 45, 46
City of Hope National Medical Center, 214
Cloyd, Gil, 9, 10 fig. 2.1, 12 fig. 2.4, 38
Coca-Cola, affinity agreement with, 170–73
Coleman, Michael B., 54, 55 fig. 5.14, 100, 101, 109 fig. 9.1, 151, 212 fig. 15.2, 223
collaboration, 80, 81, 101, 258, 270, 271
College of Arts and Sciences, 1, 24–25, 93, 115; consolidation and, 75, 80–84, 258
College of Dentistry, 79, 210, 222, 242, 260
College of Food, Agriculture and Environmental Sciences (FAES), 47, 137, 260
College of Medicine, 136, 144, 211, 213, 222
College of Nursing, 136, 210, 259, 260
College of Public Health, 22, 136, 144, 210
Columbus City Council, 151, 223

Columbus City Schools, 105, 110
Columbus Coated Fabrics, 105
Columbus Metropolitan Club, 263
Columbus Metropolitan Housing Authority (CMHA), 108, 110
Columbus Partnership, 164, 235
Columbus State Community College (CSCC), 155–56
commencement, 5 fig. 1.3, 21 fig. 3.8, 43, 44 fig. 5.2, 45, 56, 66, 119, 122 fig. 10.5, 233; speakers for/listed, 287–88
commercialization, 163–66, 195
Committee on the Physical Environment (COPE), 145
committees, 62, 63; board, 70; organizing, 60; search, 9, 12, 16, 24, 82, 239, 260, 269
communication, 70, 86, 87, 172, 208, 257, 260
community, 29, 87, 107, 108, 144, 153, 211; building, 117, 126, 240, 259; campus, 117, 127, 129, 141; committing to, 33–34; disabled, 230; LGBTQ, 230, 235; university, 40, 60
community colleges, 58, 78, 155, 156, 237, 251, 262
Community Outreach Partnership Center, 105
Community Research Partners, 104
compliance, integrity and, 140–42, 205
Compston, Michelle, 38
Construction Reform Demonstration Projects, 221
Cooper, Almeta, 217
Cooper, John, 200, 205
Cooperative Extension Service, 46–47, 105, 150, 160, 238

292

INDEX

Council of Graduate Students (CGS), 59
Covelli Center, 130
Crane Sports Medicine Center, 130
Cranston/Csuri Productions, 278
Critical Differences for Women, 235
Crowell, Becki, 48, 49 fig. 5.10, 55, 57
Culley, Chris, 9, 17, 19 fig. 3.5, 28, 29, 38, 152, 217, 258; leadership of, 176; regulatory relief and, 151
culture, 30–31, 35–36, 213, 217, 223, 230, 237; American, 139; athletics, 199; Black, 231; institutional, 255; productive, 35; student, 43; university, 16
Cummings, Brian, 17, 165
Cunningham, Merce, 112
Cunningham, Patty, 64

Dana-Farber Cancer Institute, 175
Davidson, Jo Ann, 10 fig. 2.1
Davis, Jordan, 119, 119 fig. 10.1
Dedicated Cancer Care Centers, 214
degree attainment/graduation, 285 fig.
degrees awarded, 285 fig.
Delaney, Jim, 203
deregulation, 151–52, 220
development, 57, 59, 85, 86, 95, 96, 99; advancement and, 195–96; cultural, 202; economic, 54–55, 105, 174, 195, 220, 247; mixed-use, 102; social, 202
Discovery Themes, 33, 36, 136–37, 138, 168, 239, 259
diversity, 42, 61, 63, 226, 229, 236–39; achieving, 230–33, 239–40; faculty/staff, 234–36

Diversity, Equity, and Inclusion (certificate program), 230
Dodd, Christopher, 221
Don Scott Field, 147–49
Douglas, Andrea "AJ," 22, 34
Drake, Michael, 95, 130, 137, 149, 159, 168, 177, 189, 190, 210, 223, 236, 255, 298; advancement model and, 92, 93; student quality and, 187
Drake Union, 172
Drive Capital, 173, 174
Drummond, Theresa, 69 fig. 5.4
Dumont, Ricardo, 134, 275
Duncan, Robert, 69, 69 fig. 6.3

Edwards Communities, 108
Eicher, Brandon, 26 fig. 3.11
Eicher, Michael, 17, 22, 23, 26 fig. 3.11, 70, 88; fundraising and, 196, 257; recruitment of, 26
Eminence Fellows Program, 168
endowments, 162, 195; growth of, 86, 196; parking lease and, 167–68; selective investments for, 174
energy, 63, 68, 136, 165, 145, 168–69, 256, 260
Energy Training Center, 249
engagement, 1, 97; outreach and, 150–51; rules of, 265–72
ENGIE, 169
enrollment, 149–50; counts, 284 fig.; minority students as percentage of, 227 table; total/all, 283 fig.; undergraduate, 281 fig.
Enrollment Report, 198
EPIC system, 217
ethnicity, 229, 230, 233, 238
Eunice Kennedy Shriver National Institute of Child Health and Human Development, 22
Evanovich, M. Dolan, 17, 23, 149, 150, 192, 193, 278
Executive Sponsors Group, 218
Exterior Repair Program, 110
extraordinary people: characteristics of, 35, 266–67; hiring/retaining, 35, 266–68

Faculty Council, address to, 15, 32–33
faculty governance, 60–63, 65–66
Fawcett Center, 172
Federation of the Colleges of Arts and Sciences, 81
Federation of the Colleges of Arts and Sciences at The Ohio State University (white paper), 81
Fickell, Luke, 207–8
financial aid, 129, 160, 198, 215, 237, 238
Fingerhut, Eric, 244, 245, 246; USO and, 54, 78
First Year Experience program, 190
First Year Success Leadership, 39
Fischer, Alex, 163–64, 164 fig. 12.1, 235
Fisher, John, 10 fig. 2.1
Fisher, Susan, 62
Fisher College of Business, 22, 38, 136, 143, 165
Fitch Ratings, 173
Fitzsimons, Kevin, 113 fig. 9.3
Foegeler, Terry, 102, 107
football, 2, 14, 25, 46, 71, 92, 178, 199–203, 206, 207, 208, 273, 274
Foster, Donna, 39
Foundation Board, 209–10
Fox Corporation, 203
Fox Sports Media Group, 203

293

INDEX

Frank W. Hale, Jr., Black Cultural Center, 231, 240
Franklin County Commissioners, 110
Franklin County Convention Facilities Authority, 221
Franklin County Department of Jobs and Family Services, 110
Frantz, David, 8, 10 fig. 2.1, 19 fig. 3.4, 69, 69 fig. 6.4, 115
fraternity/sorority system, 128, 129, 145
Freeman, Mabel, 190, 193
Friedman, Jerry, 211–12, 212 fig. 15.2, 221, 222, 223
Fulbright Scholars, 182
funding, 160, 193–95, 202–4, 248, 249, 251; performance-based, 252, 258; research, 183, 193–95, 198; sources of, 157, 161, 161 table 12.1, 162
fundraising, 87, 95, 195–96, 196 table 13.5, 257, 260; approaches to, 85–86

Gabbe, Pat, 25 fig. 3.10
Gabbe, Steve, 17, 25 fig. 3.10, 28, 70, 210 fig. 15.1, 213, 217, 218, 223, 224 fig. 15.5
Garland, Martha, 119 fig. 10.1, 277
Garrity-Rokous, Gates, 141, 142
Gates, Bill, 152
Gavazzi, Steve, 253, 262
Gay, Lesbian, Bisexual, Transgender Student Services, 232
Gee, Gordon, 2 fig. 1.1, 10 fig. 2.1, 10 fig. 2.2, 11 fig. 2.3, 12 fig. 2.4, 17 fig. 3.1, 18 fig. 3.2, 18 fig. 3.3, 20 fig. 3.6, 20 fig. 3.7, 23 fig. 3.9, 26 fig. 3.11, 42 fig. 5.1, 44 fig. 5.2, 45 fig. 5.2, 45 fig. 5.4, 47 fig. 5.5, 47 fig. 5.8, 51 fig. 5.11, 51 fig. 5.12, 53 fig. 5.13, 55 fig. 5.14, 66 fig. 6.2, 94 fig. 8.3, 112 fig. 9.2, 119 fig. 10.1, 206 fig. 14.2, 210 fig. 15.1, 224 fig. 15.5, 245 fig. 17.2, 253 fig. 17.3, 262 fig. 18.2; legacy of, 254–63; memo from, 273–76; recruitment of, 7–9, 11–13; retirement of, 72–73; rules of engagement of, 265–72; transition for, 13–15
Gee, Rebekah, 9, 11, 12 fig. 2.4
Geier, Pete, 217
Geldin, Sherri, 54, 111, 112–13, 112 fig. 9.2
general operating principles, 269–72
Gerber, Tim, 60, 61 fig. 6.1, 62, 63
Glenn, Anna C. (Annie), 11 fig. 2.3, 47 fig. 5.5, 253 fig. 17.3
Glenn, John H., 11 fig. 2.3, 47 fig. 5.5, 143, 247, 253 fig. 17.3
Global Gateways, 138, 139
Graduate and Professional Visitation Days, 226, 231
graduation, 43, 45, 198; percent within four years of enrolling, 285 fig.; percent within six years of enrolling, 285 fig.; rates, 127, 184, 185, 191, 191 table 13.3, 192; requirements for, 77
Grand Reading Room, 124, 125 fig. 10.9
Great Hall of the Union, 120 fig. 10.3, 121
Great Recession, 160, 173, 196, 247
Green Revolution, 137
Gregoire, Tom, 260, 277
Griffin, Archie, 89, 90 fig. 8.2, 92
Gunther, Richard, 75–76, 78

Hagerty Hall Auditorium, 39
Hale, Frank W., Jr., 226, 231, 232 fig. 16.1
Hall, Bill, 5 fig. 1.3, 118
Hanson, Pete, 204

Harding Hospital, 210
Havener Eye Institute, 211
Hawley, Josh, 73
Hayes, Woody, 199, 205
health care, 86, 110, 136, 144, 158, 211–12, 223, 256, 259–60
Health Resource and Services Administration (HRSA), 221–22
Health Sciences Academies, 110
Heinlen, Dan, 89, 92
Hendricks, Karen, 10 fig. 2.1
Hershey, Jack, 48, 220, 248, 249, 250, 251, 257, 258
Hicks, Brian, 10 fig. 2.1
High Noon: Twenty Global Problems, Twenty Years to Solve Them (Rischard), 136
High Street corridor, 99, 100, 102, 103, 106, 107–8, 116, 259
Hispanic Student Services, 232
Hispanic students, 227, 228
Hoffsis, Amanda, 102, 107
Holbrook, Karen, 4, 5 fig. 1.3, 6, 94, 100, 144, 177, 210
honorary degree recipients, listed, 286–87
Honors and Scholars program, 189, 190
Hoobler, Denny, 48
Hook, Jonathan, 17
Hopkins Hall, 116
Horn, David, 69, 122 fig. 10.5
housing, 104, 106, 223, 275; affordable, 108, 110; campus, 128; off-campus, 102
Hummer, Stephanie, 102
Hunter Heartbeat Method, 114
Hunter, Kelly, 114
Huntington Bank, 175; affinity agreement with, 170
Huntington Club, 39

iBelieve, 238

294

INDEX

inclusion, 226, 236–39; achieving, 239–40; diversity and, 240
Innovation District, 130
Institute of Medicine, 193
Institutional Research and Planning Office, 185
Integrated Financial Planning, 53
integrity, compliance and, 140–42, 205
intellectual property, 163, 166, 195
Inter-Professional Council (IPC), 59
International Poverty Solutions Collaborative Conference, 38
international students, 138–39, 140, 181, 182, 192, 225; increase in, 137, 139; number of, 284 fig.
internationalization, 137–40, 259
internships, 55, 77, 84, 142, 143, 170, 171, 189, 195, 198, 246, 252
Ireland, Billy, 113–14

James Cancer Hospital, 130, 209, 210, 211, 212, 214, 215, 217, 218, 218 fig. 15.3, 219, 222, 258; Pelotonia and, 175
Jameson Crane Sports Medicine Institute, 211
Jennings, Edward, 2, 2 fig. 1.1, 148, 155, 177, 187, 210, 255; admissions and, 188; leadership of, 1
John Glenn College of Public Affairs, 136, 142–43
John Glenn Institute for Public Service and Public Policy, 142, 143
John Glenn International, 147
Johnson & Johnson, 22
Jones, Sue, 48, 48 fig. 5.9, 49, 50

Journal of Higher Education Outreach and Engagement, 107
JP Morgan Asset Management, 22

Kaplan, Jeff, 13, 17, 20 fig. 3.6, 26 fig. 3.11, 28, 29, 38, 154; advancement model and, 96–97; alumni association and, 91, 92
Kasey, Jay, 17, 54, 217
Kasich, John, 54, 73, 163, 174, 216, 244, 253 fig. 17.3, 256, 257; working with, 247–53
Katzenmeyer, Tom, 22, 23 fig. 3.9, 29, 38, 47 fig. 5.7, 54, 87, 119; recruitment of, 27–28
Kellogg Commission, 150
Kessler, Jack, 9, 10 fig. 2.2, 11
Kids'nKamp Auction, 39
Kilroy, Mary Jo, 150
King, Lonnie, 22, 278–79
Kirwan, William "Brit," 1, 2, 4, 5 fig. 1.2, 94, 100, 177, 180, 187, 210, 255
Kirwan Institute for the Study of Race and Ethnicity, 233
Klein, Patrick, 238
Kramer, Nancy, 54
Kroger Company, 106
Krueger, Cheryl, 45
Kvamme, Mark, 174

Lake Erie Sea Grant Program, 48, 160
Lal, Rattan, 137
Land Grant Bar, 253, 262
Lantern, The, 59–60, 242
Larkins Hall, 117, 123
Lashutka, Greg, 99, 100, 102
Lawrence, Ann, 44 fig. 5.3, 69 fig. 6.4
LAZ Parking, 167
Lazarus building, 113
leadership, 74, 78, 81, 82, 84, 100, 151, 169, 176, 177, 180,

198, 209, 215, 223, 249, 265; academic, 140, 268; acid test of, 267–68; administrative, 266, 268; faculty, 62; programs, 64, 171; university, 76, 132, 138, 240; women and, 234, 235
leadership team, 34–35, 64, 245, 254; assembling, 30–31
Lee, Dawn Tyler, 108, 109, 109 fig. 9.1, 110
Lee, Spike, 112, 112 fig. 9.2
Leibovitz, Annie, 111, 112
Leitzel, Joan, 82
Lennox, Tom, 54, 175
Levy Restaurants, 172, 173
Lewis, Ben, 49
LGBTQ community, 230, 235
LGBTQ Employee Resource Group (ERG), 235
LGBTQ students/faculty/staff, 232, 235–36
licensing agreements, 133, 165, 166, 171
Limited, The (L Brands), 22, 27, 87, 175
Limited Brands Foundation, 209
Little Sisters of the Poor, 50, 51 fig. 5.11, 51 fig. 5.12, 52, 71
Llewellyn, Larry, 17
Lloyd, Patrick, 260
Longaberger, Tami, 38, 44 fig. 5.2
Longaberger Alumni House, 8, 11, 92
Lyttle, Eric, 9

MacArthur Foundation Fellowship, 112
Magrath, C. Peter, 13
Manderscheid, David, 82–83
Marbley, Algenon, 10 fig. 2.1, 27 fig. 3.12
Martha Morehouse Outpatient Care, 211
Martin, William, 22, 144

INDEX

Maymester, 77–78, 258
McCampbell Hall, 218
McCorkle Aquatic Pavilion, 123, 202
McCue, Gerald, 134, 275
McCulty, Jo, 113 fig. 9.3
McCutcheon, Kathleen, 22
McPheron, Bruce, 17, 137, 260
McPherson, Dimon, 10 fig. 2.1, 23
media, 70, 86–87, 199, 200, 208
Medicaid, 3, 157, 160, 211, 212, 224
Medical Affairs Committee, 216
Medicare, 160, 213, 214, 224
Mekhjian, Hagop, 224 fig. 15.5
Melnyk, Bernadette, 259, 260
Mendenhall Lab, 38
Mershon Auditorium, 116
Mershon Center for International Security Studies, 138
Meyer, Urban, 205, 207, 208
Michaels, Alan, 260
minority students, 226, 227, 228, 236; enrollment of, 227 table 16.1, 283 fig.
Mirror Lake, opening of, 130
monetization, asset, 166–67, 168–69
Money, ratings by, 184
Montgomery, Betty, 215
Montler, Linda, 49
Moody, Curt, 119 fig. 10.1
Moody Nolan, 119
Moody's Investor Services, 173
Moore, Allan, 12 fig. 2.4
Moore, James, III, 230–31
Moritz College of Law, 136
Moser, Bobby, 17, 18 fig. 3.2
Mount Vernon Business District, 110
Mount Vernon East, 110
Multicultural Center, 231, 232, 235

Myers, Keith, 107

Nagy, Suzanne, 69 fig. 6.4
NASA, 193
National Academy of Engineering, 193
National Academy of Sciences, 193
National Center for Zoonotic, Vector-Borne, and Enteric Diseases, 22, 279
National Institute of Environmental Health Sciences, 144
National Institutes of Health (NIH), 22, 144, 160, 164, 193, 224, 255
National Merit Scholars, 179
National Science Foundation (NSF), 164, 224, 255; funding from, 160, 193
Nationwide Arena, 172
Nationwide Children's Hospital, 223
Nauman, Bruce, 112
NCAA, 203, 205, 206, 207, 233; disqualification by, 208; recognition from, 204; recruiting restrictions by, 179
Near, Tom, 56
Near East Side, 100, 108, 110, 211
Near East Side Neighborhood Leadership Academy, PACT and, 110
Nelson, Melinda, 45–46, 57
Niecamp, Beth, 217
Nike, 203; affinity agreement with, 170–73
North Campus, 73, 259; residence halls in, 126, 129
North Campus Residential District, 100, 127 fig. 10.10, 259

Obama, Barack H., 21 fig. 3.8, 119, 121, 121 fig. 10.4, 122

fig. 10.5; commencement address by, 233
Obama, Michelle, 122 fig. 10.6
O'Brien, Colleen, 48
O'Dell, Walden, 10 fig. 2.1
Office of Academic Affairs, 46, 57, 79, 82, 143, 153, 239, 246, 260
Office of Budget and Management (OBM), 248
Office of Business and Finance, 172
Office of Disability Services, 231, 232
Office of Diversity and Inclusion (ODI), 226, 229, 230–31, 239
Office of Energy and the Environment, 146–47
Office of the Executive Dean of the Colleges of Arts and Sciences, 81
Office of Minority Affairs, 226, 229, 231, 238
Office of Research, 193–94
Office of Special Events and Commencement, 45
Office of Strategy and Innovation, 279
Office of Student Activities, 118, 239
Office of Student Life, 190, 231, 239, 240
Office of Trademark and Licensing, 172
Office of Undergraduate Admissions and First Year Experience, 149, 193
Office of University Compliance and Integrity, 140–42
Ohio Agriculture Research and Development Center, 48, 160
Ohio Capital Corporation for Housing, 105
Ohio Innovation Fund, 173
Ohio Revised Code, 151, 152

296

INDEX

Ohio Stadium, 14, 39, 43, 130, 222
Ohio State Alumni Association, 257
Ohio State Energy, 169
Ohio State Extension, 46–47, 48, 49, 105, 150, 160
Ohio State Honors & Scholars program, 190
Ohio State University Airport, 147–49
Ohio State University Alumni Association, 48, 86, 87–88, 235, 237, 257; advancement model and, 88–92, 92–93; Board of Directors, 89, 90
Ohio State University Board of Regents, 54, 78, 152, 155, 156, 244, 246, 248, 250, 251, 252
Ohio State University Board of Trustees, 8, 9, 11, 36, 38, 59, 61, 118, 130, 136, 143, 148, 152, 173, 176, 209, 215–16, 218, 219, 220, 235, 256, 259, 271; Alutto memo to, 277–79; Campus Partners and, 99, 101, 103; Gee memo to, 273–76; Gee relationship with, 68–69; geographical diversity for, 67–68; leadership of, 169; members of, 288–89; no confidence in, 73; parking lease and, 167; quarter system and, 69; regulatory environment and, 140; search process by, 6; selection of, 67–68; strategic planning and, 131–32; university governance and, 68; work of, 66–73
Ohio State University Communications, 50
Ohio State University Comprehensive Cancer Center, 175, 214
Ohio State University East Hospital, 109, 211
Ohio State University Golf Course, 148

Ohio State University Health System, 17
Ohio State University Home Ownership Program, 110
Ohio State University Marching Band, 25, 111, 201, 261 fig. 18.1
Ohio State University Medical Center, 1, 30, 166, 183, 209, 213, 214, 216, 274
Ohio State University Urban Arts Space, 113
Ohio State Welcome Leaders (OWLs), 190
Ohio Union, 38, 39, 40, 117, 119 fig. 10.1, 120 fig. 10.2, 120 fig. 10.3, 121 fig. 10.4, 124, 171; new, 118–19, 121; renovation of, 100
Ohio University, 106, 159, 174, 179
Olentangy River, 55, 130, 134
One Ohio State Framework (Framework 1.0/Framework 2.0), 36, 133–36
One University, 32, 36, 134, 153, 213
Ong, John, 10 fig. 2.1
Onyejekwe, Egondu, 38
Osmer, Pat, 278
outreach, engagement and, 150–51
Ova, 8, 14, 20 fig. 3.6, 119, 125 fig. 10.8, 261

Pan Mass Challenge, 175
Papadakis, Mike, 173
Paprocki, Ray, 9, 68
Parent University, 110
Partners Achieving Community Transformation (PACT), 100, 108–10, 223; Blueprint for Community Investment, 110
Peace Corps, 181
Pelosi, Nancy, 151
Pelotonia, 54, 175–76, 223

Pendleton-Julian, Ann, 54
Pepsi, 170, 171
Perry, Marnette, 106
Petro, Jim, 54
Pizzuti House, 38
planning, 260; academic, 132, 153, 275; capital, 136; enrollment, 149–50; integrated, 134; physical, 134; regional, 100; strategic, 36, 131–33, 135, 143, 149–50, 239, 259, 275, 278
Planning, Architecture, and Real Estate (PARE), 107
PNC Bank, 110
Poindexter Village, 110
Poon, Christine, 22, 38, 165
Port Columbus, 147
Portman, Jane, 8
Portman, Rob, 8
Preferred Pathway Program, 155, 156
President and Provost's Council on Women, 234
President and Provost's Diversity Council, 239
President's Council, 13
President's and Provost's Council on Sustainability (PPCS), 146
President's and Provost's Council on Strategic Internationalization, 138
Proctor, Allen, 275
Project One, 151, 213, 217–23, 246
ProMedica Health System, 219
public universities, 58, 140, 256; comparing, 180–81, 182–83; minority enrollment at, 228; rating, 185

QIC Global Infrastructure, 167
Quality and Professional Affairs Committee, 216
Quality and Value Initiative for Higher Education, 252

297

Index

Quality and Value report, 258
quarter system, 69, 76, 77, 192
Querry, Korenia, 69 fig. 6.4

Rainer, Yvonne, 112
rankings, OSU, 132, 173, 180, 183–87, 186 table 13.1
Ratner, Ronald, 10 fig. 2.1, 134, 218
Ray, Ed, 159
Reagan, Gerry, 62
Reasoner, Eric, 48
Recreation and Physical Activity Center (RPAC), 100, 123, 123 fig. 10.7, 124
recruitment, 7–9, 11–13, 16, 22, 23–28, 29–30, 31, 35, 87, 117, 193, 229, 237, 255, 260; restrictions on, 179; strategies for, 178
regional campuses, 153–55, 192
regulatory environment, 140, 151, 166
remediation rates, 4, 105, 188
research, 1, 15, 46, 65, 73, 82, 86, 96, 149, 225, 233, 247; agenda, 33, 76; cancer, 175, 214; collaboration on, 80; expenditures for, 194, 194 table 13.4; faculty-driven, 140; funding for, 161, 183, 193–95, 198; grants, 160; industry-sponsored, 164; medical, 214, 216–17
residence halls, 14, 259; building, 124, 126
resources, 3, 37, 170, 176, 213, 256; human, 35, 80; natural, 145
Retchin, Sheldon, 223
retention rates, 127, 184, 185, 190, 198
revenue: generating, 159–63, 171, 172, 203, 256–57; sources of, 158, 159, 160, 165, 166, 169, 176
Rezai, Ali, 216–17

Rhodes State College, 154, 211
Ries, Carol, 44 fig. 5.3, 45, 46, 56
Riggs, Xen, 172
Rischard, J. F., 136
Ritter, Gretchen, 84
Rockefeller Neuroscience Institute, 217
Ross Heart Hospital, 211, 218
Royal Shakespeare Company (RSC), 114, 115
rules of engagement, 35, 265–72

St. Anthony Hospital, 211
Santulli, Peggy, 175
Santulli, Richard, 175
Sasaki Associates, 134, 275
SAT, 187, 188, 255; average, 282 fig.
Sawyer, Tom, 253 fig. 17.3
Scarlet and Gay Society, 235
Schoenbaum Family Center, 105, 107
scholarships, 82, 96, 107, 169, 171, 235; athletic, 233; parking lease and, 167–68
Schottenstein, Robert, 10 fig. 2.1, 17 fig. 3.1, 73, 122 fig. 10.5; letter from, 72
Schottenstein Center/Value City Arena, 8, 43, 172, 173, 204
Schuller, David, 22, 219, 219 fig. 15.4, 221
Schulz, Charles, 113
Scorcese, Martin, 112
Scott, Don, 147
Scott, Madison, 69
Second-Year Transformational Program (STEP), 129, 133, 140, 189, 259
Secret Service, 119–20
semester system, 75–80, 192
Senate Steering Committee, 60, 61

Senior Management Council, 53
Senn, Larry, 34
Senn-Delaney (firm), 22, 34, 35
Shkurti, Bill, 17, 19 fig. 3.4, 53, 159, 218
Shook, Sondra, 49 fig. 5.10
Short North, 8, 108, 222
Shumate, Alex, 5 fig. 1.2, 10 fig. 2.1, 27 fig. 3.12, 38, 201 fig. 14.1; letter from, 72
Skestos, George, 39, 224 fig. 15.5
Skestos, Tina, 224 fig. 15.5
Sloopy's Diner, 118, 121, 121 fig. 10.4
Smith, Gene, 20–27, 171–72, 201, 201 fig. 14.1, 205, 206 fig. 14.2, 207
Smith, Jim, 92
Smith, Randy, 79–80, 79 fig. 7.1
Sodexo, 172
Solove Research Institute, 175, 209, 210, 214, 217–18, 218 fig. 15.3, 222
Sorenson, Andy, 22, 25, 87–88, 88 fig. 8.1; death of, 88, 96; fundraising and, 257
Souba, Chip, 53, 213
South Asian Studies Initiative, 39
South Campus, 259; residence halls in, 124, 126
South Campus Gateway, 103, 104, 107–8; revitalization of, 100, 102
Special Opportunity Hiring Fund, 239
Standup for Shakespeare, 114
Stark State College, 249–50
Steiner, Curt, 17, 20 fig. 3.7, 27–28, 29, 47 fig. 5.8, 54, 86
Steinmetz, Joe, 17, 23, 25 fig. 3.10, 260; arts and sciences consolidation and, 82–83; recruiting of, 24–25
Steinmetz, Sandy, 25 fig. 3.10

INDEX

STEM, 83, 116, 229
Sterrett, Steve, 102, 105, 107
Stevenson, Anna, 49 fig. 5.10
Stoddard, Dick, 17, 20 fig. 3.7, 29, 150
Stone, Jon, 217
Strategic Enrollment Planning, 192
Strategic Plan, 245, 246
strategies, 57, 133, 146, 178, 192; advancement, 91; communication, 257; listed, 33–34; measurement, 132
Strayhorn, Terrell, 73
Strickland, Ted, 47 fig. 5.6, 47 fig. 5.7, 220–21, 245 fig. 17.2; Fingerhut and, 246; USO and, 54; working with, 244–47
Stuck, Tracy, 41, 42–43, 42 fig. 5.1, 48, 57, 118–19, 119 fig. 10.1, 261
Student Academic Services building, 193
student groups, 63–65, 118, 240
Student Wellness Center, 123
Student Athletes Support Services Office (SASSO), 204, 205, 233
Sullivant Hall, 113, 116, 168
sustainability, 145–47, 162, 260
Sustainability Institute, 146–47
Sustainable and Resilient Economy program, 147

Taft, Bob, 47 fig. 5.6, 147
Teater, Phyllis, 217
technology, 162, 165, 247, 252
"Technology Commercialization at The Ohio State University: A Call to Action" (report), 165
Thompson, Blake, 69
Thompson, William Oxley: statue of, 125 fig. 10.8
Tiberi, Denise, 47 fig. 5.8

Tiberi, Pat, 47 fig. 5.8
Todd Anthony Bell National Resource Center on the African American Male, 227, 231
Tom W. Davis Special Events Gym, 123
Tootle, Barbie, 45–46, 45 fig. 5.4
Tootle, Jim, 45 fig. 5.4
Tressel, Jim, 71, 205–8, 206 fig. 14.2
Tucker, Ty, 204
tuition, 152, 157, 202, 248, 297; increase in, 3, 158, 197, 237; in-state, 197; lowering, 154; revenue from, 158, 159
Turner Construction, 221
two-year residency rule, 126–29
Tyson, Priscilla, 151

Under Armour, 170, 171
Undergraduate Student Government (USG), 59, 78
undergraduate students: characteristics of, 179, 188–89, 189 table 13.2; geographical home of, 228 table 16.2; quality of, 187–93
United Students Against Sweatshops, 169
United Way of Central Ohio, 110
University Area Improvement Task Force, 99–100
University Arts District, 100
University District, 99, 102, 103, 104, 107, 110, 128
University District Organization, 101
university governance, 60–63, 68
University Health System Consortium (UHC), 217
University Senate, 46, 57, 60, 61, 62, 65, 145; diversity

and, 63, 239; Diversity Committee, 239; semester conversion and, 78
University Square, 108
University Staff Advisory Committee (USAC), 60, 66
University System of Ohio (USO), 244, 245, 246–47, 252
Upper Arlington Kingsdale facility, 211
US Department of Agriculture (USDA), 160, 164, 193, 279
US Department of Defense, 160, 193
US Department of Education, 193
US Department of Energy, 193
US Department of Health and Human Services (HHS), 222
US Department of Labor, 193
US Department of Transportation, 160
U.S. News & World Report: ratings by, 132, 180, 183–87, 186 table 13.1

Van Kamp, Debra, 10 fig. 2.1
Veterans Administration, 211, 233
Vets4Vets, 233
Voinovich, George, 47 fig. 5.6, 158, 243 fig. 17.1, 247; taxation and, 243; working with, 241–44
Voinovich, Janet, 243 fig. 17.1

Wadsworth, Jeff, 38
Wagenbrenner Development, 105
Warhol, Andy, 111
Wegman, William, 111
Weigel Hall, 116

299

Index

Weiler, Peter, 17, 275
Weinland Park, 104, 105, 107, 108; Campus Partners and, 106; revitalization of, 100
West Campus, 119, 134
Wexner, Abigail, 94 fig. 8.3, 112, 112 fig. 9.2, 114, 115 fig. 9.5, 210 fig. 15.1
Wexner, Leslie (Les), 9, 10 fig. 2.1, 11, 94 fig. 8.3, 112, 114, 115 fig. 9.5, 118, 163, 210 fig. 15.1, 218; leadership of, 95, 209–10, 216
Wexner Center for the Arts, 54, 111, 112–13, 116
Wexner Center Foundation, 112
Wexner Medical Center, 95, 173, 209, 210 fig. 15.1, 211, 212 fig. 15.2, 222, 223, 225, 235; Board, 210, 216; culture/governance at, 212–17
Wexner Prize, 111, 112, 112 fig. 9.2
Whitacre, Caroline, 17, 18 fig. 3.2, 165, 193–94
Widening the Circle Initiative, 235
William Oxley Thompson Memorial Library, 100, 117, 124, 125 fig. 10.8, 125 fig. 10.9, 135
Williams, David, 22, 25, 148, 149, 200
Wolfe, Ann, 11 fig. 2.3
Wolfe, John F., 9, 11, 11 fig. 2.3
Wolford, Kate, 17, 19 fig. 3.5, 28–29, 37, 52, 53 fig. 5.13, 55, 56, 57, 146; protests and, 64–65; sustainability initiatives and, 260
Women Student Services, 232
Women's Place, 234, 235
WOSU Public Media, 86, 108

Young Scholars Program, 228, 229, 231
Younkin Success Center, 204, 231, 232–33

Zacher, Chris, 62

www.ingramcontent.com/pod-product-compliance
Lightning Source LLC
Chambersburg PA
CBHW032018230426
43671CB00005B/130